# Corporate Social Responsibility, Public Relations and Community Engagement

Diverse in economic development, political and mass media systems, the countries in Southeast Asia cast a unique light on the parallels between development-cum-participative communication and corporate social responsibility.

In our globalized environments, knowledge of power, culture and the colonial histories that influence and shape business and governance practices are increasingly important. Focusing on six countries—Indonesia, Malaysia, the Philippines, Singapore, Thailand and Vietnam—the book discusses how public relations (PR) and corporate social responsibility (CSR) discourse are constructed, interpreted, communicated and enacted in this diverse emerging region. By connecting the disparate disciplines of participatory and development communication with PR and CSR discourse, this innovative text explores the tensions between concepts of modernity and traditional values and their role in engendering creativity, compliance or resistance.

This book will be of interest to researchers, educators and advanced students in the fields of public relations, communication, corporate social responsibility, corporate communications and Southeast Asia studies.

**Marianne D. Sison** is senior lecturer and program manager at RMIT University's School of Media and Communication, Melbourne, Australia. She is convenor and founding chair of the Asia Pacific Public Relations Research and Education Network, an Urban Scholar at RMIT's UN Global Compact Cities Program and Australian lead in the Global Capabilities Framework research project. A former Deputy Dean (International) at RMIT's School of Media and Communication, she is a fellow of the Public Relations Institute of Australia and member of the International Association of Business Communicators.

**Zeny Sarabia-Panol** is professor and associate dean at Middle Tennessee State University, U.S.A. She is also the former editor of the Association for Education in Journalism and Mass Communication's *International Communication Research Journal* and now serves on its editorial board. She also sits on the editorial board of the *International Journal of Strategic Communication* and AEJMC's *Journalism and Mass Communication Educator*. An alumna of the Journalism and Mass Communication Leadership Institute for Diversity, she served as interim director of MTSU's School of Journalism in 2008–2009.

# Routledge New Directions in Public Relations and Communication Research
Edited by Kevin Moloney

Current academic thinking about public relations (PR) and related communication is a lively, expanding marketplace of ideas and many scholars believe that it's time for its radical approach to be deepened. *Routledge New Directions in PR & Communication Research* is the forum of choice for this new thinking. Its key strength is its remit, publishing critical and challenging responses to continuities and fractures in contemporary PR thinking and practice, tracking its spread into new geographies and political economies. It questions its contested role in market-orientated, capitalist, liberal democracies around the world, and examines its invasion of all media spaces, old, new, and as yet unenvisaged. We actively invite new contributions and offer academics a welcoming place for the publication of their analyzes of a universal, persuasive mind-set that lives comfortably in old and new media around the world.

Books in this series will be of interest to academics and researchers involved in these expanding fields of study, as well as students undertaking advanced studies in this area.

**Public Relations in Japan**
Evolution of Communication Management in a Culture of Lifetime Employment
*Edited by Junichiro Miyabe, Yamamura Koichi and Tomoki Kunieda*

**Corporate Social Responsibility, Public Relations and Community Engagement**
Emerging Perspectives from Southeast Asia
*Marianne D. Sison and Zeny Sarabia-Panol*

**Social Media, Organizational Identity and Public Relations**
The Challenge of Authenticity
*Amy Thurlow*

For more information about the series, please visit www.routledge.com/Routledge-New-Directions-in-Public-Relations–Communication-Research/book-series/RNDPRCR

# Corporate Social Responsibility, Public Relations and Community Engagement

Emerging Perspectives from Southeast Asia

Marianne D. Sison and
Zeny Sarabia-Panol

LONDON AND NEW YORK

First published 2019
by Routledge
2 Park Square, Milton Park, Abingdon, Oxon OX14 4RN

and by Routledge
711 Third Avenue, New York, NY 10017

*Routledge is an imprint of the Taylor & Francis Group, an informa business*

© 2019 Marianne D. Sison and Zeny Sarabia-Panol

The right of Marianne D. Sison and Zeny Sarabia-Panol to be identified as authors of this work has been asserted by them in accordance with sections 77 and 78 of the Copyright, Designs and Patents Act 1988.

All rights reserved. No part of this book may be reprinted or reproduced or utilized in any form or by any electronic, mechanical, or other means, now known or hereafter invented, including photocopying and recording, or in any information storage or retrieval system, without permission in writing from the publishers.

*Trademark notice*: Product or corporate names may be trademarks or registered trademarks, and are used only for identification and explanation without intent to infringe.

*British Library Cataloguing-in-Publication Data*
A catalogue record for this book is available from the British Library

*Library of Congress Cataloging-in-Publication Data*
A catalog record has been requested for this book

ISBN: 978-1-138-83812-3 (hbk)
ISBN: 978-1-315-73466-8 (ebk)

Typeset in Bembo
by Wearset Ltd, Boldon, Tyne and Wear

In loving memory of
*Fernando and Nieves Dayrit*
*Leonardo and Constancia Sarabia*
and
*Dr. Frank Panol*
who imbued in us a strong sense of responsibility, discipline, fairness and empathy,
who taught us to be kind and personified both kindness and tough love,
who inspired us to be our best,
who opened our eyes to possibilities and allowed us to pursue our dreams,
who sacrificed, loved, supported and accepted us for who we are,
and who kept us humble, grounded and true to ourselves,
this book is for you.

# Contents

| | | |
|---|---|---|
| *List of illustrations* | | viii |
| *Acknowledgments* | | ix |
| 1 | Introduction: exploring the connections | 1 |
| 2 | Beyond nation building: CSR and sustainability in Indonesia | 25 |
| 3 | CSR/PR discourse as advocacy and aspirational talk in Malaysia | 49 |
| 4 | CSR as social development in postcolonial Philippines | 75 |
| 5 | Singapore's strategic social enterprise and inclusive CSR | 98 |
| 6 | Sustainable community development and risk mitigation in Thailand | 117 |
| 7 | Blurring CSR/PR boundaries: transactional approaches in Vietnam | 137 |
| 8 | Conclusion: connecting the narratives | 163 |
| | *Index* | 182 |

# Illustrations

**Figure**

8.1  "*Bibingka*" approach to CSR                                      174

**Tables**

1.1  Demographic and media data of selected countries          6
1.2  Breakdown of respondents by country/group                  19

# Acknowledgments

A book project is never a single person's endeavor. A research book project is most definitely never a solo effort, regardless of who conceptualized it. There are many people we wish to thank who have collaborated with us and encouraged us through this long-winded journey.

## From Zeny

This book is my co-author's brainchild. So, Marianne, thank you, for this latest opportunity to work with you and for the years of productive scholarly collaboration. Most of all, thanks for your friendship. Our book admittedly is the most involved project we have ever done so far and hopefully it is the first of many more.

Life indeed happened while we were busy planning and working on this book. Between the book proposal approval to the actual writing of the book, we had extremely painful and sad personal losses. Marianne's mother and my husband died. There were also overwhelming challenges such as a life-threatening medical condition that required emergency surgery and landed me in the ER instead of an ASEAN-member country where I had arranged meetings and interviews for part of the book research. Then, barely 14 months after the death of my husband, I faced another health crisis this time involving my youngest sister, who was diagnosed with stage 3 ovarian cancer that required immediate surgery and months of debilitating chemotherapy. Thankfully both medical interventions saved my sister's life and she has been in remission for a year now. Meanwhile, after Marianne lost her mother-in-law and sister-in-law within weeks of each other, work-related setbacks prompted questions around the meaning of and the purpose of life and work. In all of these unexpected, beyond-our-control life circumstances, our publisher has been so understanding and sympathetic.

I am a grateful and proud daughter of Papa Leonardo and Mama Conching. Surviving the recent crises in my life would have been near impossible without the love and support of my brothers—Efrenito, Alexander, Joseph Nelson and Vincent Stephen and their families; my sisters, Arlene, Madeline, Stella Marie and her family and Myrian Zenith. Thanks to all and to my stepchildren—Jay and his family, MA, Minnette and Ace, who have been wonderfully supportive as well.

I have said that when my husband was alive, our home was my sanctuary; when he died, the office became the refuge from the storm. It was the place that provided the semblance of normalcy as my daily reality at home changed forever. So, for keeping me steady as my world went on a tailspin and for being there for me as a family would, thank you Lisa, Rachel, Ken and Peggy, Irma, Gail and Janet. During my grief-soaked years, Roy and Pam sent cards, Pat and Trish gifted me with butterfly bushes, my fellow widow, Pat T. sent me a book that helped me process what I was going through, David lent me his plumbing skill, Ping did the garage door light service, and Marc P. repaired the switch and changed the front door light. My 'Boro friends'—the Ferrers, Manacsas, Paredes, Kabilings, Akins, Omachonus and Eubanks, whose sustained kindness, help and support to this day have been immeasurable. You as well as my former colleagues and forever friends from our Texas days, Maria and Sandy, and from my Oklahoma years, Annette and Edna ... are all a Godsend. To my university classmates and friends, Adlai, Jonathan and Shirley as well as my high school/elementary pals that will remain nameless but you know who you are, my UP buddies Reggie and Helen; my former student, Dwayna, who now oversees the communication program of multibillion corporate mergers and whose expressions of what she learned in my classes and sheer thoughtfulness are heartwarming, thank you so much for confirming that what we do in academia or in industry is all worth it.

## From Marianne

Choosing the right people to work with is key to completing a project. I approached Zeny because we had previously co-authored several journal articles and book chapters. In fact, she was responsible for kick-starting my publication track with her generous offers of co-authorship and mentorship opportunities. Her journalistic and editorial experience, combined with her tenacity, were critical skills that I needed to gain the confidence to proceed with this book. So, thank you Zeny, for agreeing to join me on this cross-continental endeavor and for your continuing friendship over and beyond this partnership.

Getting this idea into a suitable proposal required the approval of the commissioning editor, Professor Kevin Moloney. When I first broached the idea to Kevin, he was rather cool about it. After working through the proposal many times with Zeny, we eventually received the go ahead, and committed to proceed. Kevin, thank you for your confidence and for your patience.

Undertaking field work in five countries involved time and resources normally funded by a grant. I had none. Fortunately, my former dean, Professor Martyn Hook, believed in and promoted the integration of research with our teaching and leadership activities. So, my previous role as deputy dean, international provided various opportunities to undertake the field research after meetings with our regional partners. To Martyn and my School of Media and Communication colleagues, thank you for giving me the space to pursue this important project.

Balancing work and play is critical to keeping one sane, especially during difficult moments. Connecting with my friends and family around the world is an integral part of my life especially as a migrant who had to start friendships anew. Aside from my fun-loving high school buddies who provide much laughter, my dearest girlfriends—Ruby, Mayang and Lilet—kept me grounded with their faith and confidence in me. And to my dear friends in the international development space—Robbie Guevara, Lilac Limpangog and Paul Battersby—thank you for allowing me into your realm and enabling me to find our common cause.

Life's challenges tend to disrupt one's equilibrium and question one's purpose. I am blessed and grateful to my siblings—Marissa, Lito, Roger, Mariel and their families—and my extended Sison family in Melbourne, the U.S. and the Philippines for keeping me grounded and for just 'being there.' Thank you for providing stability, warmth and comfort when we experienced the loss of our loved ones and for reminding me of what is truly important.

Working women, especially wives and mothers, understand the challenges of juggling many roles. Because I travelled a lot for work, my husband and two adult sons have brilliantly managed the household without me. Like the days when I was completing my PhD, they've stepped up to take over kitchen and laundry duties when I'm frantically finishing a paper or meeting a deadline. Being mother and wife is the best title I can have. Thank you, Mike, Antonio and Francisco for your enduring love, patience and unwavering support.

## From us both

To our research colleagues in the six countries included in this book—Dr. Gregoria Yudarwati (Indonesia), Dr. Cheah Phaik Kin and Yap Yee Onn (Malaysia), Dave Devilles and Gillian Cortes (Philippines), Ai Sian Ng (Singapore), Dr. Parichart Sthapitanonda and Chayanit Vivatthanavanich (Thailand) and Hue Trong Duong (Vietnam)—and our CSR and PR practitioner colleagues, we deeply appreciate all your help before, during and after the field work. Thanks to our research assistants—Dr. Rizaldi Parani, Lorelei Aguirre, Thi Hong Phuong Pham—and our illustrator—Gino Simpliciano—who generously gave their time and talent for this project.

Most importantly, this book would lose its luster and impact without the all-important stories of our respondents in the communities and villages as well as in the NGOs and companies that we interviewed. Thank you for sharing with us your narratives of courage, of resilience in the face of adversity, of humility in the willingness to yield power and control for the better good and of hope or faith in the unremitting notion that real human progress can be achieved if and when prosperity is shared and processes are inclusive. We hope that by including and amplifying the voices absent in the CSR discourse, we like you, have become agents of change.

To our patient and compassionate editors at Routledge—Jacqueline, Laura, Jess—we thank you for giving us time to breathe and to regain our bearings when we hit life's rough patches.

In the spirit of reflective practice, this book is our story too. You will hear our own voices in the retelling of our respondents' stories in the pages of this book. As we began to see the light of the long tunnel that this book took, we rediscovered and strengthened our faith in God and in the basic goodness of people. We found peace, inspiration, purpose and happiness again.

To our families, friends and colleagues, we owe you our greatest gratitude.

This book is our tribute to you all, who inspired us to do what we do and to get to where we are. *Maraming salamat po.*

# 1 Introduction
## Exploring the connections

Public relations (PR), corporate social responsibility (CSR) and community development are topics that are hardly used in the same sentence by scholars and practitioners in their respective fields. Although many scholars have examined public relations and CSR, limited attention has been given to public relations and community development, or corporate social responsibility and community development. Most scholars in community and international development are likely to scoff at any suggestion of being examined with public relations, given the general negative perceptions of public relations practice as 'spin.' Development communication scholars are also wont to possess a negative and narrow view of public relations, unaware of the growing critical public relations scholarship. A few communication-for-development scholars and many development practitioners, however, are slowly accepting the need for strategic communication, which we would argue, emerged from the public relations discipline (see Sison, 2017). Unbeknownst to many of these scholars, however, are the inextricable links between these three concepts, particularly within a Southeast Asian context. Or at least we seemed to think so, thus the exploration through this research project.

Growing up in the Philippines, both authors viewed organizations and workplaces as extensions of the home. Thus, workmates became part of one's extended family. Combining its feudalist past (although some argue that it continues) with its largely Catholic traditions, Philippine businesses, from small- and medium-sized enterprises (SMEs) to large conglomerates, are mostly family owned and have some sense of social justice and responsibility. While working in the Philippines, we have witnessed and experienced how some businesses look after their employees and the communities in which they operate from a 'paternalistic' lens through provision of cash bonuses and other financial support. This form of philanthropy and the culture of 'giving', however, are not exclusive to the Philippines.

Since we migrated to Australia and the United States, respectively, we have both experienced Western-based workplaces and lifestyles in developed economies. Our lived experiences, juxtaposed with our lives in our home country, piqued our interest in examining the perspectives of the region in which we grew up. While we take a scholarly path to this inquiry, we are also 'making sense' of the multiplicity of our experiences. As we matured in our adopted countries, we gained the courage to question universalist and Western dominant approaches to knowledge. We contend the need for a diversity of perspectives particularly from areas not previously recognized in the literature. Acknowledging our own personal and educational histories, we have evolved to embrace a multiple perspective approach.

The shifts in the global order have also shaped our commitment to diverse perspectives. Globalization and the rapid advancement and pervasiveness of communication technology created a blurry, borderless world. At the same time, global financial crises in the West demanded a refocus on Asia. Moreover, the complexity of global issues such as poverty, climate change, malnutrition housed within the Sustainable Development Goals dictated multi-sector collaboration between the government, business and civil society.

This context suggests that a singular approach to scholarship is not sufficient. A multiple perspective approach to communication, which incorporates systems/functionalist, interpretive/rhetorical and critical/dialectical perspectives, provides a richer and more realistic understanding of the context in which CSR and PR practitioners work.

Public relations scholarship's critical turn also paved the way for us to further explore a postcolonial perspective. Through a postcolonial lens that integrates critical and socio-cultural perspectives, we examine dimensions of power and culture in the PR and CSR discourse of local and multinational companies and their community stakeholders. This study answers the call of critical PR scholars for research that examines power imbalances (Coombs & Holladay, 2012; Prieto-Carrón, Chan, Thomsen & Bhushan, 2006); acknowledges the diversity and resistance of publics (Munshi & Kurian, 2005); listening to the voices of subalterns (Dutta, 2015) and for critical/cultural perspectives that "foregrounds the processes of continuously renegotiating meaning" (Curtin, Gaither & Ciszek, 2015, p. 41).

Various definitions of CSR focus on the corporation's role in society. These definitions are often framed to articulate the company's social and legal obligations to the community in which it operates and the environment in which its operations impact. Most studies have explored CSR from the perspective of the corporation and how CSR is employed as a 'strategic imperative' to legitimize its business operations.

CSR has also been referred to in terms of organizations acting as good citizens, when organizations have to interact with people and their environments (Kelly, 2001). Corporate social responsibility has often been defined based on its four dimensions: philanthropic, ethical, legal and economic (Carroll, 1991). Conceptually, corporate social responsibility refers to the "social involvement, responsiveness, and accountability of companies apart from their core profit activities and beyond the requirements of the law and what is otherwise required by government" (Chapple & Moon, 2005, p. 416).

However, CSR has moved beyond the 'corporate' world and into the realm of NGOs and governments. Furthermore, CSR has transcended its Western industrialized beginnings, and ventured into the enclaves of emerging economies. Inevitably with these transitions, the term CSR takes on new meaning. For businesses in developing countries wishing to globalize and modernize, CSR is added as a necessary requirement for the global organization. These definitions, however, become problematic in Asian contexts when CSR becomes a compliance mechanism for standards developed in the West. Some scholars argue that CSR is a Western construct that attempts homogeneity by establishing universal ethical standards brought about by globalization (Chapple & Moon, 2005). Furthermore, most CSR research tends be based in Western countries (Fukukawa, 2010).

Previous research indicated that CSR managers from poorer countries tend to focus more on community development programs especially when governments are not seen to be doing enough (Waldman, Sully du Luque, Washburn & House, 2006). Hirschland (2006) refers to this as the 'governance gap.' He posits that the gap results from absent or underperforming governments, unclear global rules, and "an increasing dependence on civil society and business to play a stronger role in global role creation and enforcement" (Hirschland, 2006, p. 18). Thus, even in developed Western countries, the private sector is often called upon to participate in nation building.

As this book will illustrate, some business practices in several Southeast Asian countries reflect elements of CSR, mostly philanthropy in all its different forms, way before the term CSR became popular. Because CSR is value and culture-laden, there will be nuances in how various countries and cultures interpret and practice CSR. In addition, as with public relations, CSR tends to be a function of a country's economic condition. This is where CSR becomes entangled in concerns of economic development.

As we explore the various pathways that CSR took, particular attention will be given to finding out and understanding the perspectives of people often absent or given limited voice in the dominant conversations and literature on CSR and PR. These two groups we have identified are: the Southeast Asian region; and community stakeholders. We also highlight how tensions between concepts of modernity and traditional values have engendered resistance and creativity.

Connecting CSR with development has emerged as a key platform within the context of the United Nations' (UN) Millennium Development Goals (MDGs) launched in 2000 and the Sustainable Development Goals (SDGs) unveiled subsequently in 2015.

As Newell and Frynas (2007, p. 669) note, international organizations and development agencies have "embraced CSR in the hope that the private sector can play a key role in achieving developmental goals aimed at poverty alleviation." However, they point out that tensions exist between the use of CSR as a *business* tool and CSR as a *development* tool. While they realize that it is unrealistic to expect businesses to prioritize poverty alleviation, they suggest that CSR initiatives can "reinforce state-led development policy" (Newell & Frynas, 2007, p. 679).

Other researchers have examined CSR in Asia (Chapple & Moon, 2005; Fukukawa, 2010, 2014; Visser, 2008; Waldman et al., 2006; Welford, 2004) in an attempt to fill the scholarship gap from the region. Chapple and Moon (2005) found that the variances were not based on the countries' level of development but based on their respective business systems. Differences in CSR practices among Asian countries were also due to differences in norms, values and local culture (Welford, 2004).

Similarly, a comparative study of social responsibility values of top management in 15 countries found that demographic, economic, cultural and leadership factors determined the CSR values of managers (Waldman et al., 2006). While it is useful to understand the regional context of CSR practice, the level of variance among different Asian countries requires a focus on how each country makes sense of corporate social responsibility based on its historical and socio-political frames. Moreover, a focus on the intersections between CSR, PR and community development have not been previously explored.

It is within this context that this book attempts to connect the disparate disciplines of participatory and development communication with public relations and corporate social responsibility discourse in Southeast Asia. With case studies from six countries—Indonesia, Malaysia, Philippines, Singapore, Thailand and Vietnam—we discuss how PR and CSR are interpreted, communicated and enacted within a national development context. We further postulate that admitting the connections between CSR and the UN development goals is profoundly germane to the book for two reasons: all six countries are UN members and therefore are keenly familiar with or have been working toward achieving the eight MDGs as well as the 17 SDGs. Besides, these countries have recalibrated their CSR along the sustainability continuum despite the differences in interpretations and implementation. Some even have pre-SDG focus on sustainability already. As the book chapters will show these countries have CSR programs aimed at addressing many of the MDGs and SDGs, such as poverty eradication, improving health and education, environmental sustainability and gender equity. Additionally, both CSR and the SDG processes share similar approaches in engaging multiple stakeholders—government, civil society and private sectors.

## Why Southeast Asia?

Public relations scholarship has largely neglected Southeast Asia often in favor of economic powerhouses such as China, Japan and India. However, the region's profile has recently increased with impressive GDP growth rates in 2017—Philippines (6.6 percent), Vietnam (6.3 percent), Indonesia (5.2 percent) and Malaysia (5.4 percent)—surpassing those of developed economies such as Australia (2.2 percent), the U.K. (1.7 percent), the U.S. (2.2 percent) and Canada (3.0 percent).[1] However, based on the United Nations'

Human Development Index, which combines life expectancy, education and income per capita measures, only Singapore (eleventh) and Brunei (thirty-first) are included in the Very High Human Development category. In the High Human Development category, Malaysia ranks 62 and Thailand is at 93. Indonesia, the Philippines and Vietnam appear in the Medium Human Development category at 110, 115 and 116, respectively.[2] Table 1.1 gives a comparative snapshot of the demographic, political and media systems of the six ASEAN countries selected for this research.

Given the disparity between economic and human development, the region also provides a platform to examine the interactions between government, the private sector and civil society within the context of participative/development communication, social responsibility and corporate communication/public relations. Moreover, Southeast Asia represents a diversity in political and mass media systems, colonial histories, culture and natural resources which undoubtedly influences how CSR and PR are perceived, interpreted and enacted.

Two recent developments highlight the timeliness of this book: (1) the establishment in 2015 of the Association of Southeast Asian Nations (ASEAN) Community that expect member countries to integrate along economic, security and socio-cultural channels and (2) the rise of populism in the West that most likely will affect the 'pivot to Asia' as a priority. Of particular relevance is the ASEAN Community's socio-cultural blueprint that indicates approaches to achieving its vision toward "A committed, participative and socially-responsible community through an accountable and inclusive mechanism for the benefit of all ASEAN peoples, upheld by the principles of good governance" ASEAN Socio Cultural Community Blueprint 2025 (2016, p. 3).

We note that the Trump administration's attitude toward Asia and the scuttling of the Trans-Pacific Partnership in 2017, on the other hand, can be worrisome as these will power more geopolitical shifts as other countries try to fill the vacuum left by the U.S. Viewed another way, however, the current U.S. stance might just be the impetus needed for the region including the ASEAN to aggressively pursue more cohesive socio-economic development and trade policies with perhaps new partners elsewhere. The shifting trade winds are, in fact, becoming real. Trade between Australia and China, for instance, has grown tremendously in recent years with Australia reporting a sizeable trade surplus. Noting the change, the media accordingly has described the land "Down Under" as "riding two horses" as it maintains alliance with the U.S. while strengthening commercial relations with China.

## Why focus on community?

Several scholars have highlighted the corporate- and Western-centricity of CSR (Prieto-Carrón et al. 2006; Blowfield & Frynas 2005) and PR (Bardhan & Weaver, 2011; Munshi & Edwards, 2011; Sison, 2016; Sriramesh, Ng, Ting, & Wanyin, 2007) scholarship. The call for a more community-centered

Table 1.1 Demographic and media data of selected countries

| Country | Population* | Urban population (percent) | Literacy rate | Per capita GDP (U.S.$) | GDP growth rates (percent) | Health expenditure % of GDP | Education expenditure % of GDP | Human dev. index HDI rank | Government structure and dominant religion | Press restriction score | CSR status | Colonial past |
|---|---|---|---|---|---|---|---|---|---|---|---|---|
| Indonesia | 260.5 million | 55.2 | 95.4 | 12,400 | 5.2 | 2.8 | 3.3 | 110 | Presidential republic Islamic | 65 Partly free | Mandated Zakat management law | Dutch Japan |
| Malaysia | 31.3 million | 76 | 94.6 | 28,900 | 5.4 | 4.2 | 5 | 62 | Federal constitutional monarchy Islamic | 45 Partly free | Islamic laws for foundations and Zakat; CSR policies for public companies | UK |
| Philippines | 104.2 million | 44.2 | 96.3 | 8,200 | 6.6 | 4.7 | 2.7 | 115 | Presidential/republic Roman Catholic | 65 Partly free | Comprehensive environmental laws; compliance a problem | Spain and U.S. |
| Singapore | 5.8 | 100 | 97 | 90,500 | 2.5 | 4.9 | 2.9 | 11 | Parliamentary republic Buddhist | 67 Partly free | CSR-related laws and incentives i.e., on environment | Malaysian federation |
| Thailand | 68.4 | 52.7 | 92.9 | 17,800 | 3.7 | 6.5 | 4.1 | 93 | Constitutional monarchy Buddhist | 32 Not free | CSR-related laws; weak implementation | Never colonized |
| Vietnam | 96.1 | 34.9 | 94.5 | 6,900 | 6.3 | 7.1 | 5.7 | 116 | Communist state Buddhist/Catholic | 20 Not free | CSR-related laws on environment, labor | France |

Source: The World Factbook, United Nations Development Program Report and Corporate Social Responsibility in Southeast Asia: An Eight Country Analysis by del Rosario, R. (2011), Makati, Phil: Asian Institute of Management.

Note
* July 2017 estimate.

approach to public relations theory and practice is not new. As far back as 1988, Kruckeberg and Starck advocated for a community-building approach to public relations. Other scholars have also discussed communities in terms of strategic cooperative communities (Wilson, 1996); communitarianism (Leeper, 1996); activism (Holtzhausen & Voto, 2002) and community relations (Heath & Ni, 2010).

Hallahan (2004) argued that a focus on community presents a viable alternative to theory development. He based his arguments on four themes: that the community construct resonates among communication and other scholars; that the construct is richer and broader than the concept of 'publics;' that there is a growing body of knowledge in public relations that crosses various research traditions; and that community building philosophically summarizes what scholars envision public relations to be. However, Hallahan's (2004) view that community building particularly "resonates with Americans" and to a lesser degree in other parts of the world is myopic. The concept of 'community' per se is not necessary culture-bound and when Hofstede's culture dimensions of 'individualism' and 'collectivism' are applied, the importance placed on community varies depending on a country's cultural values.

Heath and Ni (2010) conceptualized community relations based on the organization being a 'nice' neighbor, a 'good and generous' neighbor and a 'reflective and responsive' neighbor. Hallahan (2004) proposed three types of community building activities: community involvement, community nurturing and community organizing. In community involvement, public relations practitioners act as agents of the organization or the cause and participate actively in community events. As community nurturers, practitioners act as "facilitators, orchestrators of rituals and events, producers of information and coordinators of volunteer and philanthropic efforts" and as community organizers, they act as "recruiters and advocates" (Hallahan, 2004, p. 262).

As mentioned earlier, much of the literature on CSR and CSR communication has focused on business- and Western-centric perspectives. Given the shifts in the global economy, there is a need to examine how 'other' stakeholders such as non-governmental organizations (NGOs) in emerging economies perceive and enact CSR.

The United Nations and the World Bank define NGOs as non-profit organizations whose purpose is toward the public good. Operating at local, national or international levels, NGOs often advocate social issues such as poverty alleviation, environmental protection or undertake community development. NGO is an umbrella term that includes organizations referred to as not-for-profit organizations (NPO), or community-based organizations (CBO), grassroots organizations, or people's organizations. NGOs are still considered the most trusted institution ahead of media, government and business (2018 Edelman Trust Barometer).

NGOs often fall into two categories—operational and advocacy (Malena, 1995). *Operational NGOs*, also referred to as 'development NGOs', are involved in the design and implementation of development-related projects;

and *advocacy* NGOs defend or promote a specific cause and seek to influence the policies and practices of the private sector (Malena, 1995).

While stakeholder engagement and dialogue are deemed important in the CSR context, scholars have highlighted that these approaches have often favored the corporation (Bator & Stohl, 2011; Burchell & Cook, 2013a). Employees, governments and communities are usually defined as primary stakeholders in CSR programs and yet, NGOs are becoming important stakeholders because of their growing influence and expertise with local communities (Aras & Crowther, 2010).

Not only are NGOs growing in influence and shaping policy and practice, they are also growing in numbers. Various sources estimate over 50,000 international NGOs (Yaziji & Doh, 2009), 1.5 million in the U.S. (U.S. Department of State, 2012) and over 3.3 million just in India alone (Shukla, 2010). While most companies usually consider NGOs as secondary stakeholders, those in the resource sector identify NGOs as 'key' stakeholders (Arenas, Lozano & Albareda, 2009).

As global companies shift their manufacturing activities to Asia, and domestic companies join the global economy, corporate engagement with NGOs is becoming a necessary business strategy. The relationships between NGOs and business have generally been fraught with mistrust because the former is often perceived as anti-business or lacking in accountability and regulation. On the other hand, NGOs view businesses as capitalists out to gain profit at the expense of local and indigenous resources.

However, the relationship between the two sectors seems to be changing—from adversarial to more collaborative relationships (Burchell & Cook, 2013b; Yaziji & Doh 2009). Given the diminishing resources from governments to fund public service programs, the NGO and private sectors are finding CSR programs as a common ground for collaborative engagement.

While extant research has examined business–NGO relationships in the context of CSR (Arenas et al., 2009; Burchell & Cook, 2013a; Burchell & Cook, 2013b; Jamali & Keshishian, 2009), questions still remain on how NGOs perceive CSR and how they might participate in the design and development of CSR programs especially within emerging economies. This book will examine how NGOs enact CSR in the context of developing their corporate partnerships and in so doing locate the intersections of PR and CSR.

While increased engagement between NGOs and businesses have resulted in collaborative partnerships, there are also benefits and risks for both parties. For companies, the benefits of engaging with NGOs include risk mitigation and local access. Working with NGOs enables companies to "head off trouble, accelerate innovation, foresee shifts in demand, shape legislation, and set industry standards" (Yaziji & Doh, 2009, p. 129). Moreover, through the help of NGOs, who have established social capital through relationships with key community leaders, corporations gain access to and local knowledge of communities, who grant the social license to operate.

For NGOs, collaborating with business provides access to financial resources in an area of increased competition. Partnership with companies, who they could see as allies to their cause could provide them with much needed resources (Yaziji & Doh, 2009). Corporate engagement can provide NGOs with a broader platform for their advocacy as well as access to business expertise needed for their social programs.

Certainly, partnerships come with risks for both the NGO and the corporation. For NGOs, choosing the 'wrong' partner threatens their credibility and legitimacy especially among their key stakeholders. For corporations, the risks of partnership include security of sensitive information that is shared with NGOs, increased public scrutiny and its perceived 'public relations' advantage (Yaziji & Doh, 2009).

Thus, partner selection becomes critical to the engagement process, for both parties. Hagen (2002) suggests that successful partner selection considers compatibility, capability, commitment and control. Effective partnerships include several variables: resource dependency, commitment symmetry, common goal symmetry, intensive communication, alignment of cooperation learning capability and converging work cultures (Samii, Van Wassenhove & Bhattacharya, 2002).

As noted earlier, much of CSR scholarship has focused on stakeholder engagement but very few scholars have actually explored the perspectives of community stakeholders, often referred to as 'beneficiaries.' We would argue that even the term 'beneficiary' is problematic as it assumes that those who 'receive' benefits from a CSR intervention, such as funding, training or other resources, are the only 'beneficiaries.' We posit that corporations, who undertake these types of activities under the guise of altruistic and strategic CSR are also beneficiaries as these types of engagement and partnerships enhance and build their reputation.

In this regard, we examined how community stakeholders—who we have defined to include community residents, formal and informal village leaders, NGO representatives as well as local government officials—participated in the design, development and implementation of CSR programs. We wanted to understand how CSR is perceived and interpreted, and what communicative activities and processes occurred between representatives from local and multinational companies, local government and the community. Moreover, we are interested how notions of power are exercised and enacted during the interactions between these actors.

The findings from our four-year empirical research comprise the contents of this book. Although global politics have twisted and turned since we started this project in 2014, little has changed in the desires and aspirations of those at the grassroots and community level. While recently elected, global leaders may recast national priorities that impact the rest of the world, there is a stronger urge to articulate the voices of marginalized groups.

The book will appeal to communication scholars, students and practitioners who are interested in corporate social responsibility, international development, advocacy, civil society and public sector communication. Students

10  *Introduction*

and practitioners in international development may also find the book valuable especially if they are interested in communication for development, or communication for social change.

Strategic communication, which incorporates principles of public relations, is gaining ground in many non-profit organizations including development agencies. Previously, the private sector was the dominant employer of PR and strategic communication practitioners. That is not currently the case. More and more communication practitioners are required and employed in the not-for-profit and public sector.

A quick survey of communication jobs in international development revealed extensive opportunities that range from web development to events management to global roles such as Chief Information Officer for Oxfam International (www.devnetjobs.org/default.aspx). Business and management scholars might find enlightening the approaches undertaken toward social entrepreneurship and cooperative development.

As we expect our readers to come from different disciplines, it would be appropriate to define our terms. We then present our research approach and the structure of the book.

## Defining the concepts and exploring the connections

Public relations is managing relationships of an organization's various stakeholders (Wilcox, Cameron & Reber, 2014). Chiming along the relationship management line, Hutton (1999, p. 208) defined public relations as "managing strategic relationships." On the other hand, a 2011–2012 international crowdsourcing campaign and public vote for a modern definition of public relations undertaken by the Public Relations Society of America produced the following: "Public relations is a strategic communication process that builds mutually beneficial relationships between organizations and their publics." (http://apps.prsa.org/AboutPRSA/publicrelationsdefined/, 2017).

So, is PR about management of relations or management of communication?

The European view is that there is no dualism between communication and relationships; one is essential to the other. European scholars also argue for a "reflective paradigm that is concerned with publics and the public sphere; not only with relational (which can in principle be private), but also with public consequences of organizational behavior" (Vercic, Grunig & Grunig, 2001, p. 373).

Indeed, PR, like other disciplines and professions, possess a multiplicity of definitions that include image management and reputation management. It appears that meanings are negotiated and legitimized as organizations and publics perform PR's various roles and functions.

Corporate social responsibility is

> an umbrella term for a variety of theories and practices all of which recognize the following: (a) that companies have a responsibility for their

impact on society and the natural environment, sometimes beyond legal compliance and the liability of individuals; (b) that companies have a responsibility for the behavior of others with whom they do business (e.g. within supply chain); and that (c) business needs to manage its relationship with wider society, whether for reasons of commercial viability, or to add value to society.

(Blowfield & Frynas, 2005, p. 503)

Community development refers to a grassroots process involving the collective action of community members to solve common problems for the community's economic, social, environmental and cultural well-being. Ife (2013) integrates the individual and the collective to define community development. He advocates for change from below, which means valuing local culture, knowledge, resources, skills and processes and incorporating both the social, economic and political as well as the cultural, environmental, spiritual, personal and survival aspects to achieve balanced development. In the wake of globalization, he redirects the emphasis on community-based, indigenous alternatives and has made empowerment, community needs, human rights and participatory concepts as foundations of community development.

PR and CSR: Many scholars have examined the relationship between public relations and corporate social responsibility albeit with different positions (Bartlett, 2011; Clark, 2000; Frankental, 2001; L'Etang, 1994; Sriramesh et al., 2007). Communication, stakeholder relationships and the public good/interest are common threads in contemporary PR and CSR practice. Clark's (2000, p. 373) communication management model of CSR, for instance, proposes the use of the knowledge of identifying stakeholder groups and a corporation's responsibility to them with the ability to strengthen these relationships through effective communication.

Expanding on this research, Bruning and Ledingham (1999, p. 160) offered a definition of the organization–public relationship that refers to the "state which exists between an organization and its key publics in which the actions of either entity impact the economic, social, political and/or cultural well-being of the other entity." Furthermore, management of the communication effort relies on the quality of the present relationship with the primary or secondary stakeholder, as revealed in the communication profile and the communication effects of various methods. This type of analysis is precisely what is missing in current CSR research.

Indeed, communication managers have the ability to scan the political, social and historical environment regarding a myriad of issues; likewise, business competitiveness rests on knowing who will be affected by a company's decisions. Therefore, it is critical that these disciplines acknowledge their similarities and work toward combining their efforts. The interplay of these two disciplines with community development, however, has not been given enough attention, particularly among scholars located in the Global North.

PR and community development: Elaborating on the relationship management dimension of PR, Bruning and Ledingham (1999) stated,

> When an organization is managing a community relationship it is important that the organization be open with community members, that the organization engage in activities that can be used to improve social and economic aspects of the community, and that the organization take an active role in community development.
>
> (p. 165)

In a later study, Ledingham (2001) found public relations has a role in community building within the context of social exchange theory. He suggested that community members "seek a balance between the social 'costs' of interaction with their local government and the social 'benefits' gained in the exchange" and that the relationship declines when the costs outweigh the rewards (Ledingham, 2001, p. 292). He further argued that public relations can be a community builder only when there is a commitment to shared interests, mutual benefit and accommodating different interests (p. 292).

CSR and community development: In launching the world's largest voluntary corporate responsibility initiative, the UN Global Compact has essentially provided a strategic policy for businesses that are committed to aligning their operations and strategies within the areas of human rights, labor, social inclusion, anti-corruption, sustainable supply chains, environment and business integrity. This alignment is to help ensure the advancement of markets, technology and finance for the benefit of society. The Global Compact has reportedly resulted in extraordinary partnerships and openness among corporations, government, civil society and the UN, making it the world's largest CSR and sustainability effort. To date, the Global Compact counts 9,000 corporate participants and stakeholders from over 130 countries.

This interdependency between corporations and the communities where they operate cements the link between CSR and community development. As discussed earlier, community development involves the building of active and sustainable communities based on social justice and mutual respect. It is about influencing power structures to remove the barriers that prevent people from participating in the issues that affect their lives. Community development at its core expresses values of fairness, equality, accountability, opportunity, choice, participation, mutuality, reciprocity and continuous learning (Federation of Community Development Learning, 2009), which also is at the heart of CSR practice.

In the Global South, also referred to as developing countries, the role of international development agencies such as the Red Cross parallels that of the UN. These agencies design and develop programs aimed at improving the community infrastructure and people's well-being often by supporting education, health and employment initiatives. These initiatives require funding, previously the responsibility of national governments. However, decreasing government coffers have increased the need for the private sector to assist. It is at this juncture that community development has become associated with social responsibility initiatives by private sector organizations. Why, one might ask?

There are several possibilities and one of these reasons has to do with public relations and its community relations principles that are clearly compatible with CSR.

## Theoretical lens

Two theoretical frameworks guide this book. With the exception of Thailand, all the other ASEAN member countries in this study have colonial pasts so it makes sense to view our work through a postcolonial lens. While postcolonial analysis has its inherent limitations as no single theoretical approach can totally capture the complexity of meanings and consequences of the colonial and postcolonial encounter, we nevertheless maintain its resonance to our current endeavor. We also are acutely aware of the dialectics emanating from the book's use of Western constructs as these are interpreted and applied in Asian contexts.

Spivak's (1988) and Gramsci's (in Hall, 1996) disenfranchised, invisible "subaltern" classes reverberate throughout the book as it gives voice to Southeast Asia and community stakeholders, groups that have been relegated to the fringes of the dominant CSR discourse.

Postcoloniality according to Memmi (1968) is a historical condition punctuated by visible oscillations between freedom and the "concealed persistence of unfreedom." It is the tenacious cultural, political and psychological hold of the colonial past on the postcolonial present. Postcolonial theory therefore deals with the lingering dynamics of subordination and dominance and of historically determined hierarchies of values and experiences of the oppressor and oppressed (Gandhi, 1998).

It has been argued that postcolonial perspectives uncover the colonialist and imperialist legacies that have influenced contemporary culture and discourse. As Dutta and Pal (2011, p. 198) explained, postcolonial theory aims to "decolonize the mind at political, economic, and cultural level" with the hopes of achieving a fair and just world.

In proposing the application of a postcolonial lens to public relations scholarship, Munshi and Kurian (2005, p. 515) highlighted the need to expose extant theory and practice as coinciding "with a dominant, largely Western, model of economic growth and development."

Postcolonial approaches to public relations enable scholars to look beyond the dominant Western discourse and identify opportunities for transforming the production of knowledge. Dutta (2010) reasons that a postcolonial lens is appropriate in public relations research because it enables scholars to examine how

> (a) practices serve the interest of transnational corporation and free market logic; (b) public relations theories maintain the hegemony of West-centric articulations of modernity and development and (c) resistive politics among subaltern sectors seek to transform global inequities in knowledge production, participation and resource distribution.
>
> (Dutta, 2010, p. 3)

Using a postcolonial lens also illuminates the power dimensions in public relations scholarship. As Munshi (2005) noted, that while multiculturalism is acknowledged in public relations, power is often neglected in the study of public relations.

> Although the recognition of multiple identities, cultures, and ethnicities is a crucial first step in acknowledging demographic, ideological, and cultural diversities in the world, postcolonial scholars argue that global relationships and interactions have to be understood in terms of existing power differentials within and among nations, institutions, and organizations.
>
> (Munshi, 2005, p. 631)

The study of representation is also interested in what **is** said and what is **not** said (Young, 2001, p. 391). Moreover, postcolonial feminist scholar Spivak (1999, pp. 256–257) offers two views: representation as 'speaking for' and representation as 're-presentation' or portrayal. She hypothesizes that 'speaking for' is a political representation of the masses, who cannot speak for themselves while 're-presentation' is a cultural practice such as in art and philosophy. At the same time, Spivak (1999, p. 257) further cautions about "intellectuals or theorists who claim to 'represent' (speak for) the oppressed group" when their very position as scholars and intellectuals reflect privilege.

In the spirit of reflexivity within this postcolonial approach, both authors are cognizant that we are privileged researchers, whose inquiries and interpretations may not fully represent those of our informants. As Philippine-born migrants, who have settled in developed countries, we however are constantly in touch and visit family and friends in the region who help us understand particular worldviews and communicative practices. We therefore are attempting to leverage our 'position of privilege' in bringing to the fore the voice of a region that otherwise may be drowned in the cacophony of Anglo-Celtic accents.

This book also draws from the critical–cultural school of thought with its examination of power relationships and power dimensions. Since critical-cultural theory looks at society as a whole and in its historical specificity, we find the approach useful with efforts to derive explanatory, practical and perhaps normative ways to transform the contemporary discourse around strategic communication/public relations and CSR with a sharper focus on them as agents of change in communities and countries in the developing world that are grappling with poverty, environmental degradation, corruption, health and other problems.

As a form of social enquiry, critical–cultural thus seeks human emancipation from oppressive structures and relations. Horkheimer (1982) wrote critical cultural aims "to liberate human beings from the circumstances that enslave them" (p. 244).

One unifying element in CSR, public relations and community development is communication, and culture undergirds all human communication. This locates CSR and PR within the "culture industries," which critical–cultural scholars argue are sources of domination (Horkheimer & Adorno, 2001). Communication and all other symbolic cultural systems not only shape how we see reality, they also establish and perpetuate social hierarchies and power relations. According to Bourdieu (1987) cultural symbols, resources, processes and institutions embody functions and interests that reproduce stratified social distinctions, class-based power and privilege. These status hierarchies are competitive in nature and are therefore sites of struggle and conflict among individuals and groups as they exercise and legitimize their power.

While scholars have critiqued CSR for the power imbalances (Banerjee, 2007; Munshi & Kurian, 2007); as a PR invention (Frankental, 2001); as irresponsibility (Tench, Sun & Jones, 2012), or as a false promise of development (Frynas, 2005), it remains to be a field that needs further exploration particularly in the context of the ASEAN region. Hopkins (2007) acknowledges that views on CSR range from skepticism, optimism and pragmatism. Skeptics, he argues, see CSR as an attempt to "slow down real change, defer criticism or as slick public relations hype" (Hopkins, 2007, p. 11). Businesses and NGOs see their 'unholy alliance' as diminishing their respective purposes of 'profit maximization' on one end, and 'principles' on the other. Both parties agree, however, that "CSR efforts become stop gap measures that effectively take governments off the hook" (Hopkins, 2007, p. 11). He further notes that optimists view the relationships as 'paradigm-changing developments' that set the stage for positive action while pragmatists recognize that all agendas are self-serving and that both businesses and NGOs seek to enhance their standing and influence (Hopkins, 2007, p. 11).

In arguing for an alternative and critical approach to the study of CSR, Prieto-Carrón and her colleagues offer an agenda that they hope will facilitate deeper examinations of "what CSR can or cannot achieve in improving the conditions of workers and communities in the Global South", which include the relationship between business and poverty reduction, the impact of CSR initiatives, power and participation in CSR and governance dimensions of CSR (2006, p. 979).

These concerns about CSR combined with how PR, through its stakeholder and in particular community engagement practices, interact with community development activities in developing countries are the focus of this inquiry. We are particularly intrigued by the proposition that genuine community engagement involving participatory approaches of consultation, negotiation and co-construction, and enactment of CSR programs is vital for sustainable community development and social change. Moreover, our fieldwork discovered a strong community engagement practice within the community development context.

## Our research approach

Given the above background, questions that frame the entries in this book include: What political, economic and cultural factors affect how CSR and PR are defined in each country? How does globalization and technological advances influence how each country makes sense of CSR and PR? To what extent are Western models of CSR hindering or enhancing the country's ability to improve social services for its citizens? Aside from governments' lack of infrastructure and resources, are there other factors triggering the spread and dependency on corporate-funded community development projects? What models of corporate social responsibility are being used in each country? How do cultural values shape, promote or impede the practice of corporate social responsibility and public relations?

With the diversity represented by the countries in our study, we also thought it is important to examine how some Southeast Asian countries interpret and enact corporate social responsibility. Furthermore, various sectors in each country may have a different worldview of corporate social responsibility. For example, an executive from a transnational company may adopt how CSR is defined by the Western-based head office. How would 'local' practitioners adapt or adopt Western-style practice, if at all? How would community residents in which these companies operate view CSR? Do disadvantaged communities see CSR projects as their way out of poverty? Or do they view CSR projects as a necessary evil? More important, do they think CSR as a form of exploitation by rich, private and mostly Western multinationals?

Is public relations in the region seen as an instrument for community development? Or is community development used as a tool of public relations? From the perspective of nation building and capacity building, how do international agencies work with national and local governments and corporate enterprises? Whose agendas dominate these multi-sectoral, public–private partnerships?

To answer these questions, we employed a qualitative and interpretive approach that involved in-depth interviews, focus group discussions and ethnographic observation. We wanted to directly listen and hear the voices of the community stakeholders, NGOs, the corporate and government representatives (where possible), who have been part of a CSR program in the key countries selected. Our commitment to understanding the "human, organizational and societal communication and experiences" by our "close engagement with the voices and perspectives" of our informants in their social contexts reflects the qualitative research approaches highlighted by Daymon and Holloway (2011, p. 106). In particular, we critically examined the persuasive strategies employed by CSR and communication managers, the interactions and negotiations between community stakeholders and corporate communicators seeking to co-construct meaning, and attempted to discover the hidden voices of silent minorities, who may have been ignored in the discussions.

We used the interpretive approach in our attempt to "understand how people in everyday natural settings create meaning and interpret the events of their world" (Wimmer & Dominick, 2000, p. 103). We draw from Daymon and Holloway's (2011) position on interpretive approaches:

> Interpretivists do not seek to predict behavior or affirm laws that govern communication relationships. Instead they attempt to uncover the meanings by which people understand their own experiences, behaviors and communication. In effect, interpretive researchers prioritize understanding over scientific explanation. The notion that research can and should be 'objective' is considered illusionary by interpretive researchers, who regard themselves as a subjective, research tool, 'disturbing' not only the research setting through their presence and communication interactions, but also through introducing their own interests, biases and preferences into their construction of the research question itself.
>
> (p. 102)

For this research project, we combined purposive and convenience sampling approaches. Purposive sampling is used when individuals representing certain criteria are deemed appropriate to provide knowledge and experience (Rubin & Rubin, 2005). The criteria used to identify participants for this project included their roles in the organization/community, their involvement in a CSR program, their willingness and availability to participate in interviews or focus group discussions. In some research sites, it was more expedient to undertake focus group discussions given the limited time and resources of the researchers. For instance, in Indonesia, Thailand and the Philippines, the researchers had to travel around two hours, one way, to reach the villages.

## *Selection of countries*

We selected six of the ten member countries in the ASEAN primarily because we felt they had some developed programs in public relations and corporate social responsibility relative to Laos, Cambodia, Myanmar and Brunei. Except for Vietnam, which joined the ASEAN in 1995, the five countries were part of the original ASEAN membership in 1967. We also considered the level of economic development in the country and their status as 'developing' countries. While Singapore belongs to the group of 'developed' countries, we included it to explore whether there is indeed a different focus for CSR in more developed economies in the region.

18  *Introduction*

### Selection of organizations

For each country, we identified one local and one multinational corporation which had a CSR program that focused on community development (e.g., education, health, livelihood). It was important to explore if there were any similarities or differences between local or multinational ownership of companies with regard to their perceptions and enactment of CSR as ownership had been previously identified as an important factor in CSR practice (Waddock, 2008; Yudarwati, 2011). Local companies were defined as privately owned by individuals from the host country. Multinational companies refer to private-sector organizations, whose headquarters are based outside the host country and operate in multiple countries.

Once these organizations were identified, we contacted them by email and requested for their participation often through their communication, PR or CSR departments. In some instances, we approached the organizations through personal contacts of the researchers or their friends. This approach was undertaken for efficiency as personal contacts are almost necessary to get access to organizations and community groups. Our local research partners provided valuable assistance in identifying organizations with active CSR programs that we approached.

### Selection of respondents

We asked the participating organizations if we could interview at least five respondents based on the following breakdown:

1 Most senior CSR representative.
2 Most senior public relations manager (if not the same as the CSR person).
3 Community representative: NGO contact (if applicable).
4 Community representative: Formal or informal village leader.
5 Community representative: Local government unit/representative.

A total of 70 informants participated in the research. Table 1.2 presents the summary breakdown of the respondents in this study for each country and group.

The field work occurred between November 2014 and August 2016 and combined in-depth, face-to-face interviews, focus groups, participant observation and website analysis. Given the cultural diversity and the nature of the approach, the field work was adapted based on expediency. Some organizations were extremely helpful in coordinating with their community partners to accommodate our site visits. Most of the site visits were limited to a day so interviews and focus groups had to be scheduled. In some instances, the community partners were invited to attend the corporate offices to allow us to interview them without us having to travel far.

Despite criticisms of interview data being too subjective, difficult to replicate, problems of generalization and lack of transparency (Bryman, 2001),

Table 1.2 Breakdown of respondents by country/group

| Country (No) | MNC (Org 1) | Community | NC (Org 2) | Community |
|---|---|---|---|---|
| Indonesia (16) | Food and beverage<br>CEO (1)<br>CSR Team (3)<br>Community relations manager (1) | FGD:<br>farmers (3) + NGO (1)<br>Interview:<br>NGO partner (1) | Heavy equipment<br>CSR manager (1)<br>CSR officer (1) | Interviews:<br>Two NGOs<br>Two school principals |
| Malaysia (8) | | | University | Interviews:<br>Three community org officers<br>Two community members<br>Two elementary school teachers<br>1 university officer |
| The Philippines (20) | Manufacturing<br>CEO (1)<br>Plant manager (1)<br>CSR officer (1) | FGD:<br>Community beneficiaries (6)<br>Interview: Mayor + asst (2) | Conglomerate<br>Corporate communications manager (1)<br>Head, foundation (1)<br>CSR manager (1) | Interviews:<br>General manager, Cooperative (1)<br>FGD: School principals (5) |
| Singapore (7) | Hospitality<br>CSR manager (1) | Observation | Financial services<br>Head, foundation (1)<br>CSR team (2) | Interviews:<br>Social enterprise owners (3) |
| Thailand (8) | Food and beverage<br>CSR manager (1)<br>Property developer<br>CEO (1) | Community member (1) | Manufacturing<br>CSR manager (1)<br>Community relations manager (1) | Interviews:<br>Village head (1)<br>NGO partner (1)<br>Community leader (1) |
| Vietnam (11) | Financial services<br>CEO (1)<br>CSR manager (2) | Manager, charity organization (1)<br>NGO partner (1) | Food manufacturing<br>Executive team (3)<br>Business consultancy<br>CEO (1) | School principal (2) |

these seemed minor to the advantages of acquiring rich, sensitive and nuanced information from key community and organizational informants. Using a semi-structured interview guide, we conducted almost 100 hours of interview. During the field work and data collection phase, we worked with local research partners, who were fluent in the local dialect and familiar with the local culture, and helped us with translation and interpretation. To this end, most of the quotes from our community representatives that are presented in the book are English translations from the local language (Bahasa Indonesia, Mandarin, Tagalog, Thai and Vietnamese). In addition to providing translations, our local research partners were extremely valuable in helping us understand the nuances and local contexts of each research site.

## Structure of the book

The book is structured by country while focusing on a particular theme. Each book chapter starts with an abstract and presents each country's historical, economic, political, cultural and social contexts. We also provide a brief state of CSR and PR practice and scholarship in each country so that readers understand the various stages of development in the disciplines. The chapter then presents the key themes generated from the research interviews and focus groups. Because the book aims to provide a voice to the community stakeholders, their perspectives will be given priority. However, we also included the corporate perspective to provide a context for the CSR program and to enable a more balanced analysis.

The book is divided into eight chapters. Chapter 1 explores the connections between our key concepts and frames the approach of the book through this Introduction. Chapter 2 discusses how CSR's focus in Indonesia has progressed from nation building to sustainability. Chapter 3 presents how CSR and PR discourse in Malaysia reflects advocacy and aspirational talk. Chapter 4 examines CSR through the prism of social development, disaster resilience and philanthropy in the Philippines. Chapter 5 looks at the rise of social enterprises as inclusive channels of social responsibility in Singapore. Chapter 6 highlights CSR as a form of sustainable community development and risk mitigation in Thailand. Chapter 7 focuses on the blurring of boundaries and the transactional approaches of CSR and PR in Vietnam. Chapter 8 draws the discussion together with a summary of the common narratives, a proposed model of understanding the various powers that influence the perceptions, design and enactment of CSR, and a section on implications for practitioners.

In summary, this book hopes to contribute to the roles public relations and communication practitioners play in meaningful social transformation.

## Notes

1 http://hdr.undp.org/sites/default/files/2015_human_development_report_1.pdf
http://data.worldbank.org/indicator/NY.GDP.MKTP.KD.ZG?end=2015&start=1961&view=map
2 http://hdr.undp.org/sites/default/files/2015_human_development_report_1.pdf

## References

Aras, G. & Crowther, D. (Eds.). (2010). *NGOs and Social Responsibility*. Bingley, UL: Emerald Group Publishing Limited.

Arenas, D., Lozano, J. M. & Albareda, L. (2009). The role of NGOs in CSR: Mutual perceptions among stakeholders. *Journal of Business Ethics*, (88), 175–197.

ASEAN Socio Cultural Community Blueprint 2025 (2016). Retrieved from: http://asean.org/?static_post=asean-socio-cultural-community-blueprint-2025

Bardhan, N. & Weaver, C. (2011). *Public Relations in Global Cultural Contexts: Multi-paradigmatic Perspectives*. New York: Routledge.

Bartlett, J. (2011). Public relations and corporate social responsibility. In Ihlen, D., Bartlett, J. & May, S. (Eds.). *The Handbook of Communication and Corporate Social Responsibility*. West Sussex: Wiley-Blackwell.

Bator, M. & Stohl, C. (2011). New partnerships for a new generation of corporate social responsibility. In Ihlen, O., Bartlett, J. & May, S. (Eds.). *The Handbook of Communication and Corporate Social Responsibility* (pp. 399–421). Oxford: Wiley-Blackwell.

Blowfield, M. & Frynas, J. (2005). Setting new agendas. Critical perspectives in Corporate Social Responsibility in the developing world. *International Affairs*, 81 (3), 499–513.

Bourdieu, P. (1987). What makes a social class? On the theoretical and practical existence of groups. *Berkeley Journal of Sociology*, 32, 1–17.

Bruning, S. D. & Ledingham, J. A. (1999). Relationships between organizations and publics: Development of a multi-dimensional organization-public relationship scale. *Public Relations Review*, 25, 157–170.

Bryman, A. (2001). *Social Research Methods*. Oxford: Oxford University Press.

Burchell, J. & Cooke, J. (2013a). Sleeping with the enemy? Strategic transformations in business-NGO relationships through stakeholder dialogue. *Journal of Business Ethics*, 113 (3), 505–518.

Burchell, J., & Cook, J. (2013b). CSR, co-optation and resistance: the emergence of new agonistic relations between business and civil society. *Journal of Business Ethics*, 115 (4), 741–754.

Carroll, A. (1991). The pyramid of corporate social responsibility. *Business Horizons*, (34), 39–48.

Chapple, W. & Moon, J. (2005). Corporate social responsibility (CSR) in Asia: A seven-country study of CSR web site reporting. *Business & Society*, (44), 415–441.

Clark, C. (2000). Difference between public relations and corporate social responsibility. An analysis. *Public Relations Review*, 26,(3), 363–380.

Coombs, T. & Holladay, S. (2012). Fringe public relations: How activism moves critical PR toward the mainstream. *Public Relations Review*, 38 (5), 880–887.

Curtin, P. A., Gaither, T. K. & Ciszek, E. (2015). Articulating public relations practice and critical/cultural theory through a cultural-economic lens. In L'Etang J.,

McKie D., Snow N., & Xifra J. (Eds.). *The Handbook of Critical Public Relations* (pp. 41–53). Abingdon, Oxon UK: Routledge.

Daymon, C. & Holloway, I. (2011). *Qualitative Research Methods in Public Relations and Marketing Communications.* Abingdon, Oxon UK: Routledge.

Dutta, M. (2010). *Public relations, materiality, and marginalization in a global context: A postcolonial interrogation.* Paper presented at the International Communication Association Conference, Singapore.

Dutta, M. J. (2015). A postcolonial critique of public relations. In Curtin, P. A., Gaither, T. K. & Ciszek, E. (Eds.). *The Handbook of Critical Public Relations* (pp. 248–260). Abingdon, Oxon UK: Routledge.

Dutta, M. J., & Pal, M. (2011). Public relations and marginalization in a global context. In Bardhan, N. & Weaver, C. K. (Eds.). *Public Relations in Global Cultural Contexts: Multi-Paradigmatic Perspectives.* New York: Routledge.

Edelman. (2015, Retrieved 5 June 2015). Trust Around the World. *2015 Edelman Trust Barometer.* From www.edelman.com/2015-edelman-trust-barometer/trust-around-world/

Federation of Community Development Learning, (2009). www.fcdl.org.uk/archive/community-development-2009/.

Frankental, P. (2001). Corporate social responsibility—A public relations invention? *Corporate Communication: An International Journal,* 6 (1), 18–23.

Frynas, J. G. (2005). The false developmental promise of corporate social responsibility: evidence from multinational oil companies. *International Affairs,* 81 (3), 581–598.

Fukukawa, K. (Ed.). (2010). *Corporate Social Responsibility in Asia.* Abingdon, Oxon UK: Routledge

Fukukawa, K. (Ed.) (2014). *Corporate Social Responsibility and Local Community in Asia.* London: Routledge.

Gandhi, L. (1998). *Postcolonial Theory. A Critical Introduction.* New York: Columbia University Press.

Hagen, R. (2002). Globalization, university transformation and economic regeneration: A UK case study of public/private sector partnership. *The International Journal of Public Sector Management,* 15 (3), 204–218.

Hall, S. (1996). Race, articulation and societies structured in dominance. *Black British Cultural Studies. A Reader.* 16.

Hallahan, K. (2004). "Community" as a foundation for public relations theory and practice. In Kalbfleisch P. J. (Ed.). *Communication Yearbook* 28 (pp. 232–279). Mahwah, NJ: Lawrence Erlbaum Associates.

Heath, R. L. & Ni, L. (2010). Community relations and corporate social responsibility. In Heath R. (Ed.). *The SAGE Handbook of Public Relations* (pp. 557–568). Thousand Oaks, CA: SAGE Publications.

Herrera, M. E. B. (2011). *Corporate social responsibility in Southeast Asia: An eight country analysis.* Manila: Ramon V. del Rosario Sr. Center for Corporate Social Responsibility, Asian Institute of Management.

Hirschland, M. J. (2006). *Corporate Social Responsibility and the Shaping of Global Public Policy.* New York: Palgrave Macmillan.

Holtzhausen, D. & Voto, R. (2002). Resistance from the margins: The postmodern public relations practitioner as organizational activist. *Journal of Public Relations Research,* 14 (1), 57–84.

Hopkins, M. (2007). *Corporate Social Responsibility and International Development: Is Business the Solution?* London: Earthscan.

Horkheimer, M. (1982). *Critical Theory* (p. 188) New York: Continuum.
Horkheimer, M. & Adorno, T. (2001). The culture industry: Enlightenment as mass deception. *Media and Cultural Studies: Keyworks.* 71–101.
Hutton, J. (1999). The definition, dimensions, and domain of public relations. *Public Relations Review,* 25 (2), 199–214.
Ife, J. (2013). *Community Development in an Uncertain World.* New York: Cambridge University Press.
International Development Jobs & Consulting Opportunities. www.devnetjobs.org/default.aspx
Jamali, D. & Keshishian, T. (2009). Uneasy alliances: Lessons learned from partnerships between business and NGOs in the context of CSR. *Journal of Business Ethics,* (84), 277–295.
Kelly, K. (2001). Stewardship: The fifth step in the public relations process. In Heath R. (Ed.). *Handbook of Public Relations.* Thousand Oaks, CA: Sage.
Kruckeberg, D. & Starck, K. (1988). *Public Relations and Community: A Reconstructed Theory.* New York: Praeger.
Ledingham, J. A. (2001). Government-community relationships: extending the relational theory of public relations. *Public Relations Review,* (27), 285–295.
Ledingham, J. A., & Bruning, S. D. (2001). Managing community relationships to maximize mutual benefit: Doing well by doing good. In Heath, R. L. (Ed.). *Handbook of Public Relations.* Thousand Oaks, CA: Sage Publications.
Leeper, K. A. (1996). Public relations ethics and communitarianism: A preliminary investigation. *Public Relations Review,* 22 (2), 163–179.
L'Etang, J. (1994). Public relations and corporate social responsibility: Some issues arising. *Journal of Business Ethics,* 13 (2), 111–123.
Malena, C. (1995). *Working with NGOs: A Practical Guide to Operational Collaboration between the World Bank and Non-Governmental Organization.* Washington, DC: World Bank.
Memmi, A. (1968). *Dominated Man: Notes Toward a Portrait.* New York: Orion.
Munshi, D. (2005). Postcolonial theory and public relations. In Heath, R. (Ed.). *Encyclopaedia of Public Relations,* (2), 631–632. Thousand Oaks, CA: Sage.
Munshi, D. & Edwards, L. (2011). Understanding 'race' in public relations: Where do we start and where should we go? *Journal of Public Relations Research,* 23 (4), 349–367.
Munshi, D. & Kurian, P. (2005). Imperializing spin cycles: A postcolonial look at public relations, greenwashing, and the separation of publics. *Public Relations Review,* (31), 513–520.
Newell, P. & Frynas, J. G. (2007). Beyond CSR? Business, poverty and social justice: An introduction. *Third World Quarterly,* 29 (4), 669–681.
Prieto-Carrón, M., Chan, A., Thomsen, P. & Bhushan, C. (2006). Critical perspectives on CSR and development: What we know, what we don't know, and what we need to know. *International Affairs,* 82 (5), 977–987.
Public Relations Society of America. http://apps.prsa.org/AboutPRSA/public relationsdefined/, Retrieved May 31, 2017).
Rubin, H. J. & Rubin, I. S. (2005). *Qualitative Interviewing: The Art of Hearing Data.* 2nd edition. Thousand Oaks, CA: Sage Publications.
Samii, R., Van Wassenhove, L. N. & Bhattacharya, S. (2002). An innovative public private partnership: New approach to development. *World Development,* 30 (6), 991–1008.
Shukla, A. (2010). First official estimate: An NGO for every 400 people in India. *The Indian Express.*

Sison, M. D. (2016). Diversity and inclusion in Australian public relations: Towards a multiple perspectives approach. *Media International Australia*, 160 (1), 32–42.

Sison, M. D. (2017). Communicating development: Towards strategic, inclusive and creative approaches. In Battersby, P. & Roy, R. (Eds.). *International Development: A Global Perspective on Theory and Practice.* UK: Sage.

Spivak, G. (1988). Can the subaltern speak. In Williams, P. & Chrisman, L. (Eds.). *Colonial Discourse and Post-Colonial Theory. A Reader.* New York: Columbia University Press.

Spivak, G. C. (1999). *A Critique of Postcolonial Reason: Toward a History of the Vanishing Present.* Cambridge, MA: Harvard University Press.

Sriramesh, K., Kim, Y. & Takashi, M. (1999). Public relations in three Asian cultures: An analysis. *Journal of Public Relations Research*, 11 (4), 271–292.

Sriramesh, K. & Vercic, D. (2002). International public relations: A framework for future research. *Journal of Communication Management.* 6 (2), 103–117.

Sriramesh, K., Ng, C. W., Ting, S. T. & Wanyin, L. (2007). Corporate social responsibility and public relations: Perceptions and practices in Singapore. In May, S. K, Cheney, G. & Roper, J. (Eds.). *The Debate over Corporate Social Responsibility* (pp. 119–134). US: Oxford University Press.

Tench, R., Sun, W. & Jones, B. (2012). Corporate social irresponsibility: A challenging concept. *Critical Studies on Corporate Responsibility, Governance and Sustainability,* (4), 3–20.

Vercic, D., Grunig, L. & Grunig, J. (2001). Global and specific principles of public relations: Evidence from Slovenia. In Culbertson, H. & Chen, N. (Eds.). *International Public Relations: A Comparative Analysis.* New York: Routledge.

Visser, W. (2008). Corporate social responsibility in developing countries. In Crane, A., McWilliams, A., Matten, D., Moon, J. & Siegel, D. (Eds.), *The Oxford Handbook of Corporate Social Responsibility.* (pp. 473–479). Oxford: Oxford University Press.

Waddock, S. (2008). Building a new institutional infrastructure for corporate social responsibility. *The Academy of Management Perspectives*, 22 (3), 87–108.

Waldman, D. A., Sully du Luque, M., Washburn, N. & House, R. J. (2006). Cultural and leadership predictors of corporate social responsibility values of top management: A GLOBE study of 15 countries. *Journal of International Business Studies,* (37), 823–837.

Welford, R. (2004). Corporate social responsibility in Europe and Asia: Critical elements and best practice. *Journal of Corporate Citizenship,* 13 (31-47).

Wilcox, D., Cameron, G. & Reber, B. (2014) *Public Relations: Strategies and Tactics.* New York: Pearson.

Wilson, L. J. (1996). Strategic cooperative communities: A synthesis of strategic, issue management, and relationship-building approaches in public relations. In Culbertson, H. M. & Chen, N. (Eds.). *International Public Relations.* (pp. 67–80). Mahwah, NJ: Lawrence Erlbaum Associates.

Wimmer, R. D., & Dominick, J. R. (2000). *Mass Media Research: An Introduction* (6th edn). Belmont: Wadsworth Publishing Company.

Yaziji, M. & Doh, J. (2009). *NGOs and Corporations.* Cambridge: Cambridge University Press.

Young, R. J. C. (2001). *Postcolonialism: An Historical Introduction.* Oxford: Blackwell Publishers.

Yudarwati, G. (2011). The enactment of corporate social responsibility and public relations practices: Case studies from the Indonesian mining industry. Doctoral dissertation, RMIT University, Melbourne, Australia.

# 2 Beyond nation building
## CSR and sustainability in Indonesia

### Country context

*Historical, political and economic context*

Indonesia's colonial history started with the Dutch in the early seventeenth century. Japan then occupied the islands from 1942 to 1945, and the country declared independence shortly before Japan's surrender. It took four years, however, for the Netherlands to grant sovereignty in 1949.

The country's fledgling parliamentary democracy ended in 1957 when its first president, Soekarno, imposed martial law and established a "Guided Democracy." Soekarno, who spent two years in a Dutch jail and lived in exile for eight years for challenging Dutch colonialism, relinquished power to Suharto after an alleged communist-led coup in 1965. From 1967 to 1998, President Suharto's "New Order" government presided over Indonesia but was toppled in 1998.

The following year legislative elections took place ending four decades of authoritarian turmoil and ushering Indonesia's status as the world's fourth most populous democracy with a population of 260.6 million (July 2017 estimate), the world's largest archipelagic state, the world's largest Muslim-majority nation and the world's tenth largest economy in terms of purchasing power parity (CIA World Fact Book, 2017; World Bank, 2017).

Indonesia also holds the distinction as the largest economy in Southeast Asia. As an emerging middle income country and a G-20 member, it outperformed its regional neighbors by growing its economy during the global financial crisis. Since 2012, however, it experienced an economic slowdown mostly due to the end of the flourishing commodities export market. Its current president, Joko Widodo, who rose to political power via the slums and is the first president elected outside of Indonesia's political and military regime, has instituted economic reforms to stimulate investments through a friendlier regulatory climate (Emont, 2016).

Today, about 32 percent of the country's labor force is in agriculture, 47 percent in services and 21 percent in industry. The unemployment rate in 2016 stood at 5.6 percent with 11 percent of the population living below the poverty line. Indonesia spends the least among the ASEAN countries selected for this study on health at 2.8 percent of its GDP and second to last on education at 3.3 percent of GDP (CIA World Fact Book, 2017).

Rich in natural resources, Indonesia is a major world producer of tin, coal and copper and is generating revenues from minerals such as gold and diamonds. Its forests teem with hardwoods, which all bode well for the nation's economic buoyancy. However, with the absence of or spotty implementation of social or business ethics coupled with systemic corruption nurtured by crony and military-led capitalism, there are concerns that environmental devastation and labor problems will continue unabated (Kemp, 2001).

## *Cultural and social context*

Indonesia is a socially and culturally diverse nation. Some 16 ethnic groups reside in the archipelago although four dominant ethnicities occupy geographical enclaves in the inner islands. The Javanese, which account for 40 percent of the population, live in Central and East Java, while the second largest cultural group the Sundanese representing 16 percent of the population is found in West Java. The Madurese, on the other hand, are in Madura and in East Java and the Balinese in Bali. Of the more than 700 languages/dialects, Javanese is the most widely spoken. Bahasa Indonesia, a modified form of Malay, is the official language but English as well as Dutch are also spoken. Among the country's six religions Islam dominates at 87 percent so it is not surprising that religion would play an active role in the nation's early economic modernization especially when Islam expanded and spread in northern Java (Groeneveldt, 1960; van Leur, 1967).

As a collectivist society, Indonesians, in general, maintain strong kinships based on patrilineal, matrilineal or bilateral descent. Seniority and elder status are held in high esteem and people generally prefer stability and predictability although in some cases would leave everything to Allah. Traditional roles for women and men are adhered to with clear separation between women's public and private spheres. Women's roles are restricted mainly to the private arena, thus idealizing the role of women as mother, wife and household manager (Suryakusuma, 1996).

This heavily patriarchal society, however, had its first woman president in 2001 thrusting gender issues and politics in the public agenda. Indonesian women today who account for half of the nation's population still struggle with poverty, injustice and violence. The government and the community still routinely ignore women as political and economic agents in Indonesian society. Although slow in coming, there have been recent changes, however, in gender-related customs brought about by "rising education, rising marriage age and self-arrangement of marriages, and rising labor force participation rates" among Indonesian women (Zulminarni, 2001, p. 30).

Cultural and religious rituals, which are a mixture of age-old traditions brought in by the early migrants to the Western influences of the Dutch colonialists and Portuguese traders, abound in the country. While Indonesians adhere to practices such as consensus building through consultations or "*musyawarah*" shared responsibility and mutual assistance or "*tolong menolong*" (del Rosario, 2011), they are not particularly known for thinking ahead and this short-term perspective has reportedly impeded growth of the insurance planning industry (Mangundjaya, 2013).

Many Indonesian scholars have expressed concern about balancing culture, politics and economics for the nation's future development (Garna, 1977; Soedjatmoko, 1967; Soemardjan, 1962). Saddled with perennial issues of high unemployment, widespread poverty, corruption, inadequate infrastructure, complex regulatory environment, unequal resource distribution among its regions and terrorism, the country has set its sights on consolidating democratic gains after four decades of authoritarianism. It continues to implement economic, financial and educational reforms and has worked toward reducing corruption, reforming the criminal justice system, addressing climate change and controlling infectious diseases. Its current president, Joko Widodo, seeks to develop the country's maritime resources and increase its electrical power generation capacity since his election in 2014 (CIA World Fact Book, 2017; World Bank, 2017).

## *Public relations practice*

Public relations in Indonesia evolved over five historical periods: the formation of national identity (1900–1942), Japanese Occupation (1942–1945), Soekarno's Guided Democracy (1945–1966), Suharto's New Order (1966–1998) and the Reformation (1998 to date). The national identity period was inhabited by nationalist movements that employed propaganda techniques to resist Dutch colonialism and to build identity and public support. Of course, the Dutch used counterpropaganda to influence international public opinion and stem the momentum of the Indonesian independence movement (Kuitenbrouwer, 2014).

When the Japanese took over, they also used PR/propaganda techniques to gain the country's trust and support for Japan's economic and political programs in the archipelago. The use of one-way PR in the form of propaganda continued during the Soekarno regime as the country's first president tried to persuade Indonesians and the world of his government's legitimacy. But it was during Suharto's 32-year rule when the use of publicity and government propaganda really kicked into high gear as Indonesia's second president and longest-serving ruler promoted his development programs while suppressing freedom of speech and the press.

The fifth and final era is the Reformation period, which is characterized by the broader democratization of the country and the advancement of communication technologies that allowed opportunities for PR to thrive while facing challenges from the proliferation of public movements that demanded accountability, fairness and transparency (Yudarwati, 2014). During this period, Indonesia was led by four presidents Habibie (1998–1999), Wahid

(1999–2001), Megawati (2001–2004) and Yudhoyono (2004–2014). These leaders had varying levels of success in managing their public image with the first three on the lower end of the PR success spectrum (Dhani, 2004) and Yudhoyono on the upper end (Dhani, Lee & Fitch, 2015). Yudhoyono hired the Inke Maris & Associates PR agency to manage his campaign that catapulted him to the presidency in the 2004 direct general elections. His successor is the social-media savvy President Widodo, who is a media darling. Widodo has enjoyed high approval ratings with his reform-oriented political platform that includes free healthcare and education for the needy and a less corrupt, less complex bureaucracy (Abidin, 2013). Despite PR's great strides especially in the political arena, the long legacy of one-way propaganda dominates Indonesia's PR practices to this day (Yudarwati, 2014).

## Corporate social responsibility

CSR appeared in the lexicon of Indonesian business in the early 1990s (Lellahom & Rachman, 2017), gained traction the following decade and even seeped into the political agenda with calls for the initiation of a regulatory CSR framework for corporations (Achda, 2006). In fact, the Indonesia government has mandated CSR and has required companies to address social and environmental issues. The law, 2007 Corporate Law No. 40, includes CSR under Article 74 which specifies that "companies doing business in the field of and/or in relation to natural resources must put into practice Environmental and Social Responsibility" (Waagstein, 2011, p. 459). While the law sparked considerable debate over the nature of CSR—specifically whether it is voluntary or mandatory, it helped institutionalize CSR in Indonesia (Waagstein, 2011). In addition to the laws, the government also has programs to encourage CSR, including the national environmental reporting initiative called the Industrial Performance Rating Program (del Rosario, 2011).

Another key influence in the development and acceptance of CSR in Indonesia is religion. The Islamic practice of purification through alms giving or "*zakat*" provides the foundation for charity/philanthropy for corporations and individuals alike. Indonesia also has a *Zakat* Management Law that allowed the establishment of collection agencies such as the Badan Amil Zakat National (del Rosario, 2011).

CSR reporting is often seen as an expression of corporate commitment toward social development in Indonesia. In their CSR study of seven Asian countries, Chapple and Moon (2005) found that 12 percent of Indonesian companies did not have corporate websites in the early years of the new millennium. The country was dead last in terms of penetration and extent of CSR reporting as measured by the number of pages devoted to CSR reporting by the top 50 Indonesian companies. To be fair, the study did mention the assumption that "the emergence of CSR is a function of economic and social development" (p. 418) and that Asia as a whole lagged behind the West in CSR penetration (Welford, 2004). In April 2006, however, the Indonesia

Global Compact Network was launched in Jakarta where 22 companies and organizations committed to promote and implement the UN Global Compact Principles (www.indonesiagcn.org/about_us/overview).

A source of optimism with regard to the future of CSR in Indonesia is the growing influence of Islam, which emphasizes honesty and integrity in business. Kemp (2001) noted that Mohammed, a successful trader himself, considered honor and trust as integral to trade and business. Organizations such as the Indonesia Business Links are also leading the charge in ensuring more transparency and social accountability as well as other responsible business practices (del Rosario, 2011).

Obstacles however remain. The patriarchal, top-down management structures in both multinational corporations and domestically owned firms in Indonesia tend to impede the development of active consultation among equals, which is a *sine qua non* for sustainable CSR. Another deterrent is the push and pull dynamics of tradition and innovation, which is evident in Indonesia's modernizing urban areas while the country's business, political and community culture remains tradition bound. This tendency combined with endemic corruption and a brand of capitalism that is inextricably linked with its history of colonialism and imperialism characterized by a complex and enduring web of patronage and consolidation of power and wealth in the country's political and military elite are factors affecting the legitimacy and utility of CSR in the Indonesian context (Kemp, 2001; Wibisono 1991).

Despite the spirit of *reformasi* in government and industries, which definitely is another ray of hope on the CSR horizon, observers say that "it has not yet reached a sufficient level to bring lasting change to what is, in essence, a feudal industrial relations system reflecting *priyayi* ideals" (Kemp, 2001, p. 8; Rossouw, 1998). *Priyayi* refers to the aristocratic court culture emanating from Java's large sultanates. This gulf between the masses and the powerful elite is certainly anathema to the social motivation implicit in CSR. In Indonesia, the lingering contention seems to be—does CSR pave the way for political development or does CSR require the existence of a stable democratic government and a civil society to be effective?

The next section attempts to answer some of these questions as we present the results of our fieldwork. While we intend to privilege the voices of the community in this book, we first present the corporate voice to provide context to the programs and interactions with the community stakeholders through CSR.

## CSR perceptions

This section discusses the various perceptions of corporate social responsibility from the perspectives of corporate, community and NGO representatives. The previous literature had highlighted that differences in perspectives are influenced by whether the organization is foreign or locally owned (Kuada & Hinson, 2012; Muller, 2006).

## From nation building to inclusive business

The national company we examined in this study is in the heavy equipment industry and has been a major player in the country's nation building efforts. It has a 45-year history and operates out of the capital city of Jakarta. The corporate website highlights its vision as providing solutions and providing 'job opportunities to as many Indonesians as possible.' In addition to providing employment, the company claims that they also provide individuals with opportunities for skills training, knowledge and building character. They frame the corporate citizenship efforts, which is their term for CSR, around four pillars: Education, Environment, Health and Compassionate Relief.

One of the two corporate respondents whose role is "CSR and Corporate Communication Manager" (INDNC1) suggested that ad hoc philanthropy previously characterized the company's approach to CSR. The shift towards a more strategic CSR occurred around 2010. As a private, family-owned company, they were not obligated to adhere to global standards as such but they proudly stated that their annual reports include principles of the UN Global Compact.

She indicated that the company's CSR focus was largely dictated by the founder whose mission was "to give opportunity to as many Indonesians as possible to have good and qualified jobs". To this end, the programs are focused on education through various programs that include school renovations, scholarships for teacher training, and scholarships for student placements in vocational high school and polytechnics.

> The founder really has passion (*sic*) on education. He established the program. This is the second generation. Our CEO is the second generation. He is the youngest son of the founder. When we celebrated the 40th anniversary of (the company) he created the 40-elementary-school program. So, the number 40 came from (the company).
>
> (INDNC1)

The respondents reported that the CEO initiated the scholarships for teachers as he believed that teachers provide good role models for students. Teachers are well positioned to help students focus on character building as they see this as critical to nation building. The character building approach to education is believed to also help the sustainability of the business because "when you do a wrong thing, then it will jeopardize the business itself" (INDNC1).

The multinational company in this study manufactures products in the food and beverage industry. Initially a business started by a local Indonesian in 1973, the company has been owned by the Europe-based multinational since 1998.

Quite expectedly, respondents from this multinational company revealed definitions and knowledge about CSR that align with the Western-based literature. For example, our INDMNC respondent mentioned terms such as 'multiple stakeholder approach', 'shared value' and 'sustainability.' Interestingly, however, the respondent intimated that prior to becoming a multinational, the company was an Indonesian company whose founder believed in 'giving back to the community' while the founder of the foreign company believed that "the responsibility of the company does not stop at the factory gate" (INDMNC1). This 'shared understanding' enabled the company's transition from a domestic to a multinational company. Following this transition was an evolution of the company's perception of what CSR is. Previously, the company saw CSR as purely philanthropic, however, since the shift the company has evolved to more recent iterations of CSR such as 'inclusive business.'

She clarified the misconceptions about CSR in Indonesia. She believed that most people in Indonesia associated CSR with planting trees, which is why she preferred not to use the term. She said that,

> To me, I say it regularly to my friends, to my family, to my relatives that if you don't understand CSR, just stick it simply that CSR is responsible, it's corporate social responsibility. You are a responsible company when you use your energy responsibly, when you treat your employees decently, you are a responsible company when you treat your neighbors decently, if you have a healthy relationship with your vendors, distributors. So, in any kind of action that you do as a company, actually, that can be called corporate social responsibility. So, it does not have to be planting trees, it does not have to be co-sponsoring a sports event but from those little things that you do....

## *Livelihood and enterprise development*

Among community stakeholders, CSR was seen as a critical intervention in improving their livelihood and income generation opportunities. While there was a palpable acknowledgement of pride and local wisdom, the community stakeholders we met revealed how their lives have changed since they developed partnerships with the private sector through CSR programs and activities.

One of these activities is the INDMNC's support for farming communities outside Jakarta to shift from traditional farming to more organic farming methods.

For instance, the farming cooperative in Indonesia highlighted how the CSR program of INDMNC enabled their community to work together and collaborate. They recounted how prior to the intervention, the farmers would work individually.

> There was no togetherness. Praise to Allah, after the CSR program took place we started to organize meetings and exchanged ideas. Moreover, when there was a comparative study visit, like what the KWT (Kelompk Wanita Tani/Women Farmer's Group) did, we gathered together, having comparative study visit to Bandung or Subang. We felt unity among us. So, we greatly thank the CSR team, we really felt the impacts (of their presence). Moreover, now agricultural sector is prioritized.
> (Farmer, Indonesia)

They acknowledged that their farming was rather traditional and limited. One of the farmers said that previously, all they ever did was to farm, "Like planting on this date, harvesting on that date. But we didn't know our income and expenditure." There was no record of their inputs and outputs.

The secretary of the cooperative echoed the above statement of his colleague.

> It's true that our main attention has been to agriculture as we are all here farmers. We have been learning how to farm since childhood. Our main livelihood here is related to plantation and farming. But, since we didn't manage it professionally, investors haven't done any intervention, we managed our farming business traditionally. So, we didn't have any record on harvesting, no record on crops, no records on when the planting starts and so on. Really local, really traditional. After that (INDMNC) came in. You know (INDMNC) is still quite new here, just since three years ago. One year after its presence (INDMNC) started its CSR programs for areas around its factory. Praise to Allah, after its presence we were invited to get together and divided into groups, given guidance, invited for comparative study visit. We started to feel motivated to follow farmers, who were already successful.

Interestingly one of the things that motivated the farmers was the success of the women's farmer groups (referred to as KWT). Following KWT's lead in their village, which had 600 members, the male farmers formed their own cooperative, which has since included four villages.

> And praise to Allah, after the management was improved we are able to produce organic rice. No chemicals. We used to be like, choked by the price of chemical fertilizer because its price kept skyrocketing, but now we make our own organic fertilizer. We also try to market our products. We have sent them to Bandung, Jakarta and joined exhibitions to market our products. Now we are trying to prepare the schedule of planting up to harvesting. And insya Allah (God willing) we are heading to forming our production cooperatives. So, the cooperative will collect our products, manage them, and market them.

The women's cooperative also developed their own line of products called *Sayur Organik Pekarangan* (Home-Garden Organic Vegetables). Together they "made bamboo shelves for planting onions, egg plants, chilies. Some of the produce are used for household needs and we take the rest, pack them and market them through exhibitions or small shops." They also made rice crackers, which enable the women to generate income.

The only female farmer present during the meeting also expressed that since planting vegetables, garlic and chilies in her home garden, she was able to provide pocket money for her school children. She mentioned that if they wanted to make sambal (seasoned chili paste) or vegetable dishes, they did not need to go to the grocery stores.

The study also revealed that the role of women in improving the livelihood prospects of the community cannot be underestimated. The women in the community were more open to new ideas, especially in exploring new ways of generating household income, and were more entrepreneurial. In addition, the women were instrumental in convincing the male farmers to work with the corporate representatives in developing new technology.

While the men and women in the community were given the same materials and training at the same time, the women seemed to make progress more quickly in growing herbs. The CSR team provided everyone with polybags, fertilizer and training on planting and making liquid fertilizer to prevent pests. However, the women were

> diligent to take care of the small scale. It's unlike men, we did the planting in the field and left it. Three weeks later we came to the field again. But women at home? When there were just small grasses (in the polybags) they would clear them. When the plants looked a bit withered, they would water them. Eventually the result was better and the men were interested in following them.

The women grew herbs in their front yard which meant savings as they did not have to buy them from the grocery anymore. Moreover, they also used the herbs for medicinal purposes.

> When their children are having fever, for instance, they can take some herbs in front of their houses. If they want to make sambal, they can pick some chilies in front of their houses. So, there is no need to go to Puskesmas (Community Health Center) too often. The data said, I also happen to work at the People's Welfare Division, dealing with community health, the data shows that there is a decrease.

According to the male village leader, the local CSR liaison suggested that "the women plant specific herbs, which they can immediately use when their children get sick. So, there is a 'living pharmacy' in front of their houses."

The local CSR person agreed that it was easier to talk with the women.

> If I may speak frankly, talking to the men here is much more difficult than the women. They [women] understand quickly. Once you told them to plant, the next day they will start planting. The men usually make too many excuses, while the women will immediately give it a try. That's why garbage program, farming, and planting herbs are more done by the women.

He further explained that engaging the women started with home visits and through dialogues, the female villagers expressed their needs and their willingness to develop projects.

> From their answers, we then asked further questions: So, if you want that, what can you actually do? And they answered: well, we can do this, we can do that. Then we suggested: ok, let's do it. Then they asked: where can we get the money? I answered: I cannot give you money, but I can offer you facilities. So, we asked them to save money from collecting garbage. So, the garbage containing plastics, metals, etc. was collected. They collected the garbage and we picked it every week and paid them. From the sale of garbage ([or recycling] they started to make cookies and other snacks. We also brought their products to some exhibitions.

The social impact of this intervention also enabled the women to stay in their homes and farming communities while generating additional income for their families. According to our informants, women in their community used to leave their homes and families to work in Jakarta or abroad to look for additional income, and this brought about other social issues. Thus, the ability for women to generation additional income without having to leave their families and their homes was welcomed by the community.

In a later section, we discuss the processes of persuasion that shifted the farmers' mindsets from resistance to collaboration.

### Capacity building through education and training

While improving the livelihood capacity of the farming community is one CSR approach, another is geared toward building capacity through education and training. As mentioned earlier, the INDNC's CSR approach is strongly geared towards "character-based education." They are a signatory to the UN Global Compact.

The CSR and communication manager explained that despite being an authorized dealer of a foreign enterprise, the company's status as a family-owned business enabled it to design its CSR programs according to its own context. The education focus is underpinned by the founder's deep belief that education and character are essential in the success of the nation.

In the video shared with us during the interviews, the founder highlighted their rationale for investing in educational scholarships:

> I believe that to make Indonesia better has to start from a better education, developing qualified human resources (?) finally Yayasan ... was born. A foundation that provides scholarship for its employees, who have good accomplishment and are less affluent.

The company's CSR education activities focus on two areas: elementary school programs and coops for vocational school training. The elementary school program is an integrated program that includes school building repair or renovation, teacher training and scholarships for children from low-income families. These schools undergo a selection process, in concert with the partner NGOs and the Ministry of Education, because the company wants the selected schools to commit to the program over the three-year period of the 'sponsorship'. Part of the program investment is an expectation that the school community that includes the teachers and parents works together toward improving the learning outcomes of the students. After the three-year period, the partner NGOs assess whether the schools have met their performance indicators and they then recommend whether funding is continued or allocated to another school. In some instances, a school has achieved its outcomes and are able to proceed without further funding support from the company. So, another eligible school, which is more 'in need' is identified and provided support.

The company also offers cooperative placements for students in nine vocational high schools and six polytechnics. This coop program involves placements in the school while receiving on-the-job training (OJT). Because of the prospect of training and eventual employment with the company, placements are very competitive. Hundreds of applicants compete for a maximum of 24 slots every year. As the company informant revealed,

> The most beneficial thing here is the job training. You know that vocational schools require OJT; it's quite difficult to find industry for them. So (the company) is committed to spending time with the mentors ... for three months' time in three semesters.

The coop program demonstrates an instrumentalist approach to CSR in its alignment to the company's recruitment needs. Not only are the students targeted for potential recruitment by the company, most of the selected schools are located near the company's local plants. By providing the training while the students are in high school, the training costs are reduced. According to the CSR and Communication Manager,

> The benefit is we have qualified technicians. After they graduate we hope that we have technicians having qualified skills so that we don't

> have to train them from zero. That's the most beneficial thing because giving training like this is quite expensive for us. Let's say they have to spare minimum of 11 weeks for training, that's quite expensive for us. But if it's done during the three years at school we hope that we will have qualified graduates.

They however emphasized that the broader goal of the CSR program goes beyond recruiting their own people.

> Our goal is creating qualified technicians in the heavy equipment industry. And aside from the learning process, we give training assistance for teachers, students, OJT, literature on basic machine operations, and some basic equipment literature and also guest lectures. The guest lecturers are from (company) and they are not substitute teachers. So, the role of the teachers is to teach. So, the guest lecture is for enrichment. It's a *kuliah umum* (public lecture) on safety, environmental control, general knowledge of heavy equipment industry.

When asked later about where the selected schools were located, the company admitted that except for one school, most are located in big city areas close to a local branch.

> Yes. Most of them, yes. But in one area it's not really close to our branch. Like in Pekanbaru. We have a vocational school in Dumai, which is a four-hour drive from Pekanbaru.... Yes. But most of them are located in big cities. In ring 1.

While the Asian financial crisis affected Indonesia's employment rate, it has slightly recovered although urban unemployment remains higher than rural unemployment with more people moving to cities in search of jobs (www.indonesia-investments.com/finance/macroeconomic-indicators/unemployment). Therefore, locating schools in big cities may be a means to addressing this high unemployment especially among young males.

The corporate representatives also divulged that their company pioneered the area of 'heavy equipment studies.' They said that "Between 1996–2000 there were no standardized curricula. Then (INDNC) involved itself and contacted the Ministry of Education. They supported this kind of program." This way, the curriculum was matched with the industry's needs while meeting the government's education requirements. They worked closely with the government to get the latter's support in building the workshops, the classes and they helped in terms of the focus on the 'soft skills' and the curriculum.

Interestingly, even their employee volunteer program is focused on 'teaching.' Employees in their 40 locations are encouraged to go on rotation and volunteer to teach in the local schools. For example, "Last year we did thematic teaching, which was dental health, like teaching how to brush the teeth and the danger of using drugs." Coordinated by the head office, schools would be advised when it was their turn to teach.

> We have the teaching materials, and that now we can learn about teaching dental health. It is up to them (the branch) who will be listed as volunteers. They can do it by turn or anyone can sign up as volunteers. One class is usually taken care by three or four volunteers to teach the material.

These classes are scheduled on Saturdays and delivered in the offices to limit the travel of the employees. The respondents intimated that even "C level" executives volunteer. Given that they are not trained teachers, most of the sessions are what they called 'sharing or informal teaching.' This approach to employee volunteering straddles SDG priorities pertaining to community health and education.

## Partnership and engagement processes

Engaging partners is a critical CSR element. Understanding how corporations select their community partners is as important as knowing how community stakeholders select their corporate partners. As the next section will demonstrate, partnerships often involve corporations, NGOs, universities, local government and local community leaders.

### *Social mapping and partner identification*

Approaches to community engagement vary between organizations and often the difference lies in the extent of resources appropriated to CSR and sustainability programs. In INDMNC, for example, under the office of the corporate secretary are Sustainable Development, Government Relations and Corporate Communication. The CSR teams fall under the Corporate Communication unit.

The sustainable development manager is responsible for assisting the CSR team to develop design-specific programs alongside respective program managers. Programs may be in the areas of sanitation and hygiene, sustainable agriculture, waste management and local economic development.

Our informant is the sustainable development manager responsible for local economic development and his responsibility is to design the strategy to implement livelihood programs for areas around the company's plants. While he is based in the head office, he often meets with his potential partners outside of the capital city where it is more convenient to establish relationships.

In designing programs, he identifies the criticality of undertaking an assessment through social mapping. Social mapping involves "identifying stakeholders, potential issues, risks" and "identifying their expectations, their needs, their strengths, weaknesses, their roles and responsibilities in the community." Whether the program is initiated by the plant or by the head office, they enact participatory approaches by collaborating with an NGO or university partner and the community. The mapping exercise helps them identify who the appropriate partner is.

> Let's say, it's an NGO or university or another institution we tried to map and bring them to discussion. Usually as a program manager, we're not just sitting and then receiving proposals, but it begins with an idea, just me like, if I'm having idea about what I'm going to build in the next year about the program I will come to several parties, let's say several NGOs, make a brainstorming with them and then I share my idea, I encourage them to share, if I'm doing like this, what about your opinion. If we have a good discussion, they have their own uniqueness, their own idea and then I will tell them if I'm having a call for proposal would you like to join, like that so it is for me it is better than waiting for a proposal then we cannot do anything about, but it is better that we have clear discussion before and then they know my ideas and I know their ideas.
> (INDMNC)

In considering the appropriate NGO to partner with, he indicated that the NGO's strength and its fit to the community surrounding the plant is a key factor. Other criteria used in selecting the partner NGO include: (1) willingness to accept corporate assistance, (2) competence in the field, (3) good communication and project management skills and (4) local community base. He indicated that his previous NGO background has helped him to engage with NGOs despite their differences in ideology. While he still uses his old networks, some of whom are actively against the private sector, he confided that he maintained good relations with them by "treating them as my teacher, my master because I was learning from them."

He also revealed that although they work with community-based organizations (CBO), they prefer to work with "professional NGO, because that's the difference, because if they're CBO then they will represent the community but if they're NGO, they will try to facilitate between the community and us."

Moreover, he suggested that working with NGOs enables them to "develop a grand design, which consists of two or three years working like that and then from this NGO we could empower the CBO so they can increase their capacity." With CBOs, the activities tend to be of smaller scale and tend to be ad hoc.

Nevertheless, in their assessment activities, they encourage participation from the communities through various activities:

> Sometimes we're doing an assessment before and try to encourage people to get involved in the organizational management of the CBO, and then

we're doing some participatory workshop, which is also discussing their own result of their participatory mapping so we try to be as participatory as we can because we're working with the community, we're working with the NGO. Why we chose this participatory approach, because I think it's the best way we can absorb the voice of the people; we still have a negotiation with them, the company has to support this or you can just manage it by yourself. Sometimes we encourage their own contribution to increase their ownership. At the first stage the company puts, let's say some start-up fund and then the second year we try to reduce or we try to reallocate this fund in other forms let's say the physical infrastructure like production machine or something like that.

He admitted, however, that engaging with communities took time and required local actors to facilitate the entry before they can gain the communities' trust.

For the national company, selection processes occurred on two levels: which NGOs to work with and which communities to assist. For instance, for the educational program, the Indonesian national company initially selected two NGOs to work with. The selection was primarily based on trust, accountability and expertise. This Indonesian NGO (INDNGO1) had a nationwide reach and was well known for multiple advocacies that assist the poor in four areas: education, health, economy and social development. Upon the direction of the CEO, it was deemed more professional "because when he gave (to) charity, he got a report from [NGO]."

While the two NGOs shared in the pre-assessment activities, they later divided the work according to their respective strengths. NGO1 looked after the infrastructure and school renovation component, while NGO2 focused on teacher training and scholarship activities. Although they worked together with this company, it was clear that NGO1, which had more resources was able to generate more impact on the program. According to INDNC,

> (NGO1) puts its representatives for one whole year to assist the schools and teachers, monitor the progress of the teachers' competence in the schools. In regards to (NGO2) they didn't have representatives.

The company's selection criteria for NGO partners included the NGO's professionalism, resources and reputation. The company's representative diplomatically explained that they learned from their experience in phase 1 that NGO2's expertise was not the right fit. While NGO1 had a more extensive skillset that ranged from project management to mentoring, the CEO's imprimatur also influenced the decision to choose this NGO.

The selection of 'beneficiary' schools, on the other hand, was a combined effort of the company's representatives and the two NGOs. The company's directive was to find schools within the first ring which they can assist in a tangible manner. Initial assessment involved the local company representative visiting various villages around the plant and surveilling which school buildings may need repair.

The target schools needed to meet certain criteria: (1) accreditation by the Ministry of Education and (2) the number of teachers.

From the school teacher's point of view, the identification of his school was a "Fortune comes from Allah." As the head of the school committee, he was largely responsible for organizing the rehabilitation of the school. He narrated how his collapsed school building discouraged students to enroll, or even attend classes. With the intervention of the INDNC and their NGO partner in repairing the school building and improving the teaching program, the enrolments increased from 12 to 68 students. The school community which included the parents have since taken on fund-raising and building improvement activities while the company's scholarship assistance finished after three years.

## Power relations

### *From resistance to collaboration*

Corporations entering local communities often face various potential responses, but quite naturally it is wariness of the 'newcomer.' Many local communities likely to have rich resources especially in developing countries have been known to resist these initiatives through different means, and for different reasons. In these contexts, the means of resistance may range from more subtle approaches such as making it difficult to set up meetings with the local leader or to more active community protests.

The reasons for the resistance may also vary, from the outright disapproval with the project or as a means of negotiating a better arrangement. Some of these acts of resistance have also resulted in violence (Kraemer, Whiteman & Banerjee, 2013) while others have brought about more benefits and concessions for the local community members to be impacted by the 'intrusion' (Bebbington et al., 2011). However, there are also cases where initial resistance evolved to collaborative partnerships. The farming community in this case is one good example.

The entry of INDMNC1 into the farming community near the plant experienced initial resistance. Quite expectedly, when INDMNC1's representative first came to the town, the community leaders were immediately suspicious. He represented a company that was building a nearby plant that was perceived to use their previous water resources. As a farming community, water was extremely vital for their irrigation and general household use. According to the CSR team member, he faced resistance from everyone in the village.

> … there were men who were against us when we first came here. This village was strong, so it was quite risky here…. Even the village chief was against us. Leaders of the village, village police were also against us.

*Beyond nation building*    41

He also surmised that the drought at that time exacerbated the farmers' fear that the company plant will affect their supply. But he also wondered about other questions regarding the company's choice of the particular location to set up their plant.

> Maybe because INDMNC1 put their investment here. So, there was drought issue. They were afraid that there would be insufficient water supply for their fields. Well, maybe there was someone who blew up the issue. No one knows who blew it up.
>
> (CSR team member)

One of the groups that expressed the most vocal resistance was the young farmers. He recounted their initial stance.

> Because we were representing the youth, ma'am. So, we were the most fierce.... You see, I was part of the Karang Taruna (Youth Group), and all we knew was that our water would decrease if the company used it. That's all. But then we got explanations from (INDMNC1) that the water being taken is from a certain depth, not the surface water. We finally understood. After that the company team came here through women; yes, that's right, led by the current village chief. I was still under the authority of the former village chief.
>
> (Farmer, youth group leader)

The community relations representative recounted that in one village, the chairperson of the GAPOKTAN[1] (Association of Farmers' Groups) "rejected us. They made blood thumbprints" to demonstrate their resistance. This resistance was in fact led by another farmer, who apparently considered the corporate intervention into organic farming a threat to his own operations.

Instead of confronting the resistance head on, the company representatives applied several strategies to engage the communities. The strategies included:

1  Familial approach.
2  Mentoring and learning approach.
3  Identifying the role of women.

The respondents in the farming community all agreed that the 'familial' approach was helpful in convincing the communities to open their minds to organic farming. The community relations team admitted that the climate before was not as positive as it is now, "where you see people smile and other happy things." The familial approach involved informal meetings, some of which were undertaken secretly, mentoring farmers about organic farming. At one point, the village police stopped the meetings so they avoided working with the local authorities.

> We didn't start at the village administration level. We started from families. Then other families would join us (when we were meeting with one family). So, we started the process from the families instead of from the village administration level, not from the village chief. If we started from the village chiefs, I am sorry to say, they could have had his (*sic*) own interests. We didn't want to involve such interests. We directly visited houses, like houses of particular community figures. Finally (nearby village) joined. The chairperson of the GAPOKTAN could accept us. The key was (the chairperson of GAPOKTAN) was developing a new variety of rice, which was pandan wangi rice. We did support him. So, it would become organic pandan wangi rice. It would be more expensive. We used that opportunity to intervene.
>
> (CSR team member)

This was echoed by the youth representative, who said that

> with our familial approach, praise to Allah, most farmers joined us in our farming program. It's true that one of the challenges was to change their mindset that existed for generations; to change them from conventional farmers to organic farmers who use compost they make.

They also apply the familial approach in resolving conflict. For instance, when nearby villages questioned the resources provided to one village, some jealousy occurred.

> Here we rely on familial relation. So, we discuss all problems like a family. It's true that there was a bit friction with another village, while the core of the organization is here. The chairperson is here, the office is here. We tried to meet them with our mentors, the chairperson and we talked to discuss the problem.
>
> (Farmer, youth group leader)

One way they resolved the conflicts was to ask each village to focus on particular types of farming. For example, one village's specialty will be on chicken farming, the other will focus on goats, or sheep, and another will specialize in fishing. This avoided competition.

The informal meetings included training sessions on various skills such as planting herbs, making liquid fertilizer and waste management. Once the CSR team was accepted by the village leaders, they developed more formal skills training sessions that included marketing and business plans. The village leaders were also invited and funded for comparative study visits. These study visits also engendered confidence and pride in the successful farming communities.

While the research team (comprising two female academics) spoke to a room full of mostly male farmers and one female farmer, the influence of women in the community was mentioned several times by our respondents.

One of the informal leaders was a female community member, who convinced others to take on home gardening. As the CSR team member indicated, "lots of her constituents supported organic farming. And praise to Allah she was finally elected as the village chief. We finally have an umbrella for developing this program in this village."

The role of women in engendering change and development work has been identified in other studies (Grosser & Moon, 2006; Pimpa & Phouxay, 2017). The subtle and more informal approaches to community engagement adopted by the CSR team reflect approaches long enacted by community development practitioners (Ismail, 2009).

All the respondents agreed that the engagement process took a lot of time. When the interviews were conducted in 2015, they were on their third year in the project. The CSR team mentioned that their programs are often only for three-year periods but the farmers do not seem keen to end the partnership at that time. While the farmers acknowledge that they have learned a lot from the training and mentoring they have received especially in terms of organizing themselves, they admit their own limitations.

> We are hampered by human resource issues, ma'am, because the education level of countryside people like us, sorry to say, is only senior high school or below. Meanwhile, the CSR team's education is above senior high school. At that point, we still need guidance and mentoring from them. Maybe in terms of workforce we have more than enough. But in terms of management, business, bookkeeping we are not ready to do it alone…. But, like I said, we, including myself, are still far from hope of understanding how to market so that we can compete in this globalization era. If we just have to sell our products to our neighbors, that's out of question. We knew it well already. But I will make efforts so that (cooperative) can sell its products to other country if possible. That's our wish.
>
> (Farmer, head of farmer's cooperative)

The CSR team however reported that the cooperative has already sold their vegetable sweets overseas, but through a middle person, who brought the products to Dubai.

## *Community engagement and negotiation*

Engagement with communities undoubtedly takes time and various strategies. Critical to these two cases, and other cases in other countries, is the involvement of a local person, who is known to the community stakeholders. This person, who may be referred to as a 'boundary spanner,' straddles between the employing organization and the community group.

In the farming community's case, the company employed a local villager to be part of the CSR team. He provided the local insights and intelligence to assist the company in their engagement strategy. In addition, the female village leader became an influential person in the village's adoption of the CSR programs. In the case of the school teacher, who also headed the school committee, he was identified by both the INDNC and NGO representatives to be the linchpin to enacting the program.

These processes however also involved long-winded negotiations, which were instrumental in generating genuine partnerships. As one of the farmers reported,

> For instance, when the CSR team, or mentoring team, had an idea, then we did the planning together, made schedule together, because we have ugrem system, voluntary collective work. So, when our chairperson said, "Ok, we clean the fields on Friday." Then all of the members would gather on Friday for voluntary work cleaning the fields, then we would have another voluntary work for planting the seeds. We always do everything together, voluntarily.
>
> (Farmer, leader of cooperative)

The farmers and the CSR team described a 'synergetic' relationship that reflected "togetherness, unity and friendship."

> Usually they asked us what we wanted or what we needed. Then we would tell them what we wanted or needed, they would evaluate our ideas, then they would hold another meeting to discuss them. Then they would say that when they had the budget they would will do it. Once we told them that we needed plamet (?) for planting tobacco seeds. Praise to Allah, lots of hitachi (?) were provided by the Forest and Plantation Agency.
>
> Maybe in terms of mentoring we have got more than enough. The hardship we had at the beginning is nothing compared to the knowledge we now have. The knowledge is beyond the hardship. However, in terms of welfare and income, we are developing ma'am. Well, we are just starting. But we are not thinking of that. All of us here think that the most important thing is to start the planting first. The most important thing is we learn. At the end of the day we can consume our products too.

For the INDNC, the targeting of schools that needed repair and curriculum support avoided potential conflicts from the community. In effect, the school's vulnerability and 'ripeness' for assistance, may have been exploited by the company. As the example showed, the school had been neglected for many years and the funding support and training provided through the NGOs and the national company enabled the community to generate pride and improve its overall condition.

## Beneficiary–benefactor relationship

One of the questions we raised in both cases was at what point will the CSR program and support cease? Like with many CSR programs, there are start and end dates for projects, and budgets are reviewed annually as resources may be allocated to other communities or other priorities.

While most CSR programs espouse a goal of empowerment, many of the 'beneficiaries' expressed a wish for continued support. It must be noted that both companies do not provide cash directly to the individual community members. The 'support' is often administered through skills training, mentoring and provision of materials. As stated earlier, the approach is to enable the community to generate funds for themselves through knowledge transfer. If the communities have specific projects in mind that require resources, they have to develop proposals (in which they are also given specific training) and submit them to the CSR team for assessment.

> Praise to Allah, from the garbage sale we manage the money for business, because the CSR didn't teach us, the administration board, about how to get money. They didn't give us the money, but the knowledge. If we want to learn, that's good. When it comes to money, they never gave us fresh money directly. They expected us to be independent, to strive, and praise to Allah we're heading to that point, because as (CSR team members) said there is a demand of 30 tons organic rice, is that right, sir?
> (Leader, farmer cooperative)

While power is often ascribed to the funding organization, these cases highlight how 'power' can be exercised through the community's ability to challenge, or delay, the engagement process. Given that these two companies identified these 'success stories' also demonstrated that the notion of beneficiaries also applies to the corporation. Undoubtedly the positive relationship between the corporations, the NGOs and the local communities through the CSR programs generated goodwill, mitigated risks and eventual costs, and improved their reputation within the local region and beyond.

## Summary

The introduction of social responsibility expectations into Indonesian corporate law has undoubtedly influenced both national and multinational corporations' approach to CSR. Moreover, the UN's Sustainable Development Goals (SDGs)—and the earlier version Millennium Development Goals—have urged private-sector organizations to actively integrate sustainability into their businesses. Indonesia is no exception. However, we cannot dismiss the importance of cultural influences in how 'top-down' mandates are interpreted by local organizations and communities.

Some cultural influences on the CSR programs of the two corporate entities discussed in this chapter are unsurprising. Clearly, religion played an important role as the early CSR came in the form of corporate philanthropy. Indonesia has Zakat-mandated policies so the philanthropic aspect of CSR actually shows the synchronization of the country's regulatory and religious expectations. The strong religious undercurrents are also quite obvious from the narratives in which Allah is praised for all good things that happened not just from the beneficiary communities' point of view but also from the CSR team.

In addition to the religious influence, the country's authoritarian legacy is still apparent in the CSR realm. One of the companies reported that in the past it viewed CSR as purely philanthropic. With Zakat-related mandates, it is plainly obvious that the traditional sources of power in the country, which are the state and the religious authorities, are still very much at play in the way CSR is practiced in Indonesia.

Indeed, the CSR experience of the two companies tells us that some things have changed but some have remained the same. For instance, Indonesia just like other ASEAN countries is known to be a collectivist society but for some reason farming became an individual activity until CSR-initiated programs had the farmers working together in coops. And quite refreshingly, women, who historically were relegated to the role as home makers now assumed leadership roles such as village chief. They also exercised strong influence in the adoption of organic farming methods and recycling and their entrepreneurial skills as well as their ability to improve health and livelihood are convincingly demonstrated in the beneficiary communities.

The strategic inclusion of culturally sensitive approaches to neutralize resistance or curb suspicion such as the adoption of the familial route instead of the village administration level was very clever. It worked because Indonesians have strong familial and kinship ties. The approach also circumvented local village politics and potential gender and identity politics.

Giving agency to the villagers and other marginalized populations such as women also led to a smoother transition from tradition to innovation, and demonstrated resourcefulness through herb-growing, cash-producing waste management, school repair and educational facilities enhancement.

The stories shared by the communities and CSR respondents likewise point to the crafty mitigation of the risk of dependency and therefore the promotion of CSR sustainability because 'support' took the form of skills training, mentoring and provision of materials. Knowledge transfer undoubtedly was an empowering and long-lasting intervention. Careful vetting of NGO and community partnerships through social mapping as well as fortitudinous negotiations that allowed for subtle and more graceful power shifting among the parties involved were also key elements in this Indonesian brand of CSR.

Most important, this is also a tale of successful public–private partnerships to address gaps in education, livelihood generation, health and sustainable agriculture in a country plagued by high unemployment and poverty. This is CSR at work in the developing world.

## Note

1 GAPOKTAN refers to the *Gabungan Kelompok Tani* or umbrella farmers' association.

## References

Abidin, I. (2013). Populist politician Joko 'Jokowi' Widodo has used PR and social media to great effect to build support by highlighting his common touch. IPRA 2013 www.ipra.org/news/itle/a-new-style-of-political-communications-engaging-with-the-people-of-indonesia/

Achda, B. T. (2006). The sociological context of corporate social responsibility development and implementation in Indonesia. *Corporate Social Responsibility and Environmental Management*, 13 (5), 300–305.

Bebbington, A., Humphreys Bebbington, D., Bury, J., Lingan, J., Muñoz, J. P. & Scurrah, M. (2008). Mining and social movements: struggles over livelihood and rural territorial development in the Andes. *World Development*, 36 (12), 2888–2905.

Chapple, W., & Moon, J. (2005). Corporate social responsibility (CSR) in Asia: a seven-country study of CSR web site reporting. *Business & Society*, 44, 415–441.

del Rosario, R. (2011). Corporate social responsibility in Southeast Asia: An eight-country analysis. Research Report, Makati, Philippines: Asian Institute of Management.

Dhani, R. (2004). *Presidential Communication Management: From Soekarno to Megawati*. Jakarta: Pustaka LP3ES.

Dhani, R., Lee, T. & Fitch, K. (2015). Political public relations in Indonesia: A history of propaganda and democracy. *Asia Pacific Public Relations Journal*, 16 (1), 22–36.

Emont, J. (2016). Visionary or cautious reformer? Indonesian President Joko Widodo's two years in office. *Time Magazine*. October 20.

Garna, J. (1977). The sociocultural strategy of development in Indonesia. Gasco, Bandung.

Groeneveldt, W. P. (1960). *Historical Notes on Indonesia and Malaya*. Bharata, Jakarta.

Grosser, K. & Moon, J. (2006). The role of corporate social responsibility in gender mainstreaming, *International Feminist Journal of Politics*, 7 (4), 532–554.

Ismail, M. (2009). Corporate social responsibility and its role in community development: An international perspective. *The Journal of International Social Research*, 2 (9), 199–209.

Kemp, M. (2001). Corporate social responsibility in Indonesia. Quixotic dream or confident expectation? *Business and Society Program Paper No. 6*. Geneva, Switzerland: United Nations Research Institute for Social Development.

Kraemer, R., Whiteman, G. & Banerjee, B. (2013). Conflict and astroturfing in Niyamgiri: The importance of national advocacy networks in anti-corporate social movements. *Organization Studies*, 34 (5–6), 823–852.

Kuada, J. & Hinson, R. (2012). Corporate social responsibility (CSR) practices of foreign and local companies in Ghana. Thunderbird. *International Business Review*, 54 (4), 521–536.

Kuitenbrouwer, V. (2014). Propaganda that dare not speak its name. International information services about the Dutch East Indies, 1919–1934. *Media History*, 20 (3), 239–253.

Lellahom, M. & Rachman, D. (2017). CSR Landscape in Indonesia: The past, present and the future. http://sustainablesquare.com/evolution-csr-landscape-indonesia/.

Mangundjaya, W. (2013). Is there cultural change in the national cultures of Indonesia? www.iaccp.org/sites/default/files/melbourne_pdf/Melbourne%20Proceedings.pdf#page.

Muller, A. (2006). Global versus local CSR strategies. *European Management Journal*, 24 (2), 189–198.

Pimpa, N. & Phouxay, K. (2017). CSR and women empowerment: A comparative study of women in the mining community in Thailand and Lao PDR. *ASEAN Journal of Management and Innovation*, 4, 145–154.

Rossouw, G. (1998). Establishing moral business culture in newly formed democracies. *Journal of Business Ethics*, 17, 1563–1571.

Soedjatmoko (1967). Indonesia: Problems and opportunities [and] Indonesia and the World. *Australian Outlook*, 21, 263–286.

Soemardjan, S. (1962). *Social Changes in Jogjakarta*. New York: Cornell University Press.

Suryakusuma, J. (1996). The state and sexuality in New Order Indonesia. In Sears, L. J. (Ed.). *Fantasizing the Feminine in Indonesia* (pp. 92–110). Duke University Press, Durham and London.

The World Fact Book. (2017). Indonesia. Central Intelligence Agency. www.cia.gov/library/publications/the-world-factbook/geos/id.html.

van Leur, J. C. (1967). *Indonesian Trade and Society. Essays in Asian Social and Economic History*. The Hague: W. van Hoeve Publishers.

Waagstein, P. (2011). The mandatory corporate social responsibility in Indonesia: Problems and implications. *Journal of Business Ethics*, 98, 455–466.

Welford, R. (2004). Corporate social responsibility in Europe and Asia: Critical elements and best practice. *Journal of Corporate Citizenship*, 13, 31–47.

Wibisono, C. (1991). *Proceedings of an International Seminar on Issues of Development*, Institute Teknologi Bandung and Goethe Institute. Bandung. August 20–22.

World Bank. (2017). http://databank.worldbank.org/data/Views/Reports/ReportWidgetCustom .asp. ReportName=CountryProfile&Id=b450fd57&tbar=y&ddy&inf=n&zm=n&country=IDN

Yudarwati, G. (2014). Indonesia. In Watson, T. (Ed.). *Asian Perspectives on the Development of Public Relations: Other Voices*. London: Palgrave Macmillan.

Zulminarni, N. (2001). Indonesia: In the middle of unsolved crisis. Instituto Mundo-Control Ciudadano. www.onlinewomeninpolitics.org/indon/crisis.htm.

# 3 CSR/PR discourse as advocacy and aspirational talk in Malaysia

## Country context

*Economic and historical context*

Malaysia was formed in 1963 although its early beginnings go back to the fifteenth century in Melaka (Malacca) located in the shipping routes, which led to its emergence as a major trading port. Its history from the fifteenth to eighteenth century is dotted with various colonial occupations from the Chinese to Portuguese, to Dutch, British and then back to the Dutch. Japan briefly occupied the country from 1942 to 1945. In 1948 Melaka and Penang became the federated states of Malaya until their independence from Britain in 1957 (Liu & Abraham, 2002).

Malaysia's early years as an independent state have been challenging as it was besieged by a communist insurgency, a conflict with Indonesia and a lingering territorial clash with the Philippines involving Sabah. Its longest-reigning prime minister of 22 years, Mahathir bin Mohamad, succeeded in diversifying its export-dependent economy to include manufacturing, services and tourism although its main exports, particularly of electronics, oil and gas as well as palm oil, still account for a significant share of its economic growth.

This upper middle-income country has come a long way from being a producer and exporter of raw materials to an attractive destination for investments in technology and the services industries. Malaysia is the nineteenth largest exporter in the word (Lu & Castka, 2009). The government under Najib Razak reduced Malaysia's dependence on exports by boosting domestic demand, which accounted for more than half of its GDP. The country's 1991 blueprint for economic development called Vision 2020 articulates an ideal of prosperity that is equitable and promotes both the economic and social well-being of its citizens (Mohamad, 1991). In response to the current economic disparities, Prime Minister Najib launched the new *Bumiputra* Economic Empowerment Program in 2013 specifically to lift the economic condition of ethnic Malays.

## Political context

The Malaysian government has been seen as a "regime that combines democratic institutions with authoritarian constraints" (Weiss, 2006, p. 2). Despite the odds, the country managed to carve a long record of issue advocacy and protest movements. Along the Foucauldian vein of conceptualizing power as inherent in all social activities including ideological hegemony, Malaysia's spectrum of protests and mobilization in pursuit of or resistance to change ranges from political and electoral reform (Khoo, 2016), protection of civil rights (Soong, 2007), sexual diversity and AIDS/HIV treatment in the context of the country's Islamization (Lee, 2009), government accountability and human rights (Rodan, 2009), ethnicized divisions and economic inequalities (Carstens, 1999) and environmental conservation (Navales, 2018), among many causes.

The paradox of power as a force for domination and resistance is at play even in a country like Malaysia where the balance of power tilts heavily toward the state and manifests itself in the crafty use of propaganda and political narratives that downplay democracy, respect of human rights as well as the role of civil society for the greater good of the country. State hegemony and the suppression of dissent are justified because the state and the ruling coalition, *Barisan Nasional* and its constituent political parties, United Malays National Organization (UMNO), the Malaysian Chinese Congress and the Malaysian Indian Congress, are seen as the sole arbiter of ethnic tensions and the only entity that could best address class disparities.

Malaysians used both peaceful and radical means to resist political overreach and social injustice. The people populating the opposition groups, NGOs and grassroots organizations come from a broad cross-section of society from laborers, students, the unemployed, politicians, professionals, civil servants, the intelligentsia, etc. who held mass demonstrations and demanded reforms. In a way, defiance bred solidarity among the country's disparate groups, blurring the ethnic, class, gender and religious contours of Malaysian society.

Globally, recent years have seen a surge in youth activism and along with it the use of digital technologies in campaigns for democratic freedoms. In Malaysia, for example, the *Bersih* rallies for clean and free elections saw the use of social media to coordinate protests not just within the country but also in other cities around the world. Young women of the Women's Candidacy Initiative that wanted to create awareness and address the underrepresentation of women in Malaysia's political power nexus have also been reported to successfully formulate youth-friendly messaging across both legacy and online media platforms (Lee, 2017).

But then even virtual environments are sites of contestation. As Malaysia's activists gravitate toward social media to challenge existing power structures so did the police who used Twitter to refute accusations of brutality and to criminalize civil resistance by alleging that protesters resorted to violence.

Malaysian police also utilized Twitter to track down so-called violent protesters (Postill, 2014).

Arguably, not all protests are peaceful. The infamous but historically pivotal race riots of May–July 1969 between Malaysia's largest ethnic groups—the Malays and Chinese, dramatize the deep racial schisms in the country. There are conflicting versions of what really happened on May 13, 1969 that sparked the "worst racial riot in the history of Malaysia" (Soong, 2007, p. 34). The official account was that the Malays and Chinese spontaneously confronted each other violently in the aftermath of the 1969 elections putting the blame for the rioting on opposition parties that rejected the Malay-dominant status quo. Fingers were pointed to communists as well.

Recent declassified records, however, suggest that it was a *coup d'etat* to challenge the electoral victory of the UMNO that advanced and protected the Malay state-capitalist class. The disgruntlement of non-Malays over the discriminatory policies of the state regarding education, employment, scholarships, license permits, culture etc. reached kindling temperatures that became the fiery and deadly riots of 1969. Almost half a century after this racial bloodbath, the country's ruling political and economic elite continues to stoke fears of violent racial disharmony to warrant the tightening of their grip of the power levers of Malaysian society and privileging their own kind while completely disregarding the human rights of others (Soong, 2007). It is in the context of this milieu that the case study in this chapter is discussed.

## Cultural and social context

Malaysia is a pluralistic society. The country's Malays or "indigenous peoples" are the majority of the population at 61.7 percent. The other two major ethnic groups are the Chinese at 20.8 percent and Indian at 6.2 percent. There is also a sizeable proportion of non-citizens estimated at 10.4 percent in 2017.

Bahasa Malaysia is the official lingua franca but English, Chinese and Indian languages are also spoken. A large majority of Malaysians are Muslim at 61 percent while Buddhism is the religion of about 19.8 percent. Christians and Hindus account for 9 and 6 percent of the population, respectively.

As a multi-ethnic nation, it's not surprising that national and ethnic identity are positively correlated in Malaysia. Ethnic identity was found to be stronger than national identity in Malaysia compared with neighboring Singapore. In fact, ethnicity is more sensitive in Malaysia, particularly among Malays, than in Singapore. The dominant ethnic group tended to support more strongly the government's policy which in the Malaysian context denotes that nationalism by law means that Malay is the official language and Islam the official religion (Liu & Abraham, 2002).

Reportedly, the country's political elite is reputed to racialize issues in Malaysia (Haniffa & Cooke, 2002) but "whether discrimination is primordial" (Milne, 1981) or class-based (Brennan, 1982) is still being debated. In Malaysia, race is decidedly a marker of class relations. Haniffa and Cooke (2002), for example, found that Malaysia's corporate practices specifically regarding disclosure is influenced by culture or ethnicity and socioeconomic class. They explained that the historical hostility of Malays toward the Chinese, who are entrepreneurial and economically prosperous, can account for the mutual secretive tendencies of Malay and Chinese businesses.

Moreover, Hofstede's (1991) study revealed that the nation's two major ethnic groups were found to be low on masculinity and high on power distance. Malaysians value caring, filial piety of parents, preserving "face", loyalty and being considerate as well as respectful of others, and acceptance of social rank (Abdullah, 1992). The collectivist nature of the Malays is hugely attributed to Islam because "under Islam, social order is closer to collectivism and rights of private ownership are ultimately subordinate to Allah" (Baydoun & Willett, 1995, p. 89).

The ethnicization of Malaysia is demonstrably shown by the fact that the Malay majority has ruled the country. This ethnicization carries with it a religious dimension with the codification of social behavior based on Islamic tenets. Muslim Malays in the country therefore are a privileged group accorded preferential treatment by the government's economic and educational policies (Kortteinen, 2008). This has led to the creation of a Malay middle class and the simmering tension among the racial groups that ultimately led to the riots of 1969. Despite the socio-economic and ethnic crevasse in Malaysian society, the country has a modernizing and cosmopolitan façade with an intriguing juxtaposition of the modern and traditional, religious and secular.

## Public relations practice

Malaysian PR began as early as the fifteenth century but modern PR originated in 1945 with the establishment of the Federation of Malaya as a British protectorate. Britain liberated the country from Japan and the Department of Publicity and Printing was formed. The creation of the Institute of Public Relations Malaysia in 1962 is considered a major historical milestone. It was followed with the establishment of the first PR agency in 1965, the Eric White Associates (Gabriel & Koh, 2016).

The development of PR in Malaysia follows five epochal stages in the country's history (Idid, 2004). Phase 1, which is the period before World War II is significant, as it marked the formation of a Department of Information in 1939 and the appointment of G.L. Peet as its first director. Peet was a veteran journalist of the *Straits Times*. Then British-controlled Malaysia served as a war publicity machine operating under divergent views with the colonial master seeing Germany as the enemy while Malaysia saw Japan as the main threat.

The post-World War II period until 1957 (phase II) is noteworthy for the creation of the Department of Public Relations by the Malayan Union in 1946. Government PR efforts at this stage were centered on three goals: reputation damage control under the heels of public perceptions that Britain was brought down to its knees by Japan; restoration of public order and increasing agricultural production to stave off food shortages. Between 1948–1960 (Emergency period), the Department of PR successfully used communication in the war of public opinion against the communist threat in the peninsula. The role of PR in electoral campaigns was showcased in Malaysia's first national elections when the country gained independence in 1957. The government's Department of Public Information Services spearheaded campaigns to educate Malaysians about their voting rights and the nuances of citizenship.

Phase III (1957–1963) was a watershed in the development of PR in Malaysia. The country's independence "shifted political, economic and media focus from Singapore to Malaysia" (Idid, 2004, p. 213). This resulted in substantial growth of PR as newspapers, Radio Malaya and government PR centers moved from Singapore to Malaysia's capital, Kuala Lumpur. It was also during this period when the Institute of Public Relations Malaysia was established primarily to provide education and training (Ahmad, 2014).

Two major historical events set the tone of phase IV (1963–1980): The "Confrontation" with Indonesia that marked the use of PR in external relations and the civil riots between the Chinese and Malays in 1969 that signified the role of domestic public information to promote local peace and order. This period also saw the first entry of PR officers with academic degrees in mass communication to government information ministries in 1978. BERNAMA, the country's national news agency, was founded during this time.

Economic prosperity and Mahathir Mohamad's reign are at the heart of phase V (1980–2003). Mahathir's privatization and industrial policies led to tremendous growth in the country's economy and the PR industry ushering an era of information technology ambitions and bolstering Malaysia's emerging status in globalized markets. This northbound trajectory in socio-economic and PR advancement, however, suffered a massive course correction during the 1997 Asian financial crisis. Nevertheless, the immense change in the PR industry from a government-led public information and service orientation to a market-driven, bottom-line approach continues to define this period (Idid, 2004; Abbas, 1989; Hamid, 1990).

Among the challenges facing the industry is to effectively transition the profession from the dominant government presence aimed at nation building to a more robust corporate/private-sector practice (Freitag & Stokes, 2009). The prevailing thought is that PR's role in a multicultural society like Malaysia is as a "social engineer" to promote unity and harmony and to assist in nation building (Idid, 2004). Government control of legacy media and the resulting limits to free expression remain an issue (Gabriel & Koh, 2016). PR has been employed by elites and dominant actors in pursuit of the government's national agenda and the private sector's commercial interests (Ahmad, 2014).

*Corporate social responsibility*

Historical scholars trace the start of CSR in 1974 (Nasir, Halim, Sallem, Jasni & Aziz, 2015) when government promulgated the Environmental Quality Act that required companies to comply with environmental safety and pollution control guidelines. Indeed, Malaysia is one of the few in Asia to enact CSR reporting requirements for publicly listed companies. Since the Global Reporting Initiative (GRI) in 1999, 16 Malaysian companies published GRI reports by July 2012. Corporate CSR in the country is also incentivized through annual award programs (UNICEF Malaysia, 2016), tax breaks and a higher favorability given to businesses with CSR track records when applying for government contracts (Lariche, 2016).

Two local CSR organizations namely CSR Malaysia and the Malaysia Global Compact Network are spearheading knowledge sharing about CSR best practices. In the region's stock exchanges, Bursa Malaysia helms the promotion of CSR within listed companies and is credited for efforts in raising corporate governance standards (del Rosario, 2011). The Silver Book CSR frameworks established in 2006 and the introduction of the CSR awards in 2007 also boosted diffusion of CSR practice. The CSR frameworks particularly for public-linked corporations cover four areas: environment, workplace, community and the marketplace. The accelerated liberalization of the Malaysian economy spurred the incorporation of more private businesses that led to the expansion of CSR to help with the economic development of communities as well as addressing social needs in healthcare and education (Ismail, Alias & Rasdi, 2013).

Unsurprisingly, ethnicity and religion influence CSR practice. CSR activities also tend to be seasonal and philanthropy as well as other good deeds intersect with ethnicity and religion. For example, Malaysian companies time their CSR around the Chinese New Year, *Deepavali* and *Aidfilfitri* (Zulkifli & Amran, 2006). As the country is fast becoming an international hub for Islamic finance, Islamic principles and values are guiding banking and CSR activities of financial institutions (Darus, 2012).

A longitudinal study revealed that among Publicly Listed Companies (PLCs), three themes dominate CSR disclosures: employee relations, community development, product and the environment (Saleh, Zulkifli & Muhamad, 2010). Still CSR in Malaysia is dealing with issues such as the lack of understanding of what CSR is, confusing it with PR and whether or not it should be voluntary or mandated.

## CSR as aspirational talk

The core concept behind CSR as aspirational talk is that the lack of congruence between words and action is not always a bad thing if the potential for the discrepancies to improve exists and is realized somewhere or sometime along an organization's CSR journey. According to Christensen, Morsing and Thyssen (2013), aspirational talk is "communication, which announces ideals and intentions rather than reflect actual behaviors" (p. 373).

The conventional wisdom says actions speak louder than words. In most cases, yes, they do. That's why CSR action is treated as superior to CSR communication. However, Christensen et al. (2013) argue that "aspirational CSR talk may be an important resource for social change, even when organizations do not fully live up to their aspirations" (p. 372). In other words, it's the thought that counts. Aspirational talk may be vital to get to higher goals or for organizations to aim for excellence or far more superior performance standards and practices.

We propose to extend the notion of CSR as aspirational talk as perhaps part of the maturation or developmental process of CSR—that organizations live and learn and try to do better in synchronizing their CSR communication with CSR action. That is, the longer or the more experiences organizations have in talking and doing CSR logically, the better they become. Otherwise, credibility is jeopardized if there's all talk and no action. Truth be told there is an expiration date on the license to operate, if entities continue with unmatched CSR communication with appropriate or expected CSR action.

Given that the meaning, interpretation and enactment of CSR have evolved and expanded throughout its history (Carroll, 1979; Churchill, 1974; Christensen & Cheney, 2011), there's room to contest existing formulations of CSR. At the heart of the notion of aspirational talk is the idea that language is really performative and communication is creation (Boje, Oswick & Ford, 2004). Along this spectrum of proposition, Christensen et al. (2013) have argued that "CSR communication is essentially aspirational and therefore not a perfect reflection of organizational CSR practices" (p. 373). As constitutive of organizations, CSR communication therefore may "instigate organizational reality rather than describe it" (Christensen et al., 2013, p. 374).

This more optimistic view that allows for discrepancies between CSR communication and CSR action/practice animates the case of the university's CSR that is presented in this chapter.

## CSR in education

Corporate social responsibility for the most part has been associated with the private sector, specifically the corporate world. It is indeed rare to find universities and CSR in the same sentence. But aren't universities by the nature of their work or mission considered social institutions that produce knowledgeable and ethical citizens to help society achieve its goals or cope with or address the myriad of problems it faces and by doing so are already working for a social cause?

According to Bok (1982), the modern university has social responsibilities that span the gamut of academic freedom, students' moral development and tackling broader social issues in addition to the main service of educating students. This thought dovetails with Carroll's (1979 CSR framework particularly along the moral/ethical responsibilities as well as philanthropic activities of societal entities. Indeed Muijen (2004) redefined CSR objectives from the immediate strategic considerations to the moral and ethical realm.

Most studies have reported that among the intangible but strategic CSR outcomes are proactivity, volunteerism, value creation and media and community visibility (Burke & Longsdon, 1996; Matten & Moon, 2008). Universities as many know encourage volunteerism and community involvement as part of town–gown relationship management and as co-curricular opportunities for students. Jimena (2011) contends that universities are the new CSR frontier and that a university-based CSR culture can stimulate the accumulation of human, intellectual and social capital. In fact, for some universities it has become essential to consider CSR as a strategy for growth.

Furthermore, modelling social responsibility to the students by having their own CSR programs while benefiting the various university stakeholders is a compelling reason to integrate CSR in the overall mission and strategy of higher learning institutions. Kucerova, Fromankova and Prisazna (2016) indeed found that in Czech universities the incorporation of CSR in the tertiary sector's strategic direction is a significant indicator of their engagement level in CSR programs. But while higher learning institutions in the Czech Republic do engage in CSR, "these activities are often untargeted and representing by-products of other activities" (p. 88).

There are conditions in the university ecosystem and CSR itself that are conducive to the successful implementation of social responsibility initiatives in a university setting such as shared resources, the involvement of young people, the community orientation and that both are defined by collective responsibility as well as a responsiveness to changes in perception and circumstances (Topal, 2009). The efficacy of university CSR programs has been demonstrated in the establishment of more ecologically friendly campuses and the promotion of sustainable local communities (Mehta, 2011).

In examining the CSR of 14 public and private universities in Malaysia, Ahmad (2012) found that the undergraduate student respondents viewed that Malaysian universities in the sample focused on CSR programs that improve individuals and communities, enhance the university's reputation and maintain environmental sustainability. The study concluded that to increase student participation in university CSR activities, they have to be well informed about the beneficial impact of CSR. They must be included from the get-go such as in the planning and management stages therefore extending their participation beyond just implementation.

Mehta (2011) in an investigation of the implications on literary curricula of CSR in academia wrote: "For universities to shrug away from CSR concerns would be to deny an essential precondition of the academic framework—accountability to the stakeholder, in this case, the students and the immediate community at large." (p. 19). Yet, CSR in academia is largely underexplored. The inclusion of a university in this book is a preliminary effort to ameliorate the relatively low attention given to university CSR.

The interplay of ethnic relations in Malaysia, its authoritative culture and colonial history particularly with the British are relevant when examining the communicative CSR approaches of the university and the beneficiary villages in this study. The university is one of nearly 600 or so private tertiary educational organizations in the country (Guan, 2000), which were established in response to an ethnic community's difficulty to get non-Malay students admitted into public universities because of the quota system.

In addition to the private universities, Malaysia has about 20 public or government-funded institutions of higher learning. Of the 20, four are research universities. The university in our study is a relatively young private university.

As mentioned earlier, ethnic relations in Malaysia primarily among its main ethnic groups historically has been fraught with tension. Following the 1969 riots, the government enacted unification policies moored around the creed that a national education system and a common language constitute the elusive amalgam for the disparate groups (Abu Bakar, 2014). These national policies, however, had the unintended effect of disenfranchising other ethnic groups, who began establishing schools using English as the medium of instruction. Clearly, the English language is just one among the enduring British cultural legacies in Malaysia. Their educational system is also patterned after the British. It is in this context that the university in this study (MYNC) conducted its CSR program.

## University vision and status

This comprehensive non-profit university, ranked in the top 100 in Asia, strives for "educational excellence with transformative societal impact." It has positioned itself as one with a global outlook and with aspirations of meeting the highest international standards while creating value for society and its immediate surrounding communities.

This university aims to provide holistic, life-long learning experiences that make students conscious of their role in a digital and fast-changing world while imbuing in them "a strong sense of professional and social responsibility" (University website). Among the pillars of this university's educational mission is "humanitarianism" and social values and responsibility.

Built on a foundation of affordable quality education, this university has graduated more than 50,000 students from its 110 programs of study. Its current enrollment exceeds 20,000 students spread across four campuses. True to its global ambitions, it has forged close to 200 foreign educational partnerships in 25 different countries. It maintains ten alliances with almost ten domestic universities that include two public research universities.

### *CSR approach and initiatives: gotong royong in action*

This university defines CSR as

> The study and contribution to society where students and the university community use knowledge and skills to create value for society and to benefit others.
>
> (University official)

A mandatory community service component is this university's version of holistic education. Volunteerism and giving back to society are not only expected but required of students. There are also curricular offerings such as PR campaign courses that typically develop campaigns to benefit non-profits and internships that are often seen as mutually beneficial for students and internship employers alike. Among the compulsory co-curricular areas are Community Project, Social Entrepreneurship, Arts and Cultural Performance and Theater, which draw student volunteers from a wide swath of disciplines.

Indeed, this university is cognizant of the need for a multidisciplinary approach toward solving twenty-first century problems and has employed this strategy toward the development of a "caring community" in its campuses. At the center of its CSR is *gotong royong*.

*Gotong royong* is Malay for the joint bearing of burdens or mutual aid. Collectivist societies have variations of this concept of reciprocity and in Malaysia it is the communal way of solving problems, which this university has applied in many of its volunteer and community programs.

The overarching goal for the university's CSR is to instill social responsibility among its students, faculty and staff. A university official stated,

> We care for our students and this triggered our CSR. We want to find other ways for our students to learn, to develop empathy and humanity.
>
> (University Department of Soft Skills)

Toward this end, it has adopted a multi-pronged, multi-sectoral approach accompanied by media and public visibility. The university's division of corporate communication actively does media relations about CSR and related volunteer programs. The campus newspaper also has a regular section called *Community at Heart* that routinely features stories and pictures of student volunteer activities.

To coordinate its various community service efforts, two university divisions—Student Affairs and a special and possibly a unique element of this university—a Department of Soft Skills Competency are orchestrating all the many student-led and faculty/staff-supported CSR activities on and off campus. Through these bodies, the university has undertaken several community outreach initiatives for almost two decades now in collaboration with various student organizations, classes and multilateral partnerships with both private and government agencies as well as NGOs. With these major propellants, the university gained a foothold in neighboring small villages with average populations of about 250 residents.

The sources for volunteer or community outreach are varied. The impression the researcher got is that students, faculty, the soft skills and student affairs staff come up with ideas. Sometimes, the university is approached by entities that need volunteers or the university's expertise. In rare instances, the type/s of intervention come from the village or community.

When students and faculty/staff conduct community service, the university provides transportation and food. The university allocates a budget for CSR that includes staffing of the main administrative unit that coordinates its CSR.

The types of CSR activities this university has done can be grouped roughly and subjectively into four categories:

1  Those undertaken in the New Villages.
2  Philanthropy.
3  Community service at large.
4  Environmental related.

The succeeding section presents examples of CSR projects in each of these four groupings.

## *CSR in New Villages (NV)*

Unique to Peninsular Malaysia, the NVs were originally relocation hamlets for rural Chinese established by the British colonial government during the 1948–1960 Malayan Emergency or the Communist insurgency. This colonial legacy of the British was meant to prevent these rural Chinese living in the fringes of the jungles from supporting or being forced to support the Communist guerillas. In return for their displacement, residents of these segregated housing compounds were provided water, electricity, education and means of livelihood such as fishing, farming and tin mining. At the end of the Communist threat, many of these villages became permanent; others were abandoned. There are 450 New Villages in the country today down from 613 (Leong, 2017). These villages remain an important electoral constituency of Malaysia's political power apparatus.

Change has affected these villages. With the development of the country's economy and other social as well as political changes, the nature, number and size of the New Villages varied with the times. The most conspicuous of the transformations is demographic. In 1986, for instance, there were 478 NVs. Some of these villages had populations between 1,000–4,999, 48 of which were in Johor and 60 in Perak. A couple of villages in Johor and five in Perak even had between 5,000–10,000 people (Voon & Khoo, 1986). Low birth rates and out-migration caused these demographic changes. Other NV problems include aging population and lack of job opportunities and educational support.

During the researchers' visit to one of the NVs near campus, one male elderly village leader revealed that because a lot of people have left the village either to study or work elsewhere, they are happy to have visitors. The village welcomes the students' presence and all the volunteer work they have done for the community.

> We are a small village so we welcome outsiders coming in with activities. It's okay if they have their own agenda; we benefit anyway.
> 
> (Current village chief)

One of this university's stated CSR aspiration is to be able to reach all 450 NVs. It was not clear, however, how many NVs they have actually reached at the time of the research visit. The University President said in 2010, "It is our plan to cover all the 450 New Villages in Malaysia." He added that the university will train students to address the needs and improve the quality of life in the villages and to become social entrepreneurs by identifying business opportunities and better yet helping these communities launch business ventures. The Minister of Housing and Local Government who was present at one of the university's New Village Community Projects applauded the university's positive response to the government's effort to modernize these villages through concerted socio-economic programs.

The university's involvement with the NVs sprung from the need to provide information about these villages on a website that was created at the direction of one of the committees of the Associated Chinese Chambers of Commerce and Industry of Malaysia. The website was aimed at promoting the uniqueness of the 450 villages. However, there was a dearth of information about these new villages. The university then decided that this can be a good project for students to contribute to the community. New Village activities undertaken by this university generally fall under four categories: (1) NV tour, (2) NV survey, (3) NV community service dubbed the "We care; we act" campaign, and (4) NV collaborative project.

Consequently, in collaboration with relevant government agencies, students, faculty and staff have done free medical exams, taught villagers community composting and soap making for home use or to sell for extra income, build houses, introduced traditional Chinese medicine, beautification and cleanup drives and taught school children English, Malay and information technology study skills, among others. At one "health camp" in 2012 held to promote healthier lifestyles, the students checked height, weight, BMI, body fat, age and pulse rate of some 50 villagers, the majority were aged 40 or older. Other health-related NV community projects by students done with the help of the university's Department of Nursing include the prevention and treatment of dengue and scabies. As the village leader said,

> It is a good program for raising awareness among the villagers on holistic well-being and personal health improvement.

Commenting on the university's role in developing not only academic excellence but also social responsibility among its students, a university official said,

> Our university has always encouraged students to take an interest in the surrounding society and we believe that the university community can act as a catalyst for forging deeper interpersonal relationships and a more caring community.

In one NV that did not have a solid waste collection service from the local government, an experimental composting site was established as soon as government funding was received. The students and faculty of the university's engineering and green technology guided the village with the composting project and helped with the grant application as well. Before the composting system, village workers collected the waste from the households using a two-wheel bucket attached to an agricultural tractor. The waste was then brought to a dumpsite at the edge of the village. With the new composting system both the waste accumulated at the dumpsite and the operating as well as environmental cost of managing the dumpsite were reduced.

Another waste management project was aimed at promoting the use of organic enzymes by converting household food waste into antibacterial detergents for the home. For this project, university students taught NV primary school children, teachers and other interested locals how to produce the enzymes from household wastes such as fruit and vegetable peels. The waste is fermented in large used water bottles containing a concoction of brown sugar, bacterial culture stock and water. The end product with its germ-fighting properties can be used as floor detergent for better hygiene at less cost.

With a foundation as a co-sponsor, the university also became party of a joint venture intended to pay for English language tuition for primary school children in the new villages. In later years, the venture expanded to include the development of an IT skills program. Aside from classroom learning, this foundation dedicated to assisting needy children with their studies, has also thrown its financial support for character building and leadership development programs for NV children.

To blend learning and CSR objectives, the university conducted a field study where students examined the demography, economic development, social structure, community assets and cultural values of three fishing NVs with community development and social entrepreneurship in mind.

With technical support and access to marketing and distribution provided by civic-minded companies that the university tapped, one of the villages was able to establish commercial fish ponds with the guidance of university faculty and students. The university vice president for student development stated:

> We encourage our staff and students to assist the villages and then try to give suggestions or solutions to improve their standard of living. Besides that, we try to work with some corporations to provide some assistance to the villages especially ones that have commercializable products.

Partnering with Habitat for Humanity Malaysia, another group of civil engineering students built two NV houses. The students under the mentorship of their professor performed ground soil analysis in addition to actually doing construction work. Using the experiential learning model, the instructor of the Structural Concrete Design course articulated:

> The major aims of this problem-based community service learning assignment were to introduce student-centered learning which places greater responsibilities on the students to undertake their own learning and to meet some of the most important Civil Engineering program outcomes like the ability to formulate and solve civil engineering problems, the ability to communicate their intentions and actions effectively in written and oral form and the recognition of the need to undertake life-long learning.

Certainly, this approach was not without its challenges. For one, the students were apprehensive about their preparedness as the project required in-depth knowledge of the subject matter to be able to apply it in a real-world setting. After conquering their initial fears, the instructor reported that the students enjoyed themselves throughout the entire process.

For another NV, the students from the university's PR program did fundraising and with the proceeds built a community library. In this particular village of about 200 families a community association was organized in 2010 to have a better handle of community needs. The result of the needs assessment was the establishment of the mini library with about 500 books.

> We hope to cultivate a reading culture in the village. Without the library, villagers spend most of their free time sitting, chatting and drinking at stalls.
> 
> (Community association member)

> Without the library, children will just be playing after school and running around.
> 
> (Native village resident)

An NV housewife added:

> The library has become the best place for recreation for the villagers and for my children to do reading. It truly helps them foster an interest in reading.

The NV head and community club member elaborated that the library was the suitable place for villagers and students to do their reading and revision of class projects/homework as reference materials were available to them in addition to computer and Internet access. An added benefit was that the library now provides a more central venue for the village to meet especially for the community club meetings.

Student volunteers help staff the library and assist the village's elementary pupils with homework. At the start of library operations, it was open only once a week since the students were unable to work in the NV every day. To alleviate the staffing issue and the limitation that students face especially with their availability due to classes and exams, a village leader suggested,

> The university might consider training the village secondary school youth to run the library and help with other community activities. The university can inspire them to lead and become more engaged.
>
> (Village leader)

As expected, the process of engaging the community likewise differed. In one NV, the former village chief read in the newspaper that the university does outreach to villages so when the university students came, he didn't ask any questions. When he approved of what they were planning to do, he attended meetings and participated in the activities. He noted,

> At the completion of the CSR project, the students in his schools improved academically. The headmaster brings to me the national test results of the students in the village. I was also happy that the university raised awareness of issues around the world among the children.
>
> (Former village chief)

In the NV library case, the community engagement process began with a university lecturer who approached the community with a PR campaign idea and asked for village cooperation. In explaining the community's involvement, a village leader said,

> At the start of the campaign, the faculty and students explained what the campaign activities were and then at the end we were asked to review the campaign and provide feedback about what worked and what didn't.
>
> (Village leader)

To provide more inclusive feedback, the informal leaders, who were initially approached by the university lecturer and were mostly the elders, recruited villagers to be members of the community association. Thus, the community association was born. As it evolved, the association became more structured with officers chosen to be responsible for specific duties.

It was clear during the research interviews that the PR students and faculty took pride in their accomplishment. The NV community leaders were equally pleased although some of the villagers intimated that while the library and the help university students were giving the school children with homework were and still are all appreciated, there are other community needs such as economic development, job creation and employment. Reaching a consensus on the priority of needs is still a challenge but the library project is deemed as a momentous start of the NV and university partnership.

## *Fundraising and philanthropy*

A significant proportion of this university's CSR activities focused on fundraising and philanthropic work. Students conducted a number of fundraising campaigns for scholarships, to provide free eyeglasses to needy school children, to promote environmentally friendlier transport through bicycles and fund donations to various charities such as the Kidney Foundation, Beautiful Gate Foundation, which operates educational centers for children with disability, World Vision Malaysia and to buy books, clothes and food for orphanages, among others.

At one luncheon honoring scholarship recipients, it was revealed that as of 2015, the university has awarded 208 scholarships to qualified but financially constrained students across its campuses. Notably an additional eight scholarships went to rural high schools.

> The (name of organization) scholarship has helped me ease my family's financial burden for my education. My tuition fees are fully covered and an allowance of RM500 is given to me each month. With this monthly allowance, I have learnt to spend wisely so that I can pay my room rental, utilities and three daily meals.
>
> (Scholarship recipient)

This university has also established scholarships to give deserving students from Independent Chinese High Schools in Malaysia the opportunity to pursue higher education. In thanking the university, one of the recipient high schools with a student population of 475 commented that the university's scholarship grants and other financial aids are making a difference to their poor but deserving students.

> Some of our students are very poor and they wish to continue in their studies but they have no means to do so. Many of them end up neglecting their studies and work at the local market.
>
> (School principal)

For the Gift of Eyesight project, university students partnered with the Malaysian Association of Practicing Opticians to raise funds and provide financially strapped school children with free spectacles. So far, 1,000 eyeglasses have been given to 22 schools throughout the country. Plans are afoot to expand the program to distribute 3,000 eyeglasses.

To promote a healthier way to travel around the campus, the university has partnered with a bank for a couple of years now and together they have organized cycling events involving the university community. In 2015, the bank donated 52 bicycles to needy students. A grateful recipient said,

> I am really thankful to be one of the beneficiaries of this sponsorship. Owning a bicycle now will allow me to get to nearby places with ease.

To raise public awareness of cancer and help poverty-stricken cancer patients, students implemented a smart idea called Locks for Hope. This event solicited hair donations to be made into wigs for cancer patients undergoing chemotherapy. For this initiative, the students worked with hairstylists in the area. Students also sold plants and hand-made ring charms at a charity event to raise funds for cancer survivors in the Children's Home of Hope.

A Chinese primary school was a lucky recipient of cash donation as well. The donation was to help upgrade the school's hall and other facilities. The money was raised through ticket sales and donations orchestrated by one of the student clubs. As a pat on the back and to encourage students to carry on, the university president talked about failing at first and trying again in order to gain confidence. Furthermore, he exhorted students to

> Learn how to be charitable and also able to share. Money is just a tool. Use it to benefit others so as to make this world a better place.

True to its mission to educate for global citizenship, university students held a musical event to raise money and support the victims of the South Sudan conflict. In the wake of China's Sichuan earthquake, students sent donations of food and clothing to aid earthquake victims. They did fundraising events to generate RM30,000. All donations were given to the Chinese ambassador to Malaysia at a media-covered event.

## Community service projects

This university has a student organization called Community Service Society whose declared purpose is to inculcate social responsibility and moral values among its members. It recruits socially responsible students and engages them in *gotong-royong* activities on and off campus. Some of this group's initiatives included spreading good cheer at a children's home, repainting of a recreation park and tree-planting on campus. The society's president said,

> Tree planting is a meaningful activity. Trees would provide shade and reduce building heat loads and hence electricity bills for cooling.

To bring Chinese New Year cheer to the children at the Divine Mercy Boys' Home, senior-year communication students accompanied by their instructor and tutor visited the home and taught the children the art of Chinese calligraphy and the making of a traditional Chinese dessert. The students also donated books and shoes. The home's administrator thanked the students saying:

> It is wonderful to have students coming over to share Chinese culture with the children as these activities are educational. The visit brought smiles to the children who are either orphans or come from broken homes with little opportunity for education.

Interestingly, student community service activities are not only for less fortunate groups. Some 23 student volunteers actually went to help a single elderly Malay woman clean her house. The students also brought her food, gas, a mattress and pillow. A student volunteer quipped after recruiting other students using social media:

> I thought that the number of volunteers would be lesser as it was during exam week. It was so touching that over 20 students turned out. I hope that this will inspire more students to help the needy in the community through action.

The university's CSR in business and sustainable development center in one of their campuses also conducted a cleanliness and beautification campaign targeting the city where the campus is located. Student, staff and faculty volunteers visited business owners to promote cleanliness in their shops and their surroundings to sustain the livability of the city. This initiative according to organizers created goodwill with the business community.

In another campus, PR students through their event management class organized four campaigns to increase campus volunteerism over the years and improve the lives of neighboring communities. These campaigns used themes such as "Volunteers Work for Change" that focused on establishing a NV library; "Continuing the Legacy," which promoted the reading habit and education; "Embracing Volunteerism, Enriching Lives" and "D.R.E.A.M" which stands for Depression, Recycle, Technology Escapism, Animal Protection and Malaysian culture. All of the yearly campaigns were launched and concluded with ceremonial fanfare as media events complete with mascots that students created and were attended by government dignitaries from the home, local government and transportation ministries as well as university officials.

The hard work and creativity of the PR students under the competent guidance of their professor have received positive attention from the Malaysian PR industry. In 2015, the student volunteerism campaign clinched the bronze medal in the annual national PR excellence competition. This placed the student campaign in the same league as the winning entries of the local subsidiaries of global PR giants such as Burson-Marsteller, Weber Shandwick and Ogilvy PR.

Paradoxically, it is noted that while this university was born as a response to perceived government discriminatory policies in education against a certain ethnic group, it is still active in toeing the government line in its appreciation of cultural diversity and the importance of harmonious living. At one cultural night event organized by the Asian Cultural Society that featured the fusion beats from traditional Malay, Chinese and Indian drums, for instance, both government and university officials seized the opportunity to trumpet their respective platforms.

The university vice president acknowledged that:

> This event would help develop our students into responsible, all-round and capable members of society. We hope that our students will appreciate the importance of making contributions to society and our nation and will understand the importance of living together in harmony.

Similarly, the attending high-level government official echoed the need for unity in a multicultural society like Malaysia simulating what can be a perfectly choreographed performance:

> If our country faces unstable political conditions, our economy will deteriorate as a consequence. Investors will then stop investing, leading to the rise in unemployment. Therefore, everyone should stay united to fulfill the 1Malaysia concept.

## *Environmental-related CSR*

It's not lost on the book authors that the environment has been mentioned in other sections of this chapter. However, there is a good reason that an entire section is devoted on this university's environment-related CSR. For one, the university is in the vicinity of a former mining area and has encountered some environment issues.

For starters, the university has consistently observed Earth Hour. The entire university switches off its lights and remains dark for an hour in solidarity with other like-minded nations and people who care about protecting the planet. Started as a lights-off event in Sydney, Australia in 2007, Earth Hour has become a global grassroots movement for the protection of nature and the environment. The observance of Earth Hour has been used a platform for environmental awareness and education among the many university constituencies.

The efforts have paid off. There have been several recycling campaigns on and off campus. To clean polluted waterways, engineering students and an environmental organization made Effective Micro-organisms (EM) mud balls and threw them in an abandoned/unused mining lake. Mud balls inhibit the growth of algae and break down the sludge or silt in water. Use of mud balls is gaining wider acceptance in the aquaculture industry and because of the surrounding fishing villages, some of which are into commercial fishpond operations, this technology has great potential impact in these villages.

Responsible environmental stewardship does begin at home. As part of its environmental advocacy toward a sustainable future and its commitment to have an earth-friendly campus, the university has actively reduced its carbon footprint to match the environment awareness and action programs done by various student clubs. It has for example used more biodegradable products in its cafeterias. The university's canteen operators agreed to stop using polystyrene lunch boxes on certain days and students were encouraged to bring their own food containers.

An officer of the student club who headed the "No to Polystyrene" campaign explained:

> Polystyrene is harmful to the human health and destructive to the environment. In the future, we plan to enforce 'no polystyrene' every day and encourage students to either eat-in or takeaway using their own food containers.

## Rethinking the beneficiary concept

The conventional thought is that the beneficiaries of philanthropy and other CSR initiatives are the recipients of the charity or the communities whose lives have been impacted by CSR. Elsewhere in this book, it has been shown that corporations benefit as well from their CSR programs. The companies accrue not just reputational advantages but preferential government treatment in some countries and even favorable effects on the bottom line when consumers do pocket book activism.

In the case of the university, aside from positive image and media visibility and creating goodwill on the part of the university, students benefit as well. And it's not just developing social responsibility and compassion or a caring attitude but complementary learning as well. Students at this university for example learned how to harvest limes and other crops from an orchard in one of the NVs. The villagers taught them how to plant vegetables and do manual weeding. These students therefore learned to appreciate the hard work that goes with farming.

At another NV, the village chief tutored another group of student volunteers in organic farming in addition to showing them how to plant radishes and harvest roselle fruits (*Hibiscus sabdariffa*). For city kids, these were novel experiences. The village chief said, "I'm glad that the students handled the hot weather as well." He expressed hope that the students gained a better understanding of how agriculture contributes to the country's economy.

Certainly, students recognize the benefits of their various volunteer and CSR efforts. Aside from networking opportunities with other students, they are able to apply what they have learned from their classes, acquire leadership and organizational skills as well as time management.

> We are honoured to be given the opportunity to plan an event for the community whilst practising the theoretical and practical knowledge we have learned throughout the years of our studies.
>
> (Student 1)

> I made new friends through this event and I think I am playing my role in taking care of the environment, but there is still space for improvement in educating the public on conserving our environment and ensuring cleanliness in our neighbourhood.
>
> (Student 2)

> Being together with the villagers was indeed an enriching experience. I found that I could talk and communicate well with them.
>
> (Student 3)

All told, CSR brings benefits to many people. It expands the concept of beneficiary to undeniably include the do-gooders.

## Summary

The positive impact of the university CSR among its many constituencies is evident but is contrasted by sobering factors. It does have the breadth and variety of activities so is it time to have a more reflective stance and systematically assess its CSR programs and approach?

As the Department of Soft Skills administrator revealed, "We don't evaluate formally; informally we do through student responses to the various initiatives."

The student response part of the quote obviously explains why the campus media routinely will have some reaction from students as part of the reportage on community outreach. While completely understandable that a university will care first and foremost about how students responded to the various community outreach and other CSR activities, it behooves university officials to ask about the sustainability and long-term impact of all their efforts. If they are really serious about continuous improvement, it seems imperative to include multiple perspectives in the identification, planning, implementation and communication of CSR.

The almost negligible inclusion of community or NV voices in campus media is rather disconcerting, which is something the research ameliorated somewhat through the interviews done at the NV community level. And although it was just one instance, the villagers did have some good ideas or suggestions such as involving the youth in staffing the village library.

The one-shot, sporadic CSR approach also stands out and is worrisome due to the apparent lack of consideration of the sustainability of CSR efforts. Needless to say, a deeper dive into the assessment of all its CSR is clear, both as a learning tool or a teachable moment for its students but also for the benefit of the neighboring communities especially the NVs, who clearly need help and have expressed the need for community development intervention.

The legacies of Malaysia's colonial past are in plain sight as well. It is noteworthy that the NVs are one of the prime targets and beneficiaries of this university's CSR. Since the NV residents are Chinese, it makes perfect sense as there's alignment with the government's recent direction, on the one hand, and with one of the university's reason for existence—to serve a disenfranchised ethnic student population, on the other. This university's use of English, which is no doubt a British influence instead of Malay as the medium of instruction may be construed however as a revolt against government policy that privileges the Malay language. So, here's a university that is able to resist and cooperate simultaneously with the political authorities.

The country's authoritarian strain is likewise hard to ignore. Villagers looked up to professors and students as authorities. From the mandatory nature of their presence in the beneficiary communities to what appears to be a top-down CSR communication process starting with the recruitment by the village head of the community association members, for instance, to unverified but possible political agendas that might have driven the targeting of certain communities, Malaysia's authoritarian culture is unmistakably shown in this case. An examination of the media placements of CSR stories particularly the ones in the campus paper reveals that there's a consistent primacy given to the presence or involvement of university, government or corporate authorities. Student comments and beneficiary voices, if any, are buried in the stories. Is the university's CSR discourse a perpetuation of elite perspectives or just the use of the tried and true PR strategy of getting media attention?

All things considered, the university's CSR record to date is evocative of the main thesis of "aspirational talk" that advances the idea that language is performative and communication is really a creation process. The university's CSR communication has credibly announced its ideal of a holistic education undergirded by equal doses of social responsibility and academic excellence. It has endeavored all these years to concretize its CSR communication to actualities in the myriad of CSR projects that exemplified its declared ideal. The issue of sustainability of the initiatives remains as many appeared to be one-shot swoops into communities, families and individuals that visibly needed help and were appreciative of the help. Clearly the lack of a rigorous and comprehensive evaluation of its CSR program and the more prickly perception that what it has done and communicated so far, while beneficial, tended to perpetuate not only the dominant perspectives but also agendas of the elite are incommodious. Despite the nagging concerns, the authors submit this chapter as an invitation to have an open-minded peek into a university's journey to be a better configuration of itself. It does have the elements of a good blueprint for sustainable CSR that is matched by sincere motivations to build a compassionate university community and world. At the aspirational level, consider this as a case of a well-intentioned university's contribution to the evolving architecture of CSR.

## References

Abbas, I. (1989). Public relations in the private sector. Paper presented at the Institute of Public Relations Malaysia Seminar. May 24.

Abu Bakar, M. (2014). Education policy and ethnic relations in Malaysia: The socio-economic perspectives. *Journal of Educational and Social Research*, 4 (2), 138–142.

Abdullah, A. (1992). The influence of ethnic values on managerial practices in Malaysia. *Malaysian Management Review*, 27 (1), 3–18.

Ahmad, J. (2012). Can a university act as a corporate social responsibility (CSR) driver: An analysis. *Social Responsibility Journal*, 8 (1), 77–78

Ahmad Z. A. (2014) Malaysia. In Watson, T. (Eds.). *Asian Perspectives on the Development of Public Relations: Other Voices. National Perspectives on the Development of Public Relations*. London: Palgrave Pivot.

Baydoun, N. & Willett, R. (1995). Cultural relevance of Western accounting systems to developing countries. *ABACUS*, 31 (1), 67–92.

Boje, D. M., Oswick, C. & Ford, J. D. (2004). Introduction to special topic forum. Language and organization: The doing of discourse. *Academy of Management Review*, 29 (4), 571–577.

Bok, D. (1982). *Beyond the Ivory Tower: Social Responsibilities of the Modern University*. Cambridge, MA: Harvard University Press.

Brennan, M. (1982). Class, politics and race in modern Malaysia. *Journal of Contemporary Asia*, 12.

Burke, L. & Longsdon, J. (1996). How corporate social responsibility pays off. *Long Range Planning*, 29 (4), 495–502.

Carroll, A. B. (1979). A three-dimensional conceptual model of corporate social performance. *Academy of Management Review*, 4.

Carstens, S. (1999). Dancing lions and disappearing history: The national culture debates and Chinese Malaysian culture. *Crossroads: An Interdisciplinary Journal of Southeast Asian Studies*, 13 (1), 11–63.

Central Intelligence Agency. (2018). Malaysia. *World Fact Book*. www.cia.gov/library/publications/the-world-factbook/geos/my.html.

Christensen, L. T. & Cheney, G. (2011). Interrogating the communicative dimensions of corporate social responsibility. In Ohlen, O., Bartlett, J. & May, S. (Eds.). *Handbook of Communication and Corporate Social Responsibility*. (pp. 491–454). Malden, MA: Wiley-Blackwell.

Christensen, L. T., Morsing, M. & Thyssen, O. (2013). CSR as aspirational talk. *Organization*, 20 (3), 372–393.

Churchill, N. (1974). Toward a theory of social accounting. *Sloan Management Review*, 15 (3), 1–17.

Darus, F. (2012). Embracing corporate social responsibility in Malaysia—Towards sustaining value creation. *Malaysia Accounting Review* Special Issue, 11 (2), 1–13.

del Rosario, R. (2011). Corporate social responsibility in Southeast Asia: An eight-country analysis. *Research Report*, Makati, Philippines: Asian Institute of Management.

Freitag, A. & Stokes, A. (2009). *Global Public Relations: Spanning Borders, Spanning Cultures*. Abington, UK: Routledge.

Gabriel, S. & Koh, C.-H. (2016). Social media use by public relations practitioners in Malaysia: An exploratory study. *The Journal of Developing Areas*, 50 (5), 469–477.

Guan, L. (2000). Ethnic relations in Peninsular Malaysia: The cultural and economic dimensions. *Social and Cultural Issues*, 1, 2–39.

Hamid, A. (1990). Keynote address at the Seminar on Public Relations for Public Relations Officers in the Private and Government Sector. October 30–November 1.

Haniffa, R. M. & Cooke, T. E. (2002). Culture, corporate governance and disclosure in Malaysian corporations. *ABACUS*, 38 (3), 317–349.

Hofstede, G. (1991). Management in a multicultural society. *Malaysian Management Review*

Idid, S. (2004). Public relations in Malaysia from its colonial past to current practice. In Sriramesh, K. (Ed.). *Public Relations in Asia*. Singapore: Thomson Learning.

Ismail, M., Alias, S. N. & Rasdi, R. M. (2013). Community as stakeholder of the corporate social responsibility programme in Malaysia: Outcomes in community development. *Social Responsibility Journal*, 11 (1), 109–130.

Jimena, J. (2011). Universities: The new CSR frontier. *Canadian Mining Journal*. August 2011, p. 8.

Khoo, Y. H. (2016). Malaysia's 13th general elections and the rise of electoral reform movement. *Asian Politics & Polity*, 8 (3), 418–435.

Kortteinen, T. (2008). Islamic resurgence and the ethnicization of the Malaysian state: The case of Lina Joy. *Journal of Social Issues in Southeast Asia*, 23 (2), 216–233.

Kucerova, R., Fromankova, S. & Prisazna, M. (2016). Social responsibility in high education institutions: Evidence from economic faculties in Czech Republic. *Journal on Efficiency and Responsibility in Education and Science*, 9 (4), 88–96.

Lariche, B. (2016). CSR in Malaysia: A critique 2016. www.makeitrightmovement.com/featured-articles/csr-in-malaysia-a-critique-2016.

Lee, J. C. H. (2009). Mobilizing for social change in Muslim societies amidst political turmoil and conservatism. *Development*, 52 (2), 239–245.

Lee, J. C. H. (2017). Youth and a culture of protest in Southeast Asia. Regional Learning Hub. *New Mandala*. www.newmandala.org/youth-culture-protest-southeast-asia/.

Leong, T. (2017). Breathing life into Malaysia's old New Villages: KL is pouring RM75m into turning these sleepy towns into tourist hot spots. *The Straits Times*. November 4 2017. www.straitstimes.com/asia/se-asia/breathing-life-into-malaysias-old-new-villages.

Liu, J. & Abraham, S. (2002). Social representations of history in Malaysia and Singapore: On the relationship between national and ethnic identity. *Asian Journal of Social Psychology*, 5, 3–20.

Lu, J. & Castka, P. (2009). Corporate social responsibility in Malaysia—Experts' views and perspectives. *Corporate Social Responsibility and Environmental Management*, 16, 146–154.

Matten, D. & Moon, J. (2008). "Implicit" and "explicit" CSR: A conceptual framework for a comparative understanding of corporate social responsibility. *Academy of Management Review*, 33 (2), 404–424.

Mehta, S. R. (2011). The culture of corporate social responsibility (CSR) in the academic framework: Some literary implications. *Contemporary Issues in Education Research*, 4 (10), 19–24.

Milne, R. (1981). *Politics in Ethnically Bipolar States: Guyana, Malaysia, Fiji*. University of British Columbia Press.

Mohamad, M. (1991). The way forward. Speech to the Malaysian Business Council. Kuala Lumpur, Malaysia. http://unpan1.un.org/intradoc/groups/public/documents/apcity/unpan003223.pdf

Muijen, S. C. A. H. (2004). Corporate social responsibility starts at university. *Journal of Business Ethics*, 53, 235–246.

Nasir, N., Halim, N., Sallem, N., Jasni, N. & Aziz, N. (2015). Corporate social responsibility: An overview from Malaysia. *Journal of Applied Environmental and Biological Sciences*, 4, 82–87.

Navales, R. (2018). RFC offroaders club airs environmental advocacy. SunStar Pampanga. www.sunstar.com.ph/pampanga/local-news/2018/01/30/rfc-offroaders-club-airs-environmental-advocacy-586497.

Postill, J. (2014). A critical history of Internet activism and social protest in Malaysia, 1998–2011. *Asiascape: Digital Asia*, 1–2, 78–103.

Rodan, G. (2009). Accountability and authoritarianism: Human rights in Malaysia and Singapore. *Journal of Contemporary Asia*, 39 (2), 180–203.

Saleh, M., Zulkifli, N. & Muhamad, R. (2010). Corporate social responsibility disclosure and its relation on institutional ownership: Evidence from public listed companies in Malaysia. *Managerial Auditing Journal*, 25 (6), 591–613.

Seng, L. K. (1998). Within the Singapore story: The use and narrative of history in Singapore. *An Interdisciplinary Journal of Southeast Asian Studies*, 12 (2), 1–21.

Soong, K. (2007). Racial conflict in Malaysia: Against the official history. *Race and Class*, 49 (3), 33–53.

Topal, S. R. (2009). CSR in universities around the world. Discussion papers on social responsibility. www.socialresponsibility.biz/discuss2.pdf.

UNICEF Malaysia. (2016). Corporate social responsibility policies in Malaysia— Enhancing the child focus, www.unicef.org/malaysia/Unicef_CSR_Msia_110713_lowres.pdf.

Voon, P. K. & Khoo, S. H. (1986). The new villages in Peninsular Malaysia. *Journal of Tropical Geography*, 14, 36–55.

Weiss, M. (2004). Transnational activism by Malaysians: Foci, tradeoffs and implications. In Piper, N. & Uhlin, A. (Eds.). *Transnational Activism in Asia*. (pp. 129–148). London: Routledge.

Weiss, M. (2006). *Protest and Possibilities. Civil Society and Coalitions for Political Change in Malaysia*. Stanford, CA: Stanford University Press.

Welford, R. (2005). Corporate social responsibility in Europe, North America and Asia. *Journal of Corporate Citizenship,* 17, 33–52.

Zulkifli, N. & Amran, A. (2006). Realizing corporate social responsibility in Malaysia: A view from the accounting profession. *The Journal of Corporate Citizenship,* 24, 101–114.

# 4 CSR as social development in postcolonial Philippines

## Country context

*Economic, political/historical context*

The Philippines is the second most populous country (next to Indonesia) among the ASEAN-member nations. Three foreign powers occupied the archipelago: Spain (sixteenth–nineteenth century), the United States (1898–1946), and Japan (1942–1945). American and Filipino forces fought against the Japanese during World War II and the country gained independence on July 4, 1946. Since Emilio Aguinaldo's presidency of the revolutionary government, the republic now counts 16 presidents including Ferdinand Marcos, who ruled with an iron fist for 20 years, and two women presidents: Corazon Aquino (1986–1992) and Gloria Macapagal (2001–2010). The Marcos dictatorship was toppled by the bloodless People Power Revolution (EDSA I) (World Fact Book, 2017). EDSA or Epifanio de los Santos Avenue is a major thoroughfare in Manila where Filipinos converged in 1986 in what is historically recorded as the People Power Revolution that ousted Marcos. Filipinos stopped tanks with their bodies, prayed and demanded an end to the repressive Marcos regime. The current president, Rodrigo Duterte, elected in 2016, has waged a "war on drugs." The extrajudicial killings have raised human rights concerns and although Duterte enjoys a cult-like following among Filipinos, his recent approval ratings have plummeted as his dictatorial tendencies surfaced (Reuters, 2017).

Threats to the country's national security include terrorists, some of which are on the U.S. Government's Foreign Terrorist Organization list, the Muslim separatists in Mindanao and the Maoist-inspired New People's Army insurgency. Although the country has favorable diplomatic relations with much of its neighbors, it has a long running territorial and maritime dispute with China over the Spratly Islands. Malaysia, Taiwan and Vietnam also lay claim on these South China Sea island group (World Fact Book, 2017).

Economic growth has accelerated, averaging 6.1 percent annually during the last five years but it has not been an inclusive growth. According to the World Bank, 21.6 percent of the Philippine population live below the poverty line in 2015. More than 60 percent of the poor reside in rural areas, where severe poverty afflicts about half of the population. Unemployment hovered between 5.5 to 7.3 percent during the 2010 and 2016 period (World Fact Book, 2017). Personal remittances from Filipino overseas workers prop the economy to the tune of 10.2 percent of the country's GDP in 2016 (World Bank, 2017a), the highest percentage share among the ASEAN nations included in this study.

There are more than ten million Filipinos or about 10 percent of the population who are working or living abroad (Asis, 2017). This large migratory outflow particularly of overseas Filipino workers (OFWs) has tangible economic benefits that include conspicuous consumption and social mobility but also comes with high social costs. Temporary separation of family members has led to broken families, infidelity, dysfunctional children and changes in parenting and caregiving patterns (Vasquez, 1992; Asis, 1995).

## Cultural and social context

The Philippines is a multicultural, multilingual, collectivist, Christian society that has a high literacy rate. Education is valued and is key to social mobility for the majority of Filipinos. There are more than 80 dialects but Pilipino is the national language and English is very widely spoken. English is in fact the medium of instruction. Tagalog is the largest ethnic/language group (28 percent) followed by Cebuano and Ilocano. The country is 90 percent Christian with 83 percent of these Christians, Roman Catholics. About 5 percent practice Islam and are mainly in Mindanao in Southern Philippines (CIA World Fact Book, 2017).

One's social standing in the country is determined along economic, educational, occupational and even geographical lines. These social demarcations are largely informal and perceptual except for those based on economic factors or income. For instance, differences in status and prestige are evident based on whether one is a professional or laborer, urbanite or from the barrios (towns), the educational institution one has attended, and also on the particular province or region one hails from. Because the country is predominantly Christian and outright discrimination is not socially acceptable, these social divisions are mostly not articulated or discussed, but are real and can manifest in certain behaviors (Sarabia-Panol & Lorenzo-Molo, 2004).

The self-clustering into socio-economically homogenous tribes hits the pause button periodically when the upper-crust shares their bounty with the poor, typically during holidays or through community development projects sponsored by the churches, schools or businesses. It is quite interesting to see uniformed *colegialas* going to the slums for their annual charity or community work. Natural disasters or crises also tend to make Filipinos, much like other people, forget about class distinctions. This was observed during the People Power revolution, the deadly cyclone Haiyan/Yolanda and Typhoon Bopha or Pablo that caused deadly landslides in Mindanao, among the more recent examples.

As a collectivist society, Filipinos value the family, school and village. Two peculiar Filipino cultural traits: *utang na loob* (lifelong debt of gratitude) and *pakikisama* (cooperating with the team or group and giving importance to harmony and conformity) are manifestations of collectivism. Both are driven by the desire for social acceptance that create "complex networks of loyalties," a "hidden structure to relationships," a curiously Filipino brand of reciprocal obligations and avoidance of shame or embarrassment (*hiya*) (Bonifacio, 1977; Bulatao, 1964).

Another Filipino tradition is *bayanihan* "wherein neighbors would help a relocating family by gathering under their house, and carrying it to its new location... a communal spirit that makes seemingly impossible feats possible through the power of unity and cooperation." (http://vrplus.dswd.gov.ph/index.php/component/content/article/7-bayanihang-bayan-program-bbp-/11-what-is-bayanihan).

Hofstede (2001) found that the country exhibits many of the features of societies with large power distance such as centralized authority in organizations, reliance on rigid, formal rules, top-down management decision structures where subordinates expect to be told, wide disparities in salaries between management and the rank-and-file, and the existence of huge numbers of supervisory personnel. In such an authoritarian leadership setting, power has its privileges and status symbols. Those in authority such as the boss, parents, clergy and other formal and informal leaders are treated with respect and obeyed. The ideal boss is described as a "well-meaning autocrat or good father," one who sees himself as a "benevolent decision maker" (Hofstede, 2001, p. 107). Under this setup, communication tends to be formal and hierarchical, approval systems long and time-consuming, and there's a general reluctance to share information without expressed approval from superiors. In other words, organizational behavior is steeped in protocols.

The country's feudal history continues to permeate in contemporary society where power is perceived to be in the hands of the few, mostly among politicians and the wealthy 10 percent of the population. The disproportionate gap between the rich and poor also accounts for the vast power distance.

## Corporate social responsibility

The inception of corporate social responsibility in the archipelago can be traced to the seventies with the establishment of the Philippine Business for Social Progress (PBSP). About 70 founding corporate members committed 1 percent of their post-tax earnings to CSR to help end extreme poverty and stem environmental degradation (Lorenzo-Molo, 2009). At about the same time the PBSP started, the Association of Foundations (AF) was also established. As the first network of NGOs, AF members include corporate foundations, not-for-profit institutions and small organizations based in the rural areas. It was set up to enable its member foundations to develop sustainable programs that serve their communities.

In 1991, a sub-sector of the AF set up the League of Corporate Foundations (LCF). The LCF's mission is to "promote CSR and to contribute to its practice by enabling effective and strategic corporate social investments among our members and the larger business community" (www.lcf.org.ph/aboutthelcf/mv).

Naturally, CSR development in the Philippines is influenced by its collectivist culture and Christian tradition. Being the only predominantly Roman Catholic country in the region, the Catholic church played a major role in "developing the early concept and value of CSR" (del Rosario, 2011, p. 35). The church and non-governmental organizations focused CSR initiatives on poverty alleviation, environmental protection, health, education and social development. Philanthropy continues to be a hallmark of CSR programs although corporations are increasingly integrating CSR into business strategies.

Another national distinction is the existence of a strong civil society. Two "People Power" revolutions, the first in 1986 and the second in 2001 demonstrated to the world the power of civil society in mobilizing the peaceful end of corrupt and despotic Philippine rulers.

The country has strong environmental and labor laws although enforcement remains an issue. Maximiano (2007) found that among 166 respondents representing micro, small, medium and large businesses and who are members of the Philippine Chamber of Commerce and Industry, regulatory and legal compliance is a CSR motivator along with the satisfaction of public expectations.

Some of the large local corporations in the country are owned by families of Spanish and Chinese lineage. These companies remain the biggest CSR spenders, typically through the foundations that they establish. Two business organizations—the Philippine Business for Social Progress and the League of Corporate Foundations, are instrumental in promoting sound and sustainable CSR practices (del Rosario, 2011). Scholars and policymakers alike say that with a weak economy and a government plagued by corruption and its inability to alleviate poverty, CSR and other private–public partnerships are imperative to fill the gaping holes that impede the country's progress.

## *Public relations practice*

Filipino public relations practitioners consider 1949 as the year PR began in the country (Lorenzo-Molo, 2006; Nieva, 1993, 1999; Sarabia-Panol & Lorenzo-Molo, 2004). Historical accounts, however, indicate that the profession actually began as early as colonial times with the country's national hero, Jose Rizal (Sarabia-Panol & Lorenzo-Molo, 2004). In 1882, Rizal campaigned for the Filipino cause by harnessing anti-clerical feelings in Spain in what was later called the Propaganda Movement.

Sison and Sarabia-Panol (2014) structured the historical narrative of Philippine PR around five key periods: Spanish colonial (1521–1896), characterized by propaganda for domination and for emancipation; American occupation (1896–1946), still propaganda-driven but this time the goal was to promote U.S. policy of "benevolent assimilation"; post-war Philippines (1946–1972), considered the period when modern Philippine PR was born and the concept of development communication emerged as different from pure propaganda because the purpose was the advancement "of greater social equality and larger fulfillment of the human potential" (Manyozo, 2012, p. 199); martial law period (1972–1986), which saw the tightening of thought control by the Marcos dictatorship and the non-violent triumph of People Power that ousted Marcos; and post-dictatorship (1986–current), which has as its centerpiece the gaining of more traction of corporate social responsibility and its role in national and social development particularly in the eradication of poverty.

Current PR practice in the country can be described as modernist, media-driven with a strong focus on CSR and a functionality derived from a socioeconomic context that continues to be feudal, capitalist and paternalistic.

The presence of active industry associations such as the Philippine Public Relations Society of the Philippines (PRSP), International Association of Business Communicators Philippines (IABC Philippines) and International Public Relations Association (IPRA) reflects the energy and interest in growing PR in the country. The drive to expand the industry comes from several factors: a robust media system, a democratic government, a young population of early adopters and a global outlook. This global outlook stems from economic reasons but also from colonial history (Sison & Sarabia-Panol, 2014).

Educational institutions continue to provide formal socialization and training of PR professionals, who either practice PR in the private or public sector.

## CSR and social development

Corporate social responsibility and public relations in the Philippines seem to be more intertwined than other countries in the region. Many of the public relations and communication practitioners tend to be comfortable with this connection as shown by the number of CSR programs submitted to and awarded by PRSP and IABC-Philippines. For instance, the 2016 winner of the Grand Anvil award was an educational program, "You For You (U4U): Educating the Youth About the Risk of Teenage Pregnancy," which was a partnership between an NGO and a media agency (http://adobomagazine.com/philippine-news/prsp-awards-top-firms-51st-anvil-awards). Another awardee that year was the telecommunication company PLDT's *Gabay Guro* program on educational advocacy (http://adobomagazine.com/philippine-news/pldts-gabay-guro-bags-major-wins-education-advocacy-52nd-anvil-awards), which was also billed as a 'nation building initiative by empowering teachers.'

Many corporations in the Philippines have established corporate foundations as their CSR arm. Part of the reason for this is economic. The other part is governance. In 2011, the Philippine legislative assembly passed Senate Bill no. 2747 known as the "Corporate Social Responsibility Act." The bill refers to corporate social responsibility as "the commitment of business to behave ethically and to contribute to sustainable economic development by working with relevant stakeholders to improve their lives in ways that are good for business, sustainable development agenda and society at large." The law mandates all 'large taxpayer corporations whether domestic or foreign, doing business in the country' to allocate a 'reasonable percentage of their net income to CSR,' SB 2747, p. 1 (retrieved from www.senate.gov.ph/lisdata/109799357!.pdf November 27, 2017).

Yet the Philippines is still considered a 'developing' country, despite its stellar 2017 growth rate of 6.7 percent (https://psa.gov.ph/regional-accounts/grdp/highlights), surpassing that of Western countries. Because of their emerging economy status, Philippine CSR is intricately related to social and community development. Moreover, the Philippines' complex political and social contexts engender a need to practise multiple stakeholder engagement as a matter of course.

We delve into these intricacies by examining how the multiple stakeholders of two companies, one multinational and one national, perceive and implement CSR and PR in the name of social development. We present excerpts from our interviews with the corporate (and corporate foundation) representatives, a local mayor and community leaders.

To provide context and a common reference point, we adopt the definition of social development as follows:

> Social development is about putting people at the center of development. This means a commitment that development processes need to benefit people, particularly but not only the poor, but also a recognition that people, and the way they interact in groups and society, and the norms that facilitate such interaction, shape development processes.
> 
> (International Institute of Social Studies, 2017)

The World Bank (2017b) states that:

> Social development focuses on the need to 'put people first' in development processes. Poverty is more than low income—it is also about vulnerability, exclusion, unaccountable institutions, powerlessness, and exposure to violence. Social development promotes social inclusion of the poor and vulnerable by empowering people, building cohesive and resilient societies, and making institutions accessible and accountable to citizens.
> 
> Working with governments, communities, civil society, the private sector, and the marginalized, including persons with disabilities and

Indigenous Peoples, social development translates the complex relationship between societies and states into operations. Empirical evidence and operational experience show that social development promotes economic growth and leads to better interventions and a higher quality of life.

Inherent to the idea of social development is social change, which has been defined as "multidimensional, but is ultimately contingent on a change of mentality, both for individuals and collectives" (Castells, 2009, p. 299). Castells argues that social change results from the "interaction between cultural change and political change" where cultural change involves changes in values, beliefs and behavior of individuals, and political change involves "an institutional adoption of the new values diffusing throughout the culture of society" (2009, p. 300). Social actors aim for a change in cultural values through developing movements. Based on this definition, we submit the parallel argument that CSR and PR practitioners are 'social actors' who are involved in social change.

With this conceptualization of social development and social change in mind, we demonstrate how the CSR programs of the two Philippine corporate entities promoted social development by an inclusive and participatory approach to engaging the communities as they respond to expressed community needs that range from livelihood generation, education, land ownership, disaster relief, etc. In so doing, communities were empowered thereby benefiting both the corporations and the village communities and creating a more sustainable model of economic and social development. By teasing out the varying interpretations of CSR and PR through a discussion of the community-based programs that flourished as a result of collaboration and power negotiation among the stakeholders, we are able to present a compelling narrative of how CSR has either contributed or has the potential to contribute to social transformation in the Philippines and perhaps the ASEAN region.

## Stakeholder perceptions of CSR

### Sustainable development: enterprise and education

The first organization we examined in the Philippines (PHNC) reflected that their CSR activities are focused on sustainable development, social enterprise and education.

The Philippine company (PHNC) started in hemp trading in the 1800s. Since then the family-owned business has expanded to the financial services, power, food, land, construction, shipbuilding and infrastructure industries.

The company's CSR communication declares its sustainability and goals on its website and collateral materials. In particular, it claims the business "looks beyond profitability and explores better ways to integrate social development and responsible environmental stewardship" in their operations.

The organization views sustainability "not as a cost but as a way of doing business" and as such, integrates the "people, planet, profit" framework in their operations. Although they continue their commitment to 'sharing,' the company's initial foray into CSR primarily involved philanthropy. They since have shifted to more sustainable community projects that are aligned with their business.

To manage the company's CSR activities, it organized a foundation in 1988 to complement the founder's foundation established in 1965. Aside from developing a more formal and systematic approach to the company's charitable activities, the Foundation focused its CSR on three pillars: education, enterprise development and environment.

Grounded on the dual purpose of 'helping people help themselves' and becoming a 'neighbor of choice,' the company works with stakeholders mostly in areas where they have a business presence. Corporate representatives stressed that their current CSR, which they refer to as CSR 2.0, must link projects with specific community needs.

> We need them to set parameters. It has to be a community need, it has to be aligned to the business, it should help or provide competitive advantage to the business. It should provide capability built within the communities, promote volunteerism for team members and team leaders, and it should be nationwide in scope.
>
> (Representative, Corporate Foundation)

One of the company's beneficiaries is a cooperative based in a remote village in central Philippines. The cooperative's general manager is an unassuming elderly man, we shall call Jose, who also works for the local municipality in the Cooperative Development unit. He intimated that the cooperative's initial engagement with the corporation was as a recipient of microfinance packages and grants to kick-start livelihood projects such as a bakery and a convenience store. Basically, the cooperative offered community members credit to start up their businesses. Under new management, the membership grew from 17 to 300.

The cooperative was so successful that they needed extra space to house their increasing inventories and to provide a safer environment for their microfinancing services. Jose revealed that prior to his arrival five years ago, the cooperative had difficulties collecting loan payments from its members. Many were defaulting on their loans so he was brought in from the municipality to manage the cooperative. Along with the seven-person board (five women and two men), he has been able to make members pay their loans in a timely manner.

To help fund the multipurpose building, the cooperative in partnership with the Philippine Business for Social Progress approached the company. In addition to funding the building construction, the company also assisted the cooperative in training and development as part of the compliance process. The Foundation validated this:

There are people from the business units who train the local government or local community to have the capability to write, prepare proposals and develop them to have a linkaging (sic), a networking capability so that they would know who to talk to, how to talk, and how to get the facts, how to implement it, and liquidate because otherwise if the LGU[1] does not liquidate, they will be barred from dipping into the pot.

(Corporate Foundation manager)

The relationship between the cooperative and the corporation involves both financial literacy and social development. At the time of the interviews, Jose advised that they were submitting a loan application to the company for an agricultural development project. The cooperative acts as a 'community bank' that approaches the private sector and then manages the funds on behalf of the community with appropriate interest accrued on the loans. Using this model, the cooperative delivered half a million pesos (approximately US$100,000) in dividends, which was then shared by the 300 members. This amounted to a dividend of about P50,000 (US$1,000) for that year for each member and an additional P5,000 (US$100) every December for each family.

Jose alluded that part of his goal is to further develop the livelihood in the community so they can just stay in the Philippines and enable them to own land to build their houses.

I told them (other members) if you develop your business here, your children will not have ambitions to go abroad. As an example, they don't have to spend a year in Saudi Arabia like I did (to earn an income) then afterwards, nothing is left to buy land and build a house, nor to educate the children.

(Jose, general manager, local cooperative)

When asked about the relationship between this cooperative and corporate entities, Jose confided that other corporations have approached their local community but they have been selective in their choice of corporate partners. He cited one company who offered them P100,000 (approximately US$2,000), which they declined because they found that the company had vested interests, particularly as the elections approached. So, their diplomatic response was that they did not have a project to which the monies will be allocated.

When asked how they chose which projects to pursue, Jose replied that some members were requested to submit proposals during their meetings. Other times, Jose said that he had to come up with solutions because some of the farmers, who are given land before the elections end up being unable to keep the land as unscrupulous politicians or their operatives would ask them to leave after the elections. Or if the lands are sold, they put fences on those lands right after they're sold, making it difficult for farmers to access them. So, he thought,

> what if we have the resources to buy, why not buy those lots and give that back to the farmer. They will be the land owners, they are members of the coop and they will not be separated from their land because they are members of the coop.

In terms of identifying projects, Jose reported that members are also encouraged to propose and their suggestions are evaluated by the seven board members, who then make the final decision.

> We often negotiate and ask for some authority because it is difficult if we are called 'dictators' so we can have healing and also have shared success.

With regard to the project proposed by PHNC, they felt that there was no issue and nothing was questionable (unlike the others). "We saw that the project was really going to help out the community, so why not?"

According to Jose, both the companies and NGOs, who provide funding and support also expect them to deliver progress reports. He laments that often times, those who help him locally do not know how to write reports and that the burden of reporting is left to him.

> We just give them reports as required and it's up to them to do what they want with it. They've told us we are the 'most progressive' and they're the ones who tell us, not us, that we're the most successful.

The company has assigned a staff member, a community relations person, to liaise with the cooperative. Her role is to facilitate community and company needs. This relationship management strategy between the company and community stakeholders seems to augment effective listening.

In another southern Philippine community, PHNC's CSR program reflected sensitivity to community needs and a strong awareness of the broader social issues while simultaneously being strategic. Because of the Department of Education's shift to a K-12 school curriculum, the schools examined ways to broaden student skill sets and recognized a need for vocational education pathways particularly for students, who are not college bound.

Since the company owned the local power facility, they supported several public schools to develop vocational training programs for future electricians and dressmakers. The support came in the form of electrical circuit boards and equipment to assist teachers through hands-on training for a course on Electrical Installation and Maintenance (EIM) or sewing machines for a course on dressmaking.

The school principals, especially those located in the mountains where some rebels operate, were extremely appreciative of the company's EIM lab donations. Not only did the company demonstrate courage in going to the deep rebel-infested hinterlands but it also represented the company's willingness to provide the same opportunities to all students in both urban and rural areas.

School principals acknowledged the company's sustainable approach and regular communication.

> What I appreciated most with (Company) ma'am is the sustainability of the program. They always contact past school heads what is happening in the program especially in the tracking. Very effective *ang* communication from the (company). Usually once in a month there will be a text, there will be a call.

The assessment visits are often unannounced to enable more robust evaluation. The company admits that their CSR program does not only deliver reputational benefits but also enables them to identify potential scholars, who they support through a university degree, then employ them as electrical engineers. They then ask these former scholars to visit the schools to inspire and mentor high school students.

In both these cases, the company's approach to CSR manifested a sensitivity to community needs. While the company retains veto power in project selection, the community also exercises power. The community is the source of ideas for potential projects especially those that address national concerns, such as K-12 transition or poverty reduction. For instance, they recounted the time when they suggested training programs based on the needs of the community:

> We really requested TESDA to come up with a community based training program for them so that it would not only benefit the teachers but also the entire community …We said you're not helping local economy in that area so it's better that we see the people from them so we came up with the ideas of a different training … we call it project basic electrician CIS training for the out-of-school youth or those who are farmers who while waiting for cropping season want to have a sideline as an electrician.

The school principals also narrated how they do not submit proposals but that the corporation would approach them with particular ideas in mind. However, when they are consulted, they would provide their input and negotiate with the company representatives. As one principal said:

> If we can't give two classrooms (for the project), we'll just get one classroom with dividers. So when it comes to giving of support, it is the donor who will look for alternative just to give, to push through with the project … because the donor wants to give two rooms but the principal can only provide one classroom. We find a way.

Community stakeholders are also very aware of how community programs become political platforms for those in government at local, provincial and national levels. Since power resides among the multiple actors in these CSR initiatives, community engagement involves consultation, negotiation and co-construction of the programs with multiple stakeholders. Very often the community and corporate representatives would express the term *"gawaan ng paraan"* which means "we will find a way" as a matter of compromise.

## CSR and community development as risk mitigation

The second company in the study, PHMNC, enacted their CSR activities from a framework of community empowerment and resilience. We interviewed the Philippines CEO, the local mayor of the Southern Philippine city involved in disaster rehabilitation and reconstruction, the plant manager, CSR manager and a focus group of community leaders.

The private-sector organization is a multinational company with head offices in Europe. It is a manufacturing company in the construction industry. In the Philippines, the company operates in four key areas and we visited their offices in the Southern Philippines. We also visited the community that experienced a natural disaster (a landslide), which has been the focus of the company's CSR efforts.

The perspective of the country CEO about CSR was rather enlightening. He disclosed that his CSR value formation and strategic direction started in the 1980s "when CSR has not been spoken of yet in many businesses." He narrated how in his former company, they were the only employer in the community so "everyone looks (*sic*) up to us. Almost for everything—employment, education, water source, electric source and even some of the community now, is still top in our plan for providing electricity."

He highlighted the philosophy of the Philippine Business for Social Progress which combines CSR as a form of community development and risk mitigation:

> As the owner believes that if you cannot be the only one in the community, and the only one eating and the rest are all very poor so you have to prove to the host community that it is getting more benefits of your presence so in such communities they started the CSR in early 80s and that was also the time when the insurgency in all of these areas are really at a high-level ... and they (companies) think that, rather than hire an army or security force, to really strengthen the defences in the community so the community will provide that for us. And they put our community relations initially towards more livelihood, then went into education and infrastructure.

The CEO brought this philosophy to his current company and reported that despite the strong insurgency in the southern city where his plant is located, they have not been asked for revolutionary taxes. He said that the seven-kilometer stretch between the quarry and the plant was free from unwanted rebel attention:

> From the mountain to the plant ... and we were not asked for revolutionary taxes so, I think in a way the community, the CSR program that we put together proved to be very effective and that is from providing water to the community which is sometimes very basic but obvious. You see children being used to fetch water, kilometers away and they couldn't study and you know when the organizers-cooperatives put the pump in and put running water into their houses that changes the lives of a lot of people, very simple.

However, he argued that their approach was more out of a moral obligation to help the community rather than a risk management strategy. Neither were they compelled to do anything by any one, not the government, the community nor the insurgents. As far as he's concerned, paying the right taxes to government is all that they need to do and maintaining a philosophy of helping others.

> If we can do more we want to do more. It's not like as if we put a number on what we can do, if it changes the communities' lives to a certain extent. For example, lately in (southern city) where we saw people living along the river close to our plant and they were like putting their houses close to the wall and it can collapse and there are quite a lot already. What to give up three to four hectares of our prime property to transfer them there and coordinate with the departments also wherever together with the National Housing and us to put together housing for these people. Is that something required of us? No, but it is something morally required for a company like us. Yes, because any accidental death within that area we think we're partly responsible for that.
>
> I don't think it's just a risk management or strategy. It's being like anyone else being concerned with society as we said the philosophy is people, planet and it doesn't mean our own people. It means the people whether it's customers, stakeholder of some sort. So, is it just a risk? You can say that. Is it part of strategy? You can say that but in the end, it's actually how a company really operates within its community, where it gets profit you want them to be looked at and looked up *di ba*?

When asked if the philosophy was reflective of Filipino or Christian values, he responded by first saying that the southern city is 95 percent Muslim. Then he continued,

> Being human is something with us as a people and you see a lot of people suffering and you're enjoying so much you should be able to share it. It has nothing to do with being Filipino, it is something of being human.

However, he acknowledged that they do have a process that enables communities to assist. For instance, the community relations managers, who are in the area discuss with the local community members their needs and ways in which both parties can contribute to the solution. These community members can include church leaders, NGOs in the area and school principals. They can make requests but it does not

> necessarily mean that we will say yes immediately. We have to say there are ways to do that. For example, an alternative fuel (source) or where we look at your plastic recycling and so on ... you can give it to us and in exchange we can give you rice ... so it's not automatic. Of if you want us to fix certain things in the schools, collect the garbage and leave it to us. It has always to be a give and take....

The community relations managers then identify what the priorities are and how much they will cost, and what their legal obligations are as well. Then they prioritize according to their consonance with the three pillars—education, infrastructure, livelihood. "So, if it falls under one of those three categories, yes. So then we automatically look at how much we budget as a company for you."

The CEO also reiterated that unlike other companies, who operate CSR programs based on their proximity to their company operations, they do so based on 'need.'

> We don't really put a ring. We look at the need of the community then there are communities that are already self-sustaining. You see that kind of houses that they have, right? I think the important thing is that you bring the necessary help for those who really need it most. Like for example the IPs (indigenous people) in the northern part of Davao that's even farther. You can reach it by riding on a horse, there is no motorcycle. Nothing. But we still engaged them *di ba*.... So that has nothing to do with being close to us and I think it has something to do with who needs it most.

This philosophy is exemplified in the community, which the company assisted after the devastating landslide caused by Typhoon Bopha (locally known as Typhoon Pablo) in 2012. The affected community is located about 120 kilometers and about a 2.5 hour drive from the city-based manufacturing plant. In this next section, we discuss the perspectives of the local plant, the local mayor and community leaders as they worked together in disaster rehabilitation and economic recovery.

### Rebuilding communities through collaboration

According to the plant manager, Typhoon Pablo wreaked so much havoc and damage to the hillside town that they could not sit in the city and not do anything. Even if she was not from that town, she felt the need to offer assistance initially just as a fellow Filipino. So, she ventured to the site with her friend (who happens to be the CSR manager) and offered help of any kind: food, clothing and just being available.

After seeing the devastation, she then asked the local community leaders what other assistance they needed. It was only then that she put on her hat as 'factory plant manager' and explored the possibilities of assisting with the rehabilitation. After discussions with the local mayor and the provincial governor, they identified that alternative housing is a priority for the affected residents.

The mayor said that 3,000 houses were totally damaged and 5,000 were partially damaged. About 300 casualties were reported but a total of 12,000 residents were affected. He recounted how many international NGOs, multinational and local companies arrived as well as individuals arrived to offer help.

> I received everything (that was offered). Even individuals with means, they brought food here. Others offered their heavy equipment for the deep clearing because that was what was needed.

Initially the mayor asked for food and water through media interviews he conducted. Even the then President (Aquino) arrived. Within a day of the typhoon's aftermath, the Red Cross and the Philippine military arrived whose help was really valuable as they were not from the local area. All the residents including the mayor were affected, but he knew he had to focus on his constituents first.

The Philippine Department of Social Work and Development (DSWD) was responsible for assessing which houses and agricultural properties were damaged and they classified them as either totally damaged, or partially damaged. However, the mayor added that some houses, which were not damaged were located in a 'fragile' location so DSWD put them in another category.

The mayor recounted that he met with the provincial governor to ask for further assistance. The governor advised that he had been approached by the local plant manager, who offered to help build houses for the affected families. However, they needed land in which to build the houses. Because the lands are owned by the local government, the mayor required a resolution authorizing him to sign the necessary documents.

> Actually, one of the requirements is land to put the houses on. Since the company will build housing there and the owners of the land is us, the local government unit (LGU) ... so I was involved because the LGU as owners of the land need a resolution authorizing me to sign any needed documents.

So, the process involved working with cluster (or committee) meetings such as shelter protection, water sanitation and health and these clusters included community leaders as well as international humanitarian and private-sector organizations. For this particular organization (PHMNC), they committed to building 100 houses, a training center and a gymnasium plus livelihood generation. Other organizations such as the Red Cross committed to building the other housing requirements.

For PHMNC though, providing housing was not a just a matter of building houses and donating them to those whose houses were totally damaged. The 'CSR package' involved providing materials and training for the residents to build their own houses. Male farmers and their wives were taught skills in carpentry, masonry, basic electrical insulation, welding, hollow block production and roof tile making, which were certified through the government agency, Technical Education and Skill Development Agency (TESDA). The mayor also acknowledged how the PHMNC has continued its community development engagement long after the others have gone.

> They've been here a long time, until now, they are here. That's the beauty. If it's them, they haven't turned their backs on helping out.

The mayor also reported that the disaster following the typhoon gave him the inspiration to transition from rubber plantation to cacao farming. He realized that there was more money to be made from selling cacao in the global market, compared to rubber, and the turnaround time was quicker. So, with the assistance of the government departments (Agriculture and Science and Technology), the farmers were provided training and this enabled them to be generate better revenue more quickly.

While the mayor acted as a 'conductor,' orchestrating the various private-, public- and civil-sector organizations and individuals, who wanted to help in the disaster rehabilitation efforts, they were always consulting various stakeholders especially the affected community leaders.

Collaborating with disaster victims was not easy and took a lot of time. As many of the disaster survivors revealed, they were not that interested in attending meetings as they were still reeling from the loss of their homes and their neighbors. We spoke with six of the local village leaders, who now comprise the 'leadership team,' and who initially were not big fans of meetings and training sessions. In addition to their leadership roles, they held daytime jobs as a beautician, an engineer, school teachers (two) and local government employees (two).

### Community empowerment and resilience

One of the village leaders recounted that it took them at least a year before they woke up to what laid ahead of them. She said that they would attend meetings and training but they would not even dress up or they would not respond. They would not even organize the children so when they are in the training, there is no parent, who would tell the children to keep quiet.

> Couldn't do it immediately. It was like we were sleeping and only woke up after more than a year. So in the beginning when we would meet or go to training, the women don't dress up or even respond. They just go there as 'audience', to watch but with no response. And even the kids were not looked after. We'd have our meetings, our training and the children were just there, left on their own and no parent would tell their kids to behave.

Eventually they were able to convince the trainers to relocate the meetings to the town and then to a hotel in the city to give the villagers a fresh outlook away from the devastation of their own environment. It was only when they were taken to the municipal hall's conference area that they were able to start the business of developing policies and their mission and vision, which was at the heart of their leadership training.

> What we got we brought back to the community. Now, we have a very collaborative community that responds quickly for any calls to attend meetings. If you want to meet, just go to your block leaders and the block leader will disseminate the communication. So, organizing meetings are like that now because communication is easy.

The leadership training arranged by the company involved bringing social work consultants from Manila-based universities whose interventions involved various stages. The initial stage included organizing themselves, identifying the leaders and their respective skill sets. For instance, one of the leaders is an engineer, who chaired the infrastructure and property development committee so all the houses they built were pretty solid. They also had a liturgy committee, who was able to work with the PHMNC and the local government to provide materials to build a chapel and a basketball court. Once the local village had their 'leadership team' organized, then they proceeded to developing the training program.

Before the village had settled into their 'new' housing community, there was a lot of resistance from the community members to move from their temporary housing. After being displaced once and moving their families to the temporary communal housing, the residents found it difficult to move again to the more concrete housing offered by PHMNC. They felt they have just bonded with their new neighbors in the communal housing and were unsure of re-establishing themselves.

Not all however resisted another move. In fact, some had very good things to say about the new houses. For example, one of the residents felt that the communal housing was not appropriate for her family. According to her, it was very crowded for her four children and two grandchildren as they were located in the middle of the building. It was hot, and also the bath and toilet facilities were shared with others. So, when she moved to the new housing, she told the others how the air was different, like it was air-conditioned, "*Parang aircon doon kasi ang hangin, wow iba*", and how the new houses had their own rest rooms. The others followed suit, including the engineer.

To be eligible to move to the housing, however, required the residents to help build their houses, so part of the selection process was to assess how much involvement they provided. The company provided basic structural materials and a basic house design, and the residents were given the latitude to upgrade or improve the basic structure. For instance, one family wanted to have a mezzanine so they did that at their own expense. Another placed a bamboo gutter from the roof tiles to collect water and avoid roof leaks. The company also provided the beneficiaries with electrical lines, but each family had to organize their own electricity.

The provision of leadership training and building and construction skills created a sense of pride and empowerment in the community. They also recognized that they were already given so much in terms of basic housing, training and hope, they felt it was now their responsibility to make things happen: "We would be a bit embarrassed (to ask for more) because they already gave us everything. It should just be up to us to find a way to get things done."

The village leaders repeatedly expressed their gratitude to PHMNC, through the interventions provided by the two consultants, for the numerous training programs that enabled them to organize themselves into committees, develop a mission and vision and move them out of their depressive conditions.

They highlighted how the CSR program provided major assistance in transitioning them from being disaster victims to productive citizens and leaders of their communities. They felt that the interventions raised their living standards, broadened their horizons and developed their families and communities.

They were extremely grateful that PHMNC offered a program that included two social workers:

> At first it was DSWD who helped but in the long run (PHMNC) gave people who helped us—Ma'am Thelma and Sir Joshua. They were the ones who greatly helped us to improve our livelihood, if not to broaden our horizons, so we can think about development for family and community. And for the community base, for the many many trainings including leadership training so we can organize ourselves, until we can put up a mission, vision … until we were able to form eight committees including a board of directors.

As one of the community leaders said,

It's difficult if no one is teaching you because if you're experiencing stress, especially from a calamity, your brain function is limited. It's just like a dot and your brain will not broaden up if there is no one doing the intervention.

This reflection highlights the need for the intervention of responsible external actors equipped in psycho-social healing. So, while the members of the disaster community are keen to learn, their mental and emotional states can be highly vulnerable to exploitation and manipulation.

The community leaders then feted the research team to a lunch in their basketball court where they also displayed their catering skills and musical skills. We were also invited to walk around the neighborhood and visit houses where some enterprising residents also established herb gardens. It was evident from the interaction with the other community residents that this community of 'disaster survivors' have since transformed their lives through their collaborative efforts with local and provincial government officials, national agencies, national and international NGOs and the private sector.

## Summary

The cases from the Philippines signify that corporate social responsibility is an integral, almost intrinsic, component of Philippine business. The establishment of the PBSP in the late 1960s/early 1970s emerged from the business community's realization that "urban poverty became more widespread and the ineffective land reform program failed to alleviate rural oppression" (Tan & Bolante, 1997, p. 5). The rising poverty fed the insurgency and "drove fear into the hearts of the rich and powerful Filipino business community—which was regarded as one of the perpetrators of the lopsided distribution of wealth" (Tan & Bolante, 1997, p. 5). Business leaders then formed the PBSP as a way of demonstrating their commitment to social development, and following the Venezuelan model "*Dividendo Voluntario Para La Comunidad*" contributed 1 percent of their pre-tax income to the organization.

Undoubtedly the establishment of PBSP as with the more contemporary CSR programs reflects a risk mitigation for businesses. While corporate representatives articulate their 'humanistic' and 'moral responsibilities' to the communities, they also demonstrated that the goodwill they generate with the communities result in a form of 'social fencing.' By empowering and enabling the communities to generate livelihood, they become protective of the corporation and their assets. In effect, the communities, who wish to protect their livelihoods become protectors of the corporation. While this approach may be viewed as an instrumentalist approach by corporations, it can also be seen in reverse: that the community stakeholders are 'using' the corporation's resources and assets to improve their livelihood. While this power dynamic is not present in all community–corporate relationships, there is scope to further explore these types of relationships.

Because of the country's developing economy status, social development programs and subsequent development communication activities have been a natural imperative in the country. This history of communities helping each other out, of private enterprises filling the gaps left by government has evolved to what is now known as corporate social responsibility. Although Philippine business leaders do not see that Western-style CSR has been fully integrated in the business, the principles of CSR seem to be already embedded in the psyche of the Filipino employee. The question however remains on how to translate and integrate the individual's natural intuition to do good to a more institutionalized level.

This chapter also provided glimpses of the social transformation of individuals, who developed into leaders of their communities. Turning indifference into engagement and eventually into personal and group leadership was as convincing as the broadening of the horizon of possibilities made possible through study visits or brought about by necessity. Economic betterment awaited, for example, rubber farmers who became cacao farmers and simple *barangay* folks who acquired construction skills to rebuild houses destroyed by a typhoon. In these cases, the emerging value differentials indeed resulted in corresponding behavioral changes, which bode well for CSR as a catalyst for social change and development and the effectiveness of CSR as social actors in a developing country like the Philippines.

Furthermore, this study shows how the Philippine practice of CSR requires the involvement of various sectors of the society. The complexity of relationships demands businesses to engage not only with the government at national, provincial and local levels but also with the Church, NGOs and people's organizations to initiate and implement CSR projects. While multi-sectoral involvement is critical in generating buy-in for CSR among key community stakeholders, it could also pose difficulties and challenges especially if many perceive public servants as mostly corrupt (Transparency International, 2009). How businesses navigate through the maze of political and cultural systems is by itself a challenge in relationship management.

The cases also reveal that CSR programs require a deeper level of engagement with the community to be feasible and meaningful. While corporate representatives acknowledged that their programs required the approval of their CEO or Chairman, identifying the needs of the community from the ground up was critical in their implementation. Working with the local community leaders or *barangays* was key to ensuring that the CSR project was not merely a 'public relations stunt' but rather a genuine effort to address a real need within the community. In some cases, the need was determined at the national level. Finding the happy medium between the national and local agenda is the task of the CSR practitioner, who in most cases works in the corporate affairs department of the organizations in this study.

While power dynamics still manifested traces of feudalism especially in the countryside, the cases also tell how valuable public–private partnerships, multi-sectoral coalitions and advocacy are in CSR and social change. Given the enormity and scale of the problems, the Philippine government has no choice. While previous studies (Waldman et al., 2006) suggest that CSR in Asia thrives when government is weak, it could be argued that these cross-institutional relationships are relevant to CSR practice in any country.

In this regard, we would argue that there is value in revisiting the term 'beneficiaries' to also refer to the corporations, and not just the communities, who are often seen to be at the 'receiving' end of corporate largesse. As these cases show, the corporations involved with these empowered communities are also 'beneficiaries' in that the positive engagement has generated positive benefits to their organizational reputation. As a corporate representative previously mentioned, the local community representatives in the Philippines are highly aware of their rights, and quite politicized because many have learnt to rise up against exploitation by some corporations. The Philippine experience of resistance during World War II and the Japanese occupation continuing through the Marcos dictatorship generated a sense of activism and social justice among local community leaders. This historical experience taught many local community leaders to fight, mobilize, leverage and negotiate with the private sector and exercise the strength of the 'community power.'

Part of the complexity in Philippine CSR is that while there are many individuals, and companies, who have a desire to do good, once they have to deal with the public-service system, their good intentions hit a brick wall. The 2009 Global Corruption Barometer cited that of the 1,000 Filipinos interviewed, 35 percent found that public officials/civil servants were most affected by corruption (Transparency International, 2009). Other sectors deemed as corrupt were political parties (28 percent) and parliament/legislature (26 percent). Thus, the discourse on CSR will continue to be regarded with much skepticism until integrity and trust in the systems are in place. The 2017 Transparency International Corruption Perceptions Index ranked the Philippines 111 out of 180 countries (www.transparency.org/country/PHL).

While the current Duterte administration attempts to address issues of social inequality and reduce the prevailing corruption in the system, the spirit of community and '*bayanihan*' within the private-, public- and civil-society sectors underpin the enactment of CSR. Regardless, the paradox of communicating and maintaining visibility vis-à-vis the credibility of CSR programs remains. Despite criticism that Philippine CSR tends to be merely for show, there is still a group of grateful scholars and aid recipients, who may not otherwise have had the opportunities for education and new means of livelihood. For businesses, it may be a case of "damned if you do, and damned if you don't" but they don't seem to mind being damned for doing good.

## Note

1 Local Government Unit (LGU) is the official nomenclature that encompasses three levels of local government authority or jurisdiction, namely: the provinces and independent cities, municipalities or towns and the barangays in that hierarchical order based on geographic and population size.

## References

Anonymous. (2009). *Global Corruption Report*: Transparency International.

Asis, M. (1995). Overseas employment and social transformation in source communities: Findings from the Philippines. *Asian and Pacific Migration Journal*, 4 (2–3), 327–346.

Asis, M. (2017). The Philippines: Beyond labor migration, toward development and (possibly) return. Migration Policy Institute: www.migrationpolicy.org/article/philippines-beyond-labor-migration-toward-development-and-possibly-return.

Bonifacio, M. (1977). An exploration into some dominant features of Filipino social behaviour. *Philippine Journal of Psychology*, (10), 29–36.

Castells, M. (2009). *Communication Power*. Oxford: Oxford University Press.

CIA. (2017). The World Fact Book. Philippines. www.cia.gov/library/publications/resources/the-world-factbook/geos/rp.html

del Rosario, R. (2011). Corporate social responsibility in Southeast Asia: An eight-country analysis. *Research Report*, Makati, Philippines: Asian Institute of Management.

Department of Social Work. (2017). Bayanihan. http://vrplus.dswd.gov.ph/index.php/component/content/article/7-bayanihang-bayan-program-bbp-/11-what-is-bayanihan.

Hofstede, G. (2001). *Culture's Consequences. Comparing Values, Behaviors, Institutions and Organizations across Nations*. Thousand Oaks, CA: Sage.

International Institute of Social Studies. (2017). Indices of social development. www.indsocdev.org/defining-social-development.html.

Lorenzo-Molo, M. (2006). Understanding the reputation and image of the Philippine public relations industry. *Public Relations Review*, (33), 58–67.

Lorenzo-Molo, M. (2009). Why corporate social responsibility (CSR) remains a myth: The case of the Philippines. *Asian Business & Management*, 8 (2), 149–168.

Manyozo, L. (2012) *Media, Communication and Development: Three Approaches*. New Delhi: SAGE India.

Maximiano, J. (2007). A strategic integral approach (SIA) to institutionalizing CSR. *Corporate Social Responsibility and Environmental Management*, (14), 231–242.

Moss, J., Hoffman, J. & Lipton, S. (2016). The South China Sea: The Spratly Islands dispute. http://asiahouse.org/the-south-china-sea-the-spratly-islands-dispute/.

Nieva, R. (1993). Public relations in the Philippines, *International Public Relations Review*, (16), 5–7.

Nieva, R. (1999). PR is alive and well and moving forward in the Philippines. *PR Net*, 9–11.

Reuters Staff. (2017). Philippine president sees biggest ratings dip, but popularity intact. www.reuters.com/article/us-philippines-politics-duterte/philippine-president-sees-biggest-ratings-dip-but-popularity-intact-idUSKBN1CD0NJ.

Sarabia-Panol, Z. & Lorenzo-Molo, C. (2004). Public relations in the Philippines: A cultural, historical, political and socio-economic perspective. In Sriramesh, K. (Ed.) *Public Relations in Asia: An Anthology*. Singapore: Thomson Learning.

Sison, M. D. & Sarabia-Panol, Z. (2014). Philippines. In Watson, T. (Ed.). *Asian Perspectives on the Development of Public Relations*. UK: Palgrave Macmillan.

Tan, V. & Bolante, M. P. (1997). Philippine Business for Social Progress, *The Synergos Institute Voluntary Sector Financing Program Case Studies of Foundation-Building in Africa, Asia and Latin America*.

Vasquez, N. (1992). Economic and social impact of labor migration. In Battistella, G. & Paganoni, A. (Eds.). *Philippine Labor Migration: Impact and Policy*. Quezon City: Scalabrini Migration Center.

Walden. (1999) *Walden Country Reports*. Philippines: Walden Publishing.

Waldman, D. A., Sully du Luque, M., Washburn, N. & House, R. J. (2006). Cultural and leadership predictors of corporate social responsibility values of top management: a GLOBE study of 15 countries. *Journal of International Business Studies*, (37), 823–837.

World Bank. (2017a). Personal Remittances received (% of GDP). https://data.worldbank.org/indicator/BX.TRF.PWKR.DT.GD.ZS, https://data.worldbank.org/country/philippines?view=chart.

World Bank. (2017b). Social development. www.worldbank.org/en/topic/socialdevelopment/overview.

# 5 Singapore's strategic social enterprise and inclusive CSR

## Country context

### Historical, political and economic context

Singapore has deep historical ties with Malaysia. Both were British colonies during the late eighteenth and nineteenth centuries and gained independence from Britain in 1957.

Japan occupied both countries from 1942 to 1945. Considerable socio-cultural and ideological differences as well as ethnic tensions led to the political separation of the two countries.

Singapore's historical narrative, which can be traced back in the fourteenth century, has been described as a journey from the "emporium to a world-class city state" (Kwa, 2009). The island known then as Singapura had Temasek, a Malay trading port. Temasek's glory days as an entrepot ended in a conflagration in the seventeenth century. Historians credit the British to have founded Singapore as a trading colony in 1819. It became part of a single federation with Malaysia but the tumultuous merger terminated in 1965. The rest of Singapore's story is about nation-building and its rise to an economic powerhouse with a stable political and market-based, export-oriented system with a GDP matching that of prosperous Western European countries (CIA, 2018).

This parliamentary republic has very low unemployment and is attempting to reduce its dependence on foreign labor. It remains as Southeast Asia's premier financial and technology hub with a reputation of a graft-free business environment, low barriers to foreign investment (Robertson, 2009) and sensible as well as consistent government regulations. Some of the challenges of this "smart city" or "intelligent city" are industrial pollution, limited natural freshwater and land resources and waste disposal problems.

### Cultural and social context

Singapore is ethnically diverse. The country's cultural make-up consists of Chinese at 74 percent, Malay, 13.4 percent and Indian 9.1 percent. Both

Mandarin and English are the official languages. About a third of the population are Buddhist, another 14 percent are Muslim and 11 percent are Taoist. Catholics represent 7 percent of the population; Hindus, 5 percent and those with no religious affiliation, 16 percent.

Given the racial and religious composition of Singapore, its government has made the promotion and preservation of racial harmony a top priority. In this country, multiculturalism as an official, state-sanctioned policy means that no cultural group is superior or is a majority or a minority (Huat, 2009).

Quite adept and effective in social engineering, the Singapore government, particularly the Political Action Party (PAP), has forged through policy, propaganda, planning and regulations a national culture and identity that is "hierarchical, disciplined, repressed and materially successful—a show house of technocratic, authoritarian, dependent capitalism" (Haley & Low, 1998, p. 531). Yes, Singaporeans enjoy high standards of living but their freedom from the economic yoke of material poverty may have come at the cost of other personal freedoms. It seems that Singapore society places a higher premium on discipline and harmony rather than personal freedom.

Vulnerability, a result of PAP propaganda, is observably ingrained in the nation's psyche (Seng, 1998). The state has crafted a "survivalist" culture by equating social cohesion with national survival and economic progress. It has promulgated the following shared national values:

> 1. nation before community and society above self, 2. family as the basic unit of society, 3. community support and respect for the individual, 4. consensus, not conflict; and 5. racial and religious harmony. The adoption of English as the official language and Chinese, Malay and Tamil as secondary languages unified and integrated Singaporeans. Its language policy is likewise seen as instrumental in the understanding and appreciation of the country's various cultural elements.

Indeed, after several decades of strong state influence on society, multicultural Singapore with its brand of ethnic hybridity has flourished as a cosmopolitan city-state that blends Western modernity and pragmatism with Asian values such as communalism. It is a meritocracy that believes in charity and collective well-being and values education and gender equality (del Rosario, 2011).

## Public relations

Public relations in Singapore started during colonial times with the Department of Publicity and Printing under the British Military Administration. Expectedly, PR was mainly in the form of propaganda aimed at building credibility and support of the colonial government. The industry received a boost in the 1950s with the influx of multinational corporations especially oil companies who established in-house PR departments (Beng, 1994).

Government PR efforts continued soon after the country's 1965 independence but this time the goal was to rally citizens in the formation of a stable and prosperous nation (Nair, 1986). The then Ministry of Culture and the Information Division oversaw the government's public education/information program, which included public campaigns on anti-littering, anti-spitting and other government policies. In the 1990s, the primary government PR apparatus was the Ministry of Information and the Arts, which like its predecessor used not only the in-house PR staff but both local and international PR agencies as well. As Singapore became the leading financial nucleus in the region, more MNCs began establishing regional headquarters in the country which in turn attracted the major international PR firms such as Burson-Marsteller, Hill and Knowlton, Ogilvy and Mather, etc. to follow suit. Local PR agencies in increasing numbers also took their slice of the persuasive industry pie (Beng, 1994).

While much of the focus of PR activities in Singapore revolved around media relations and marketing support as well as government relations in the early days as well as today there's movement toward more strategic PR (Beng, 1994). A peculiar challenge facing Singapore PR professionals is the monopolistic structure of the media system that limits diversification of coverage. Misperception of the field that plagues PR in other countries as well and ethical problems due to the stiff competition among firms are some of the unflattering spots of Singapore's PR industry. Lwin and Pang (2014) highlight that public relations in Singapore suffers from: negative public perceptions, difficulty in quantifying its value, and focus on traditional (media-oriented) competencies.

Efforts to combat these problems are in place and spearheading industry professionalization is the Institute of Public Relations of Singapore. Founded in 1970, it has an accreditation process and an annual Prism awards for the best PR programs in the country. IPRS also conducts certification courses and training workshops. Educational institutions are certainly doing their part in the formal training of strategic communication practitioners as well. The introduction of full degrees in public relations in three well regarded universities—Nanyang Technological University, National University of Singapore and the Singapore Management University—has aided in the value of public relations in the country (Lwin & Pang, 2014).

Logically, in a diverse society like Singapore, cultural values inevitably impact PR practice. Yeo and Pang (2017) have found that because multiculturalism is a state policy, managing diversity often means that "all racial representations that included translation of languages took precedence even over the success and effectiveness of the intended message to persuade" (p. 117).

### *Corporate social responsibility*

According to popular media, CSR in Singapore officially started in 2005. This happens to be the year when the Global Compact Network Singapore, which encourages multi-sectoral collaboration between corporations, government and civil society to advance responsible business conduct and CSR particularly in the protection of human and labor rights as well as the promotion of environmental conservation and accountability/transparency in business. It has been proposed, however, that the concept and practice of CSR actually began in the 1960s when the government instituted Singapore's labor policies (Cheam, 2015).

A 2004 CSR survey of 450 companies in Asia, Europe and North America indeed disclosed that Singapore had the highest number of policies not only on labor standards, but also trade, stakeholder engagement and local community development (Welford, 2005). With the country's plurality of religions, it was also not surprising for a study of the role of religion on consumer support for CSR to find a positive relation between religiosity and CSR support in Singapore (Ramasamy, Yeung & Au, 2010).

Another important milestone in the evolution of CSR in Singapore is 2011 when the Singapore Exchange released sustainability reporting guidelines. Since then a CSR component has been integrated in the business reports of many major companies in Singapore. Tan (2011) suggests the following drivers of CSR in Singapore: (1) the government as agenda setter and manager, (2) CSR as a strategic differentiator in the economic realm, (3) Singapore's export economy, (4) CSR as a catalyst for self-regulation, (5) ISO 26000 as standards, and (6) CSR as social innovation.

As mentioned above, the strong hand of Singapore's government clearly extends to CSR, which appears to bode well for the city-state. Because corruption is extremely low, the need for watchdogs is not at the level as it is in other countries in the region. Besides, the government is very well able to "control and regulate corporate behavior effectively" (Robertson, 2009, p. 627). In addition to the Singapore government, the other key lever in the country's CSR is globalization. With an economy that relies on foreign trade and investment, Singapore is inextricably linked with the international system and expected to conform to global standards (del Rosario, 2011). As such, the government sees itself "as the promoter and practitioner of CSR" (Tan, 2013, p. 185).

The country's leading organization in the promotion of CSR practice is the Singapore Compact for CSR. Composed of corporations, the government and NGOs, the Compact was founded by the National Tripartite Initiative for CSR, Singapore Employers Federation and the National Trades Union Congress. Diffusion of CSR among small and medium firms as well as the expansion of CSR objectives beyond business competitiveness are in Singapore's to-do list (del Rosario, 2011). The 'tripartite' approach has somehow moderated the CSR environment with the absence of "overt contention, a general reticence in pushing the CSR agenda, non-existent employee activism, wariness with excessive government regulation and enforcement" (Tan, 2013, p. 190).

## Perspectives on CSR enactment

As a developed economy, Singapore's approach to corporate social responsibility takes on a different flavor compared to the other Southeast Asian countries mentioned in this book. Several scholars have examined CSR in Singapore in terms of SMEs (Lee, Mak & Pang, 2012), religion and values (Ramasamy et al., 2010), its emerging state of play (Tan, 2011, 2013) and more recently, for enhancing corporate image (Pang et al., 2017). Earlier studies indicate a low level of awareness of CSR among company employees in Singapore and Malaysia (Ramasamy & Ting, 2004). While the awareness seems to have increased since then, the practice of CSR in Singapore is emerging in various ways.

For this study, we interviewed four representatives from the corporate sector (3 SGNC, 1 SGMNC), and three representatives from social enterprises in Singapore who are partners of SGNC. Our interviews and observations point to variations in the focus and approach to CSR by the two corporations included in the research. Both national (SGNC) and multinational (SGMNC) companies employ a strategic approach to CSR but each has a different focus. Both companies have established corporate foundations to handle most of the CSR activities although the SGMNC Foundation was relatively new at the time of the interview.

The SGNC foundation is the implementation arm of its CSR programs and projects but its CSR activities also sit under the Strategic and Marketing Communications group. Working within the financial services industry, the company started out as a community business and grew to become a national corporation that also operates outside Singapore. They claim that the company is rooted in a deep community orientation and has focused its programs to address three groups: elderly, people with disability and out-of-school youth. Their programs however are underpinned by a strong approach to employee volunteerism and social entrepreneurship.

In this chapter, we present the voices of the SGNC corporate foundation representatives and their partners who identify their organizations as social enterprises and social organizations. The SGMNC's CSR approach meanwhile may be characterized as underpinned by a shared values approach. As an outcome of this audit, which involved consulting with their partners worldwide, SGMNC identified three focus areas for their CSR: (1) environmental sustainability, (2) skills training, and (3) disaster relief.

### *CSR as employee volunteerism*

SGNC prides itself with being involved in the community long before CSR was fashionable because its history as a company is tied to Singapore's economic development. The organization's history and size enable it to tap on its resources for its social responsibility activities. Like in other countries, SGNC has established a foundation arm to handle its CSR programs.

The head of the corporate CSR department, who is also the SGNC Foundation head, clarified that their CSR activities are

> very much centered around our corporate resources in terms of our people, and our products and services making a difference in the community ... that allows us to very holistically support the communities that we operate in toward the outcome that we seek.

While the company is a for-profit, commercial organization, she emphasized that her company is

> more than just a corporate entity. We actually have a role to play in society. We assist in society, with license from the economy, with license from communities. We need to identify how our work can benefit communities in the future.

The company views that their greatest contribution to the community is through their resources—human and other materialities. As such, the CSR program is primarily focused on volunteerism.

> The (company's) resources are what we bring to the table. Some of that may include also inviting our networks whether it's clients or otherwise to join us. But it is really the (company's resources) that is making a difference. I mean we have 22,000 employees worldwide, half of that is in Singapore. So, we have quite a bit of resources that we can tap on.

The company has introduced a volunteer policy that allows each employee to take two days of paid volunteer leave to serve their communities. While they encourage their employees to volunteer in their existing and long-standing partner programs, they are also open to other opportunities suggested by their employees. However, there are 'core principles' that their partners are encouraged to abide by:

1 alignment with corporate values: PR ideal, purpose-driven, relationship-led, innovative, decisive and fun;
2 initiatives are sustainable and impactful.

They report that close to 18 percent of their employees have availed of their volunteer program which accounts to about "almost 1 million-dollars-worth of time within the year. Half of that is coming from Singapore." They have integrated their volunteer program as part of their corporate culture so that employees see the program not just as an incentive but also part of their leadership training.

She further added that they assimilate and promote the volunteering opportunities in their staff recruitment. They assume that the "younger workforce, millennial workforce actually do prize this kind of sustainable and corporate citizenry stance by the employers." The organization has also incorporated the CSR volunteer program as part of their on-boarding process of new employees to enable early engagement.

Employee volunteering has also been employed as an employee engagement mechanism. So, in addition to the CSR team designing the activities and mobilizing employee volunteers, they have established "over the past two years, a corps of what we call 'volunteer leaders' so they are themselves ambassadors and champions in their own business units." The team members found that as the employee volunteers engage in the process, they are also undergoing a learning and development process themselves—the more they know about the community issues, the better feedback they provide to identify particular priorities and issues. This employee engagement process is similar to the community engagement process previously discussed in the farming community in Thailand. In both cases, the 'engagement as research' process emerges out of the CSR programs and activities.

The enactment of this company's CSR activities addresses the objectives of employee engagement, internal communication and marketing. Employees who participate in the volunteer program are encouraged to tell their stories, take photos and videos and share these with their colleagues inside and outside the organization.

The other aspect of their corporate citizenship is through their foundation. She admitted that the CSR and Foundation teams work hand-in-hand on projects, although the foundation has a particular focus on social entrepreneurship.

## Enabling social entrepreneurship

As previously mentioned, the corporate arm started off as a company during Singapore's early years of economic development. As such, working with small to medium-sized enterprises (SMEs) was an integral part of their core business.

> So, when it came to orienting our resources and our expertise to want social good, it was a very natural extension to look at social entrepreneurship because these are small businesses just like the commercial ones we're working with but they are established and oriented towards achieving a social outcome. So, it allowed us to very naturally extend what we were already doing as part of our business to also be more beneficial towards the country.

While the "foundation is a grant-maker and deploy funds," the foundation head also stressed that they take an active role in "co-creating, designing and executing" the programs. In addition to mobilizing their employees as volunteers, they can also activate "other resources whether for branding, facilities, networks to impart the programs that the foundation is actually running."

She believes that social entrepreneurship is still at a nascent stage in the country and in the Asia Pacific region:

> Social enterprises are an exciting structure and business mode of operation which we see as bringing great potential to what the future can be ... we think they can play an important role in more sustainable and inclusive communities in the future.

She then recounted that the focus on social entrepreneurship came from a team within their operations that actively engaged with SMEs. These activities eventually evolved into a CSR focus area and when they realized the area needed to be nurtured and developed, which "can benefit commitment and a longer-term strategy," the company established the foundation.

The SGNC Foundation comprises board members of the company, executive leaders and senior managers who meet regularly. They involve their social enterprise partners in the businesses as their suppliers as well as being customers of the social enterprise. In some instances, they also provide mentorship and skills training to their social enterprise partners.

The two foundation program managers indicated that the company had a program, which for this study we will refer to as "People with Dreams" (pseudonym) that started about the same time as their CSR programs. Interestingly like in Indonesia, these two managers come from an NGO background and have since moved into the CSR departments of a corporation.

The program managers report that their main objective is "to raise awareness of social enterprise and we nurture them and we also support them financially" through grants. The grants scheme involves applicants submitting proposals and they evaluate the funding request proposals based on the foundation program objectives. They also host an online platform "to showcase social enterprises ... and we hope to encourage people to live a more inclusive lifestyle...." They echo their supervisor's comment on the non-financial contributions of their colleagues to various social enterprises.

For instance, their colleagues in the accounting department ran a clinic with social enterprises on accounting and tax policies, or made themselves available for informal chats. Other examples include senior executives providing mentoring and strategic advice to social enterprises, or setting up online donation platforms to help in disaster relief.

The foundation's social entrepreneurship program has identified partnering with organizations that assist three key marginal groups: the elderly, people with disabilities and marginalized sectors of society. We then inquired about their process in selecting these priority groups.

The foundation head said they looked at the research undertaken by the "social sector including unmet needs in Singapore. What are the more important issues currently that matter to the country? For example, we've identified seniors, the aging society, especially senior disability and low-income families." While they have identified key areas, they are also open to take up causes that resonate with their employees. So that the priority issue areas will be driven by what employees are also interested in. "It's more of an operations manager decision about where we go in terms of the partners that we engage and the programs that we undertake."

They focus on the three main groups of people because they are viewed as "underserved." The respondents indicated that Singapore is faced with an aging population and dementia among the elderly is a real problem. They assert that, "One in ten seniors will have a chance in getting dementia and it is a very real thing." As such they work with various partners such as specialist NGOs that focus on the elderly, hospitals who have resources to assist in this area and even food banks who are able to provide affordable and nutritious food.

While the corporation's history is indeed tied in with Singapore's economic development and SMEs, its focus on social entrepreneurship also reflects a strategic approach to CSR. The company belongs to the financial services sector and as such offers technical knowledge and opportunities to grow their business while helping others. Because of its maturity as an organization with extensive resources and a solid reputation, the SGNC is in an enviable position of somehow influencing the business community in effecting social change.

We met with three community partners of SGNC, two are social enterprises (SGS1 and SGS2) and another is a social service organization (SGS3). SGS1 is a fairly new and small social enterprise whose focus is on creating programs that may include events to increase awareness about people with disabilities. The two founders started the organization as a personal journey given that they had family members with intellectual disabilities. Realizing that there were limited opportunities for physical exercise for disabled people, the pair conceptualized a start-up and leveraged on their respective skills and knowledge in marketing and communication. The relatively young founders started their social enterprise as part of an incubator program with SGNC and from joining competitions.

> We didn't get any money out of our (incubator) pack, but we got a lot of business knowledge and access to materials. We also joined competitions such as the Singapore International Foundation Social Entrepreneurship program and we were one of the winners so we got $10,000. Last year, November, we won the President's Challenge start-up of the year so we have like a $40,000 cash prize.

They admitted that winning competitions made their name "move very fast in the scene" and more people wanted to be associated with them. The three-person team develops and designs programs mostly for corporate organizations that include indoor or outdoor team-building activities that involve working with, or learning how to work with, people with disabilities. These activities can include sports events or simulation exercises, learning sign language, or undertaking blindfolded tasks that allow able bodied individuals to understand the world of visually impaired people. At the time of the interviews, this social enterprise reported 28 to 30 corporate clients.

In addition to the start-up support provided and the designation as a 'preferred community partner,' SGNC has also identified employee volunteer opportunities at SGS1. Often the social enterprise submits a proposal for events lined up in the year where they'll need SGNC support. In the process, SGNC will provide feedback and SGS1 will revise accordingly and so the program is co-designed. The proposal typically will include events lined up for the year which will need volunteers. SGNC then promotes these opportunities to their employees and registers their interest. The employee volunteers then assist in various tasks at the events such as registration or being the liaison, video operators, etc.

According to the SGS1 founder, critical to their success thus far was their partnership with SGNC.

> We really benefit from their marketing of the events and we benefit based on growing our contact base ... especially last year (company) really expanded our contacts with VWOs (Volunteer Welfare Organizations) and it helped us to form more credible partnership ... because the first introduction to us is already via them ... who are very credible sources.

Moreover, the partnership with a highly reputable organization has reaped flow-on effects for this new and emerging social enterprise.

> We definitely benefit in terms of the name and branding as well, just like saying that (company) is our client gives us the whole reputation out of that. Whereas, (company) I think how they benefit from doing this, it's really more fulfilling their KPIs like in their CSR goals, and I guess giving People of Dreams more avenues to volunteer and different ways and channels of volunteering.

While they appreciate the corporate sponsorship and the reputational benefits that accrue for their affiliation with the company, the social enterprise founder suggests that there are still many areas for improving the partnership arrangements.

> A shorter work time. So, when we give a proposal and then they give us feedback and everything, that whole back and forth process usually takes quite a huge amount of time ... it will help us to be a lot more efficient ... if we can actually have a shorter turnaround time. Also, some of our other clients still come to us and ask, "oh but you know if you're doing good, why should I pay you?" because people still associate social enterprises with charities. So, a lot of corporates don't really

understand what is a social enterprise and why should social enterprises charge money, and why there is a need for social enterprises to be sustainable.

There is no doubt that a small and lean operation like SGS1's corporate partnership is reaping benefits that will enable them to be a sustainable business. However the founders' personal motivations that drove them to establish the social enterprise must not be overlooked. Their personal commitments to inclusion is not too different to the motivations of the second social enterprise.

The second social enterprise (SGS2) was founded by a young woman who believed in the "very powerful medium of business to do good to help people and to create positive change." When asked what made her establish her business, she observed the increasing income inequality in Singapore was causing more people to be marginalized. She said that "in Singapore if people are not academically strong, the pathways are very limited." While social services and skills training were offered to marginalized communities, she believed that the core issue of 'managing their challenging lives' was not being addressed. As such, she established a 'holistic' social enterprise that included physical and emotional well-being with livelihood development, and skills training. Her social enterprise generates revenue through a professional training academy, government-funded training, corporate events, workshops and retail services. The training academy offers several courses that range from basic skills to certification of individuals for a fee. And the revenue generated from these enrolments subsidizes 'holistic training programs'—or the 'social program'—geared toward vulnerable women and at-risk youth.

The six-month social program includes an international standard training academy, emotional resilience and physical training (such as yoga, self-defense training, rock climbing). The program involves three months of learning in the academy, paid internships around Singapore and "if they survive those first 12 weeks, then we put them out for full-time work for another three months. If they survive those three months, then they graduate."

Participants in the social program are referred to them by the Singapore National Social Service organization as they need to be genuinely in need of support as the program also works with social workers to support the participants' families. Moreover, this social enterprise supports graduates of these programs to establish micro-enterprises to enable them to generate a livelihood.

The corporate partnership with SGNC started with the latter hiring the social enterprise's mobile crew for their corporate event. Because of the social entrepreneurship thrust of the SGNC Foundation, the social enterprise was asked to cater the corporate's major events and later provide technical support. The social enterprise was also provided a grant by the foundation to "increase its manpower capabilities." The founder highlighted the SGNC Foundation's approach to the grants:

> ... what I liked about the (company) grant and the way they approached it was it wasn't very prescriptive. It was, what does your organization need, and how can the money help you get there? So, the key things were really more organization specific rather than (company) saying these are the 3 things you need to hit regardless of your model....

While the company was still committed to meet the goals in their five-year plan as part of the grant conditions, there was also an expectation that the company was going to leverage on the social enterprise's good work. This was another example of strategic, mutual benefit partnership approach.

> In a way, it's great because we get I guess visibility and marketing to their channels, and their reach. And they get to use the brand and brand story to display their commitment. I'm not saying this because we're partners ... I'm saying this generally as they do really try and walk the talk.

Because of the increased visibility and improved social enterprise's reputation, they also undertake a process of partner selection, similar to the way corporates select community and NGO partners.

> I think we've been lucky we've had people come to us but obviously assessing who to work with and how to work with them is very important. I think for us it's really just, are they in it for the right reasons, are they generally interested in helping, are they generally interested in the process? Yeah so there have been organizations which you engage once and after that, you know what, you guys are just not genuine about this so we disengage.

The third community partner (SGS3) is a social organization whose work focuses on providing support and friendship for the elderly. Established in 1995, the organization works with community and corporate partners who provide volunteers. The program involves volunteers to commit to a one-year plan to visit and establish a relationship with an elderly person near their community. Because of the expectation of a long-term relationship, a rigorous matching process is undertaken that includes considerations of language/dialect spoken, preferred location, availability and most crucial of all, interest.

Similarly, the nature of the partnership between this social organization and the corporation is through the provision of employee volunteers, technical support and advice. For instance,

> they are looking into our handicraft project and they gave us feedback on the products and they even helped us with the seniors who do the handicraft items that we will be showcasing this October. Because this is a very new initiative for us.

The respondent from SGS3 reiterated the collaborative nature of their corporate partnership as they co-create and co-design program activities. "We appreciate the insight from the various departments in (company) who specialize in these various functions, (they're) very helpful."

She attributes this type of relationship from its being a long-term commitment and regular communication: "Every month there will be interactions between us and the company, whether it is with the community center or our organization."

While they have other corporate partners, this social organization has a preference for strategic long-term relationships and partnerships. While they also do half day "CSR events," they use these opportunities to discuss longer term volunteer opportunities. Ensuring that their corporate partners align with the needs and services of senior citizens reflects how a social enterprise also exercises strategic partnerships.

The narratives of the social enterprises reveal that SGNC has made strategic investments into building partnerships through their CSR programs. All partnerships are selected and leveraged to maximize their assistance to the community and extend their reputational clout. The next section presents the shared values approach to CSR employed by the SGMNC.

### CSR as shared values

SGMNC is a global brand within the hospitality industry and operates in over 100 countries. According to its website, the company is committed to engendering a culture of 'responsible business' by minimizing its environmental impact, providing training and support to its communities, enhancing employee diversity and selecting ethical suppliers.

The respondent representing the SGMNC is the director for corporate responsibility responsible for two of the company's four regions. While each of the company's operations around the world had been doing its own form of CSR or advocacy (e.g., AIDS, Down's Syndrome, breast cancer prevention)—often as personal initiatives of the general manager—the head office realized that they were spreading their resources too thinly. According to him, there were 2,000 charitable projects in a given year and each charity was receiving US$100–200, but "we didn't have a story to tell about our global impact."

So, they undertook an audit around the company's worldwide charity and fundraising activities using the shared values framework. Shared value is defined as

> policies and practices that enhance the competitiveness of a company while simultaneously advancing the economic and social conditions in the communities in which it operates. Shared value creation focuses on identifying and expanding the connections between societal and economic progress.
>
> (Porter & Kramer, 2011, p. 66)

He shared that they had to ask themselves these three questions:

1 Does the community and environment need this thing we're doing?
2 Does the business need this?
3 Is this something we're uniquely good at doing well?

They layered the above questions on the 2,000 activities they were doing worldwide and concluded that they could reduce them to three key themes: environment, skills training and disaster relief. These three themes anchor their strategic CSR programs.

Environment. As part of their operations, one of their biggest costs is the utilities bill so decreasing consumption of energy and water makes the business profitable. At the same time reducing their carbon footprint and waste is good for the environment. To enable their global operations to achieve this, they developed an online tool with over "200 green solutions ... to help them think about what they can implement ... to reduce their consumption that's at a brand standard to ours."

Skills training. Their global operation employs half a million people and they recognized their strength is in skills training for their industry sector. Consequently, they established academic programs in specific locations, and worked with local vocational schools, high schools, community organizations, and schools for the deaf, the blind and mentally disabled.

> Through these partnerships, they will bring in a number of people to get work experience so essentially, we are making local people more employable but at the same time building a pipeline for our business, reducing recruitment costs, because many of these people after they do their work experience, will get hired into full time positions.

He intimated that this program, particularly the one that operates in Singapore, works with different schools for people with disabilities. The disabilities range from hearing or vision impairment to "different sorts of mental disabilities or physical disabilities." They work closely with the schools to "identify different roles" that are required that can be "well matched and suited for their physical abilities, bring them in, train them, do work experience with them and then hire many of them into full time roles."

Given Singapore's regulations around employment quotas for local and foreign workers, this 'inclusive workplace' strategy was able to address not only the business imperatives but also the employability concerns of people with disabilities and their families. He cited that for this particular business in Singapore, 20 percent of its workforce are people with disabilities.

Disaster relief. The third pillar of SGMNC's CSR program centers on disaster relief primarily because of their experience in providing assistance during these calamities. They leverage their resources and facilities, including their access to their supply chain. They have established partnerships with relief organizations in different local communities ... adapted us to preparedness plans so that when a typhoon happens, everybody knows what to do and the (business) general manager knows the point of contact that the local let's say Red Cross organization, or Care International or World Vision ... so they can immediately jump into action.

While Singapore itself does not experience disaster of the magnitude seen in the Pacific islands, or the Philippines, the office coordinates these operations for the region.

Like other private sector organizations in the region, SGMNC also has a foundation which shares similar focus areas as the corporate organization. They can fund grants to organizations doing skills training in their sector, for development research in products or services that are useful in their business operations or for disaster relief and preparedness.

For this SGMNC, the foundation is managed by the corporate CSR team. Interestingly though, the nature of our respondent's role revolves around coordinating with colleagues around the region and developing stories about the company's corporate responsibility activities. For example, he recounted the use of the company intranet.

... usually I draft the story for them (CSR team) and say 'hey look it's ready to go' and just upload it and push it out to all of our properties. We also have a weekly email bulletin that goes out to all of our properties across the organization and so that we'd very regularly do stories and information usually if I require their action. If I need them to do something, then I'll use that bulletin....

The respondent discussed CSR operations mostly from a regional and global perspective because that is his remit. The research team managed to visit and observe one of the local properties run by SGMNC and saw an employee with Down's Syndrome. As our respondent mentioned, employees with disabilities are integrated within the workforce and not 'identifiable' as part of increasing public awareness and reducing the stigmatization.

## Summary

As this chapter reveals, CSR takes on a different flavor in Singapore as it reflects a more strategic, albeit government promoted, approach to CSR. The focus on social entrepreneurship, employee volunteerism and shared values indicates the country's economic development status. While it was unfortunate that we did not get to speak directly to any of the program 'beneficiaries,' our observations of their onsite operations and visits to their websites provided equally valuable insights. One website in particular featured video testimonials from several students who proclaimed how their lives were transformed by their involvement in the social enterprise.

Two features of the CSR cases in this chapter are worth noting: the 'engagement as research' process and the strategic, mutual-benefit aspect of the partnerships created in the enactment of the various CSR activities. The immersion of corporate staff in their partner communities enabled new learning that led to better understanding and prioritization of community needs. Also, the partnerships forged through the various CSR initiatives produced win–win relationships for all involved. The skills training, for example, developed a pipeline for competent, future or potential corporate employees, which even if it was not originally intended is a welcome benefit for sure. The push for a much lesser environmental footprint hoists the benefits to a planetary scale way beyond just energy savings for the company that undoubtedly help the corporate bottom-line.

The inclusion of people with disabilities, vulnerable women, the elderly and other populations living in the margins of Singapore society makes the CSR of the companies, their foundations and partners merit considerable notice. Addressing the needs of an aging population also sits well with the government agenda, and at the same time enhances the corporate image as previous research has indicated (Pang et al., 2017).

Indeed, Singapore's regulatory environment somehow dictates the CSR approaches of private-sector organizations. So, the focus on social inclusion of marginalized sectors of the community is not necessarily accidental. In 2007, Singapore launched its first Enabling Masterplan aimed at building a more inclusive society. Run out of Singapore's Ministry of Social and Family Development, the Enabling Masterplan "is a five-year national roadmap to build a more inclusive society, in which persons with disabilities can be integral and contributing members, empowered to reach their potential" (www.msf.gov.sg/policies/Disabilities-and-Special-Needs/Enabling-Masterplan-2012–2016/Pages/default.aspx).

Drawing from its experiences in the first two iterations of the masterplan, the third edition (2017–2021) focuses on four areas: improving the quality of life of persons with disabilities, supporting caregivers, building the community and building an inclusive society (www.ncss.gov.sg/NCSS/media/NCSS-Documents-and-Forms/EM3-Final_Report_20161219.pdf). The Enabling Masterplan defines disabled people as those "whose prospects of securing, retaining places and advancing in education and training institutions, employment and recreation as equal members of the community are substantially reduced as a result of physical, sensory, intellectual and developmental impairments."

The government has allocated about SG$1 billion for this program since 2007. This financial commitment from the national government is a practical move to demonstrate Singapore's efforts to improve the social well-being of its people. It also somehow explains the CSR focus of the corporate sector in developing programs for social inclusion.

While the government's role is critical in the promotion and implementation of CSR in Singapore, the case studies also reflect the *seemingly* 'collaborative' and 'harmonious' approaches between business, government and society. Singapore's growth as a developed economy has been attributed to its stability and orderliness, due in large part to the controls set by government. This means that activism and protests are discouraged, and quelled immediately.

As Tan (2011, p. 7) admitted "undue CSR activism on the part of NGOs and civil society is not encouraged as it is seen to detract from Singapore's branding as a business-friendly place." This statement suggests that Singapore's authoritative power pervades over the enactment of CSR and engagement with community stakeholders.

Moreover, the cases confirm that while CSR in Singapore reflects a top-down approach, the spread and adoption of CSR initiatives accrue to SME business leaders as well as MNCs who balance the commercial operations with the social needs of the local community. In particular, engaging employees in CSR activities as part of 'team-building' efforts is a strategic yet subtle imperative that comes from top management.

In the same manner, the values of harmony and consensus have been embedded in the Singapore psyche that initiatives from the government and top management are often left unquestioned.

While the cases discussed in this chapter reflect positive outcomes of social inclusion through CSR programs, they could also be a way of "redressing some of the excesses of capitalism" (Tan, 2013, p. 194). Nevertheless, whether MNCs and SMEs undertake CSR for compliance, strategic advantage, altruism or guilt, the cases demonstrate how CSR programs can make a major difference to the lives and futures of marginalized individuals and communities.

In terms of communicating CSR, the cases in this study confirm previous studies that found word-of-mouth an effective means of spreading the corporates' CSR message (Pang et al., 2017). By engaging with community partners, both local and foreign-owned corporations are able to reduce public skepticism of their CSR activities and instead gain traction through 'third party' endorsements and strategy alignment. As the respondents mentioned, designing CSR programs and activities that fit with their brand values generates more credibility than 'gimmicks' that do not have any connection with their company goals.

While strategic engagement with their employees, partners and suppliers may indicate a risk mitigation approach, the inside-out CSR approach across the range of organizations in Singapore seems to be underpinned by a regard for control and respect for hierarchy. Although Singapore is a multicultural and cosmopolitan global hub, its population is predominantly Chinese and Buddhist. CSR activities and communication require a deep understanding of the whole range of cultural, and religious, values (Pang et al., 2017; Yeo & Pang, 2017; Ramasamy et al., 2010). Undoubtedly, local culture and wisdom are integral to the effective enactment of CSR activities and practitioners are well placed to invest time and energy in understanding these cultural nuances.

The totality of the CSR narratives in this chapter points to the indisputable fact that being good corporate citizens brings a pot of golden benefits to the companies themselves, the communities, partners, the government and in maybe smaller measure, the planet. Enlightened self-interest in the form of strategic social entrepreneurship works.

## References

Beng, Y. S. (1994). The state of public relations in Singapore. *Public Relations Review*, 20 (4), 373–380.

Central Intelligence Agency. (2018). Singapore. *World Fact Book*. www.cia.gov/library/publications/the-world-factbook/geos/sn.html.

Cheam, J. (2015). The evolution of CSR in Singapore. *The Straits Times*.

del Rosario, R. (2011). Corporate social responsibility in Southeast Asia: An eight-country analysis. *Research Report*, Makati, Philippines: Asian Institute of Management.

Haley, U. & Low, L. (1998). Crafted culture: Governmental sculpting of modern Singapore and effects on business environments. *Journal of Organizational Change Management*, 11 (6), 530–553.

Huat, C. B. (2009). Being Chinese under official multiculturalism in Singapore. *Asian Ethnicity*, 10 (3), 239–250.

Kwa, C. G, Heng, D. T. S. & Tan, Y. (2009). *Singapore, a 700-Year History: From Early Emporium to World City*. Singapore: National Archives of Singapore.

Lau, A. (2005). Nation-building and the Singapore story: Some issues in the study of contemporary Singapore history. In Gungwu, W. (Ed.). *Nation-Building Five Southeast Asian Histories*. Singapore: ISEAS Publications.

Lee, M. H., Mak, A. & Pang, A. (2012). Bridging the gap: An exploratory study of corporate social responsibility among SMEs in Singapore. *Journal of Public Relations Research*, 24, 299–317.

Liu, J. & Abraham, S. (2002). Social representations of history in Malaysia and Singapore: On the relationship between national and ethnic identity. *Asian Journal of Social Psychology*, 5, 3–20.

Lwin, M. O. & Pang, A. (2014). Singapore. In Watson, T. (Ed.). *Asian Perspectives on the Development of Public Relations: Other Voices. National Perspectives on the Development of Public Relations*. London: Palgrave Pivot.

Nair, B. (1986). *A Primer on Public Relations Practice in Singapore*. Singapore: Institute of Public Relations and Print N Publish Pte Ltd.

Pang, A., Lwin, M., Ng, C., Ong, Y., Chau, S. & Yeow, K. (2017). Utilization of CSR to build organizations' corporate image in Asia: Need for an integrative approach. *Asian Journal of Communication*, 1–25.

Porter, M. E. & Kramer, M. R. (2011). Creating shared value: How to reinvent capitalism—and unleash a wave of innovation and growth. (The Big Idea), (Cover story). *Harvard Business Review*, 89 (1–2), 62.

Ramasamy, B., & Ting, H. (2004). A comparative analysis of corporate social responsibility awareness: Malaysian and Singaporean firms. *Journal of Corporate Citizenship*, 13, 109–124.

Ramasamy, B., Yeung, M. & Au, A. (2010). Consumer support for corporate social responsibility (CSR): The role of religion and values. *Journal of Business Ethics*, 91, 61–72.

Robertson, D. (2009). Corporate social responsibility and different stages of economic development: Singapore, Turkey and Ethiopia. *Journal of Business Ethics*, 88, 617–633.

Seng, L. K. (1998). Within the Singapore story: The use and narrative of history in Singapore. *An Interdisciplinary Journal of Southeast Asian Studies*, 12 (2), 1–21.

Tan, E. K. B. (2011). The state of play of CSR in Singapore. Singapore: Lien Centre for Social Innovation, Singapore Management University.

Tan, E. (2013). Molding the nascent corporate social responsibility agenda in Singapore: Of pragmatism, soft regulation, and the economic imperative. *Asian Journal of Business Ethics*, 2 (2), 185–204.

Welford, R. (2005). Corporate social responsibility in Europe, North America and Asia. *Journal of Corporate Citizenship*, 17, 33–52.

Yeo, S. L. & Pang, A. (2017). Asian multiculturalism in communication: Impact of culture in the Practice of public relations in Singapore. *Public Relations Review*, 43, 112–122.

# 6 Sustainable community development and risk mitigation in Thailand

## Country context

### *Economic, political/historical context*

Thailand is the only Southeast Asian country that never became a European colony. It was however under the control of the Khmers until its independence and was invaded by the Japanese during World War II. Since its establishment as a united Thai kingdom in the mid-fourteenth century, the world knew it as Siam until 1939. A constitutional monarchy was formed following the 1932 bloodless revolution that ended the absolute monarchy. King Bhumibol Adulyadej reigned from 1946 until his death in 2016. His only son, Crown Prince Maha Vajiralongkorn succeeded him (CIA, 2017).

The country, which is the only constitutional monarchy among our six-country sample, has been through a period of political instability since 2005. Its Prime Minister Thaksin Chinnawat was ousted in 2006 by a military coup. There were massive street protests by rival political parties from 2008 until 2010. The following year Thailand saw the election of its first female prime minister, Yinglak Chinnawat, Thaksin's youngest sister. She was however removed from office in 2014 after exacerbating the political turmoil with her amnesty bill that excoriated her brother's crimes. Another coup led by Royal Thai Army Gen. Prayut Chan-ocha led to his appointment as prime minister. His reform-minded interim military government drafted a new constitution, which was passed in a national referendum in August 2016. The new king signed the new constitution in April 2017 paving the way for the national elections in mid-2018.

The World Bank (2017) classified Thailand as a middle-income country. It has adopted Western economic tools for development and has managed to grow its economy at a healthy clip of 7.5 percent on average from 1960 to 1996. The growth rate went south during the Asian financial crisis (5 percent) and further slid down to 3.5 percent during the 2005–2015 tumultuous political period. This economic contraction continued in 2016 with a sluggish 2.3 percent growth rate. The economy, however, recovered somewhat in 2017 with the relative political stability that has been achieved.

Thailand has reduced the country's poverty level from 67 percent in 1986 to 7.2 percent in 2015. However, 7.1 million Thais still live below the poverty line and like other ASEAN countries, 80 percent of the nation's poor are in the rural areas. Attaining a more inclusive economic prosperity is at the heart of the country's 20-year national development strategy (2017–2036) along with regulatory reforms, infrastructure projects and improved educational system.

The country wrestles with environmental problems ranging from deforestation, water shortage, soil erosion, pollution (including agricultural chemical pollution) and loss of biodiversity (Forsyth & Walker, 2008). The tug of war between economic development and environmental protection is a Thai reality much like most countries in emerging economies or in the developing world.

## *Cultural/social context*

Thailand expectedly is 97.5 percent Thai with a minuscule coterie (1.3 percent) of Burmese people. Thai is the official language and Buddhism, particularly Theravada, is the dominant religion accounting for 94.6 percent. Muslims are at 4.3 percent and Christians at 1 percent.

In describing countries like Thailand that have been spared direct colonization, Michael Herzfeld (2002) coined the term 'crypto-colonial' to capture the societal changes brought about "by the global projection of Western imperial and neocolonial power" (p. 13). Among the manifestations of this semi-coloniality is the tension between the modernizing Thailand with the associated influences of a capitalist-driven market economy and the traditional teachings of Theraveda Buddhism (Jackson, 2005).

No other everyday practice nets the intricacies of Thai culture and its dominant religion than perhaps the *Wai*, Thailand's most common social greeting. According to Powell, Amsbary and Hickson (2014), in addition to the greeting's utilitarian, status, nationalistic and personal enhancement functions, *Wai* likewise expresses respect for monks, religious statues of Buddha and royalty (since the king is seen as a deity), hence a religious function. In other words, in a high-power-distance society (Hofstede, 1991) like Thailand its signature greeting conveys the Buddhist belief that one is born to a status based on karma. This religious belief evidently makes Thais more accepting of power differentials in their social relations. Another normal feature of this elaborate hierarchy is *greng jai*, which means "self-effacing, respectful, humble and extremely considerate, as well as the wish to avoid embarrassing other people, intruding or imposing upon them" (Servatamorn, 1977, p. 13). In a sense, Thais share the value of 'saving face' with many Asian cultures.

And like other collectivist and agrarian cultures, Thais historically are members of extended families where interdependence and collective work are common (Hallinger & Kantamara, 2000). As a people with high uncertainty avoidance, Thais also prefer stability where "order depends on people's knowing and accepting their proper place or rank and on not disturbing the proper order of things" (Hall & Hall, 1987). The maintenance of harmonious social relations and the familiar is paramount, which creates "a communal security blanket" (Redmond, 1998, p. 62) but can be hazardous to the idea of accountability, innovation and the entrepreneurial spirit (Hallinger & Kantamara, 2000).

## Public relations practice

The origins of public relations in Thailand coincided with the country's switch from an absolute to a constitutional monarchy in 1932. The government under the new political system recognized the need to keep its subjects informed so it created a Publicity Office, which later became the country's first public relations department (Ekachai & Komolsevin, 1998). Like other Asia-Pacific countries, the historiography of Thailand's public relations is located at the "emergence of the governance expert systems during nation building" (Halff & Gregory, 2014, p. 401) to unify the country as it transitioned from absolute to constitutional monarchy.

The government therefore was the primary PR operator and as such used one-way, persuasive communication or propaganda to inform the people of government activities, which for some critics were considered deceptive. In fact, the government had the second largest PR budget next to the telecommunications industry. Other state agencies like tourism and petroleum also had large PR budgets. In 1980, Thailand's government instituted a national policy for the PR industry and a national PR plan in 1988 (Ekachai & Komolsevin, 2004; Halff & Gregory, 2014). The 1980 policy enunciated five principles including the need for PR at the grassroots level. Two-way PR however began to materialize only when the country became more democratic with an emerging emphasis on planning and research (Ekachai & Komolsevin, 1996).

In the private sector, PR mainly performed image building and maintenance in addition to marketing support. Some of the PR industry problems cited were the lack of skilled practitioners in both the government and business sectors. Thai universities have responded to this need with PR curricula patterned after the U.S. and have since played an "indispensable role in the production of quality practitioners and the development of the profession" (Ekachai & Komolsevin, 1996, p. 233).

In addition to universities establishing degrees to assist in professional development, the Public Relations Society of Thailand, established in 1965, provided training for the private sector (Tantivejakul, 2014). While its code of conduct mostly drew from that of the Public Relations Society of America (PRSA), it also contained one that distinctly reflected Thai cultural values—"respect for Thai social order and moral standards" (Tantivejakul, 2014, p. 136). Despite the advent of globalization, Thai public relations practice and education mirror the country's respect for the monarchy, Buddhist and relationship orientations.

## Corporate social responsibility

Thai media first mentioned corporate social responsibility in 2003 (Prachachart, 2005) and in 2006 the Thailand Research Fund reported, based on qualitative data from CSR early adopters, that the country has two CSR management types: the in-process type in which companies integrate CSR into the organization's production and profit-making apparatus and the after-process type in which corporations manage profits for the benefit of society (Yodprutikarn, 2006).

After the 2004 tsunami that devastated Thailand's southern region, the Stock Exchange of Thailand established the Corporate Responsibility Institute in 2007. It was the CRI that proclaimed the need for businesses to address community and societal needs including environmental conservation. Another attempt by Thailand's public sector to diffuse and implement this Western concept particularly in corporations was the establishment of the Thai Industrial Institute and the Kenan Institute of Asia, which published a draft of ISO 26000 containing guidelines for manufacturers to meet new CSR industrial standards (Srisuphaolarn, 2013). The Thai government has recognized that CSR can be a strategic economic engine (del Rosario, 2011).

In response to the public push for CSR, companies began appropriating a "social tax budget." Through this mechanism Thai enterprises support religious causes, educational scholarships, hospital funding and disaster relief through direct financial donations.

In discussing the national profile of Thailand's CSR, Chapple and Moon (2005) confirmed that for issues involving education and environmental conservation the main CSR delivery modes are philanthropy and government codes. But as multinational companies in the country respond to global market demands, they have gone beyond compliance as part of their CSR initiatives particularly in terms of labor and environmental practices and consequently influencing local Thai companies to do the same (del Rosario, 2011).

Indeed Srisuphaolarn's (2013) CSR study of 30 Thai companies in 2009 and 2011 found that the main driving force of Thai CSR is solving social and environmental problems through management of corporate profits as a way of paying it forward to society or integrating CSR into business strategy through the development of products to benefit consumers as well as the larger society. There is a strong cultural element to the practice as these approaches were attributed to Thai social and Buddhist values that can be summarized in the truism *Pid Thong Lang Pra* (placing the gold in the back of the Lord Buddha image), which means that doing good without announcing it is a personal virtue. Thais believe that once good deeds are advertised, they lose their virtue. This was reported as a reason why companies in the study carried out CSR projects to improve the living standards in surrounding communities or chose activities that have little or no direct relation to the products produced and marketed.

However, a perceptible surge of media reporting about corporate philanthropy and other social marketing activities has occurred since the 1990s and this has prompted concerns on whether Thai companies know and understand the distinctions between CSR and PR. Critics also raised questions regarding the sustainability of Thai CSR programs (Business Thai, 2007, 2008; Pratchachart, 2005).

Other scholars have examined CSR in Thailand from a variety of angles such as the organizational perspective like the shift from an altruistic to a more strategic approach (Srisuphaolarn, 2013), as a form of competitive advantage (Kraisonsuthasinee & Swierczek, 2009), as a poverty alleviation strategy (Pimpa, 2013) and the relationship between corporates and NGOs (Sthapitanonda & Watson, 2015).

## CSR perspectives and practices

As mentioned earlier, many of the CSR studies about Thailand have highlighted various cultural values such as Buddhism and *pid thong lang phra* (Sthapitanonda & Watson, 2015) which underscores giving without the need for recognition. Because the vast majority of the Thai population are Buddhists, the notion of giving and philanthropy are intrinsic in their nature. Another factor that shapes CSR practice in Thailand is the practice of patronage where members of the ruling class provide welfare for those less fortunate, who in turn provide service and respect. The power imbalance created by differences in one's class and economic status seems to be addressed by attempts to undertake CSR activities.

While the existing research is valuable in understanding how CSR is perceived and practiced in Thailand by different stakeholder groups, very little attention has been given to the perceptions and voices of the community 'beneficiaries.' While corporates are often seen to have overriding power in determining CSR policy, we argue that community stakeholders also exercise some power over corporations. That is why corporations invest time and resources in gaining their 'social license to operate.'

This chapter will discuss the perspectives from these different stakeholder groups. For this study, we conducted several interviews that included: the corporate communication manager and community relations manager of THNC, three community leaders (one village leader, the local NGO leader, and one informal leader), one manager and one employee of a THMNC, and the CEO/managing director of an industrial estate.

### Sustainable community development through enlightened community relations

The THNC was established in 1913 under the decree of King Rama VI to support the country's modernization and infrastructure projects. Its philosophy of "doing business with righteousness" has continued with its more recent commitment to be a leader of sustainable development in the ASEAN region. The company is a manufacturer of building and construction materials and its plants are spread around the country.

The company prides itself in integrating its social responsibility and sustainable development in its philosophy and vision. Aside from looking after the well-being of its employees through various sports programs, the company has adopted environmental sustainability as a key platform with its three stages of 'green implementation:' green manufacturing, sustainability supply chain and eco-value labels and products (Leelakulthanit, 2014).

One of its key projects was conceived in 2003 after the King remarked that 'water is life.' The project is underpinned by a belief that water conservation is critical to a better environment and quality of life. They adopted the business concept of 'where our factories are, there's lush green forest.' Part of this approach included ensuring that the forest areas surrounding their factories were safe from forest fires. One such plant is located in Northern Thailand and the company (THNC) initiated a project to restore degraded forests "aimed at preventing fires around the plant" at a time when the "community was not aware of the problem, nor how to deal with the potential fires," according to the company's communication manager.

The project started with tree planting in the nearby forests but extreme drought reduced the foliage and caused forest fires. Aside from the farmers in nearby rice fields, many of the plant employees also lived in the surrounding communities affected by the fires.

The company decided to learn about watershed management in one of the King's study centers in 2003. Company representatives learned to construct small 'check dams' made of locally available materials such as rocks, logs, branches and soil. Check dams are "temporary or permanent linear structures placed perpendicular to concentrated flows such as in drainage ditches, channels and swales to reduce flow velocities and prevent channel down-cutting." A range of materials can be used to construct check dams including rock, fiber logs, triangular sediment dikes, sand bags and prefabricated systems. Check dams are used mainly to decrease water velocity but sediment capture and increased infiltration are added benefits (Minnesota Stormwater Manual, 2017). Since this 'technology' can impact the surrounding communities, and is relatively easy to teach, the THNC saw an opportunity to engage the community and approached them to join the project.

> THNC initiated the check dam project to solve the fire problem. In the beginning, the community didn't care about building the check dam perhaps because they cannot see its benefits.
>
> (Corporate communication manager)

So initially, the community resisted and was distrustful of THNC's intent. The village leader was concerned about the company's pollution. About 40 percent of the community refused to cooperate and participate in the 'dam building activity.'

> I am an elected village leader. My role is to take care of the people in every way. About THNC, I was concerned about the pollution in the beginning.

The NGO leader echoed his distrust, "My NGO was skeptical as the thought is that industry is an evil to the environment." The village leader added,

> But THNC showed their readiness in green business, explained and communicated for mutual understanding with the people. And supported the knowledge of conserving the water and forest which was necessary for the livelihood of the community.

In addition to the knowledge learned from the company, the village leader recounted that the community's survival from a storm five years ago demonstrated the benefit of the dam as their village was the only one in the district that was saved from the floods. The NGO leader also said that "since the water came back from the droughty (sic) land, it brings back natural resources and wild animals. The people see the benefits with their own eyes."

This show-and-tell approach was part of the community engagement strategy developed by THNC's community relations manager. As someone who grew up in the area and spoke the language, he persisted and developed a relationship with the NGO leader. To establish trust, the community relations manager patiently explained their green concept and organized a community trip to their plant in the central region. They showed how their plant was designed with a semi-open-cut system with environmentally friendly technology imported from Germany. The system has won best practice awards and the company organized open houses so the community can visit when they want.

According to the NGO leader,

> ... organizing the trip inspired people's imagination although there was skepticism about reality and the possibility of building the dam. Some villagers questioned the allowance for building the dam and how much money they will get. So, I organized the trip to another village which was successful in building the dam. Villagers need to be conscious that the dam is their issue.

Once the NGO leader was on board, the community relations manager brought a few of the village leaders to the King's study center to show how check dams are built and what the result can be. To empower them in water conservation, THNC acted as mentors while the community was made to run and manage the project, exploring and testing their ideas. The project implementation was neither designed nor implemented, nor dictated by THNC. While the company suggested the idea to the community, the community developed the project and now hosts an annual community event with farming and non-farming families, THNC employees including executives and the media.

Since 2003, there are now more than 70,000 check dams in the area, of which 55,000 or 79 percent were built with THNC involvement. The company's community relations manager, who we shall call Mr. Nattapong, admitted that they changed their paradigm from 'giving' to 'participation' in 2008. The community project not only increased the knowledge of the village members but also restored the forest's biodiversity. THNC then commissioned Chiang Mai University to survey the flora and fauna and found that the number of bird and plant species increased, enabling local residents to collect mushrooms and other plants for their consumption.

Another benefit to the community was access to clean water. The improved condition of the forests allowed water to be collected, stored and used by the nearby communities through the installation of pipelines from the mountains to the lowlands. One female, informal village leader we interviewed, revealed how the return of the water to the forests brought water to her house through pipes set up as a partnership between the local district and THNC with the villagers putting in the labor. Her face and eyes lit up as she narrated, in the local language, how the forestation and water project provided her with physical relief as she previously had to walk many kilometers, hiking up and down the mountain, to collect and carry buckets of water on her shoulders for her family to use in their daily activities. Not only was she relieved from the physical burden of collecting and carrying water downhill, but her access to clean water has also allowed her to use the time she saved to focus on her family activities and their small family businesses—a local store, a frog farm and a rooster farm.

> The project outcome brings back the natural water. Before there is no water in this droughty (*sic*) land. I had to walk for kilometers to get the water. It was a tough life. Nowadays we have water pipe from the forest to our household. The water is used to feed the chickens and frogs. Natural water has no chemicals so the frogs are growing better and faster, when compared to government water.
> 
> (Informal community leader)

Her farms have generated sufficient income for her family after her husband passed away. She said the secret to her successful business was "good water, good environment, good teaching about techniques, local herbs and honey." She also proudly intimated that her good fortune has enabled her to offer home stay accommodation as she showed us around her home and backyard garden. She stated that in addition to the closer relationships among the villagers, the reforestation and the water project really changed her life in significant ways.

> Water is the most important. Before I used to do agriculture by moving from place to place. I had to barter my crops with the rice from other hills. It was a tough life. Now I buy vegetables and sell to those who work in the factories from here.
>
> (Informal community leader)

Both the community leaders all agreed that the project has strengthened the community. By building the dams together they have developed another level of friendship among the villagers. When asked about the benefits other than economic, the NGO leader replied, "People are more united, (gain more reputation, received many awards), (there's a) richness in culture, and the transmission of local wisdom from generation to generation."

They further indicated that by involving the children to participate in the reforestation efforts and stopping the bushfires, some children are now interested to stay in the village and do agriculture. "We persuaded the kids to invest in the future by planting teak. Later in their life, children can use the teak wood to build their house," said the NGO leader. However, he clarified that not all children will stay in the farms as other children will work in the city or do industrial work. The transfer of local wisdom to the next generation is also one way toward sustainable development.

In addition to the physical benefits accrued to the reforestation project, the community engagement activities have also provided a platform to transfer knowledge and empower the communities.

## *Empowering communities through capacity development*

The village leader told us that some projects required knowledge and the company invited experts to the area to provide training: "For example, before we were buying grains, but now we can produce it in our village." With 80 percent of the villagers working in agriculture, it was important to develop their capability which involved knowledge transfer.

The community empowerment process was confirmed by the NGO leader who said that "Knowledge was provided in order for the community people to think and analyze information in a proper way. Now, the community doesn't ask (the company) for financial support. Highest achievement is to build knowledge as community intellectual weapon." He then announced that the "locals could apply for funding from the UN for an organic plantation project" with little to no help from the corporation, because the locals are already equipped with the knowledge.

Engendering self-sufficiency and confidence is a critical component in community development. And this often involves training and education through various approaches. In community settings, these interventions are referred to as 'extension' work and take a long time to achieve.

As the community relations manager said,

> They have the knowledge from learning process and can survive without our guidance. It was difficult to change the locals' attitude when THNC changed its paradigm. It took three years for (the) community to understand but seven years for full participation. Now the locals can do the research. The community's success has also enabled them to share their knowledge to other nearby villages.

The village leader said that "My village is their role model. We are open for them to learn from us. Then they will do the project for their own village." The villagers are working together and undertaking the research on the water quality and quantity. THNC provided and installed equipment around the village so the locals are aware of their own resources.

The NGO leader explained that while each village is undertaking the research together, "each project is based on the needs of each area. So, the 'success' is different." However, the village's current ability to manage their resources with minimal to no help from the company is a testament to the successful partnership between the community members, village leaders and the corporation.

Unlike in the Indonesian farming community, this community has gained a level of confidence that the corporation can now move on to the next project which may need their help. When asked how they felt about being independent, the village leader humbly affirmed that while the people in the community will miss the support of the community relations manager, they understood that he has to move on to other communities.

## *Negotiating with communities*

As indicated previously, the 'success' of the community partnership did not happen overnight. Even for Mr. Nattapong who was well-known and regarded in the community because of his local roots, reaching this level of community engagement required patience and the use of various communicative and persuasive tools. He recounted the work he did with the local community.

> The factory is built on land that is considered National Conserved Forest Zone E. This meant that because of the deteriorated forest, they are able to use the land to build an industrial factory. But when the company started in 1998, "one of the executives promised the community that THNC would bring back the green forestry. We started by planting 1000 acres of forest together with the Ministry of Forestry.

He explained that his job was to make the "community understand about our green factory. The community faced the polluted air problem with sulphur contamination." So, he went to the community in 2002 to undertake some knowledge exchange activities. However, the restoration was too slow. "So, in 2003, we went to learn from the Royal Project and brought back the idea of the dam."

Then in 2007, they initiated the water conservation project but "my team didn't know how to persuade and approach the community. Eventually, we cooperated with the NGO." Moreover, he admitted that the head office asked him to build several dams. He and his team decided however that for the dam project to be sustainable, it needs to be passed on to the community. And this is what triggered the development and design of the community-based project.

He confessed to experiencing some resistance from the community and the NGO leaders. To soften the resistance, he expounded on the steps he took as follows:

> I explained about our green concept. I showed the green plant model. I organized the community trip to our plant in the central region. They got to see how our management cares about the environment. Our plant's design has received the best practice award. Our machine was imported from Germany and its technology is friendly to the environment, and performs better than the law regulation (*sic*). Moreover, we have an open house concept where the community can visit our plant whenever they want.

As previously mentioned the notion of experiential learning through show-and-tell, or what the Thais refer to as developing 'learning centers' has been instrumental in gaining the support of the community for THNC's CSR activities.

In terms of communication processes, the THNC community relations manager said that he employed both formal and informal communication.

> Formal communication is usually a meeting, which is based on the project that THNC supports. We have to collect the data for the research so we communicate about two times a week. Informal communication occurs by talking on the phone, using social network application and visits to villagers' house.

He disclosed that he worked with many organizations such as forestry groups, youth networks and other community-based associations. He said that he often ensured that everybody works together in their respective activity in some form of 'give and take' approach. "We are working together to help each other. My activity, they help. Their activity, I help."

The types of support that the corporation give are based on the needs of the local people. Mr. Nattapong described four categories of corporate support to the community:

> First, creating jobs. We spend 20 million baht per month on staff allowance. Next, creating prosperity to the province: we register our company to this province. The tax we paid (500 million baht per year) will go to the locals. Third, conserving environment. Fourth, being a good citizen of the town will make the third person talk about our good behavior.

However, Mr. Nattapong revealed that corporate support to communities had previously been based on giving equally to villages. But in 2008, they changed the paradigm of 'giving' to that of 'participation.' This meant that:

> (1) We won't let money come first. (2) We don't hire the villagers but instead provide the equipment and knowledge. (3) We encourage data collection by the community. (4) There is no commitment from the community. They can stop whenever they want to. (5) They have the knowledge from the learning process and can survive without our guidance. It was difficult to change the locals' attitude when THNC changed its paradigm.

Part of the community relations/engagement also entailed employee participation in any CSR project. So, for "every project the staff need to be involved. For example, the check dam project, the staff have knowledge in how to build the dams so they had to lead the building efforts."

He attributed the success or failure in their community relations/engagement to three factors: internal persuasion, research question development and time. For the internal factors, he acknowledged the importance of getting the village leader to agree and provide buy-in to the project, otherwise they won't give their full cooperation. He also emphasized that the community "creates the question (focus), which benefits the community as a whole." He said that no matter what interventions or external actors are thought to be needed, the community identifies the key issues that they wish to resolve and put their efforts into. Then the community feels ownership of the project. The third factor he highlighted is the amount of time required to work with the community members. As indicated earlier, Mr. Nattapong had invested over seven years to get the community to this stage of self-sufficiency. During that time, he worked with the NGO, the village leader, other villagers as well as his colleagues in the plant and head office to generate the level of goodwill they currently have with the community.

The success of the highly participative projects was attributed to an integrated communication process, which targeted the needs of each stakeholder group. Moreover, involving media practitioners, spiritual leaders and NGOs to join employees, residents and other volunteers in building the dams enabled them to experience the process 'hands-on.' At the same time, they launched a public awareness campaign on water conservation using TV, radio commercials, print ads, articles and an illustrated guidebook. In addition, THNC collaborated with a production company to develop a four-episode music documentary featuring well-known Thai musicians.

These media and communication activities are the public insignias of the project's success. Many of THNC's communication sites highlight this project as a tangible sign of the company's CSR efforts. However, the project has generated success in other intangible, more important ways. The project has empowered the village community toward self-sufficiency and contributed to the sustainable development agenda not only of the corporation but of the country.

When asked how the villagers might feel if Mr. Nattapong returned to Bangkok, the NGO leader replied,

> Of course, the villagers wouldn't want their mentor to leave them. But because of the process of learning, the villagers now have knowledge as their intellectual weapon. They can survive without their mentor. The process of learning will stay with them.

## *Employee engagement and social enterprise*

In addition to the focus on community development, we also observed other approaches to CSR in Thailand. Although still tied to sustainable development, other organizations concentrated on social enterprise development and inclusive approaches to employment. One such organization is the multinational company whose retail outlet we visited during our field work. This retail outlet (THMNC) was chosen as a site because it has been dubbed as the "Community Store." The concept of the community store comes from the overseas head office where part of the proceeds go back to the farming community. After launching in 2013, the outlet has raised about US$50,000 from the partial proceeds and this amount has been transferred to the NGO that works with the hill-tribe farming community. According to our respondent, the NGO then gives the funds to the community "without any reduction." The NGO also earns money from selling the produce so "they wear two hats: as an NGO and as a supplier."

Aside from this endeavor, the THMNC has also enabled its staff to undertake part of their management training through immersion in the communities that they are helping. For instance, the assistant manager we spoke with recalled her experience in visiting and living in the farming community in northern Thailand.

> It was a tough journey to reach the (produce) village. I learnt how the locals lived, their lives, and how they collect the (produce). The locals taught the (THMNC) team about their process of collecting the (produce).

During that time, she lived with a family in a house without any doors, just a door frame. She played with the hill-tribe children, "some of whom can't go to school because their parents can't send them to school."

The community immersion trip is optional and employees can volunteer to join in the trip. Volunteers however go through a selection process based on how much profit each store generates from selling the product. So, for example, one staff is allowed from each branch, but two are allowed if the branch generates a higher profit.

The trip allowed the assistant manager to have a greater appreciation of the products they sold and the project they promoted, enabling her to share her experiences with their customers and her work colleagues.

> Before attend (ing) the trip, I have no imagination about the community and the local people's livelihood. I only heard stories from others. I felt so happy that THMNC build the learning centre for the local kids. It took 45 minutes for the children to commute from the village to the government school at the bottom of the hill ... I shared my experiences about the local people's difficulties in living their lives with my customers ... I shared the (produce) story with my colleagues. I let them know the effort that has been put to get the (produce). I encouraged them to value the (produce) and try not to waste it. I suggested to spread this experience with others.

Another CSR approach employed by this company is their inclusive recruitment strategies. For this visit, we also met one of their special employees, a young female with Down's Syndrome. According to the assistant manager, employing people with disabilities (PWD) was a directive from the MNC's head office. However, like most recruitment tactics, she had to take a test about working with others and show her competency. At the time of our visit, she has already worked in the store for three years and was happy to continue working there because she was able to look after her family.

> I am happy here. Everybody is friendly. I get to help my colleagues and I can make my own (products). I want to continue working here. I am happy that I can take care of my family. My salary is the main income in my family.

Although she is the only PWD employee in the store, her contributions to the store have been much appreciated. The assistant manager said that May helps the shop by observing.

> She will tell when she notices that something went wrong. For example, if something is broken, run out of supplies, or some area is dirty, she reports to the manager. She also remembers all the names of the frequently-visiting customers.

The assistant manager reported that this store has generated much media attention because of its 'community store' concept and that many customers appreciate the 10-baht contribution to the farming communities. This approach to CSR has enabled the company to also gain reputational and commercial benefits from this program.

## Risk mitigation and compliance

While other corporations attempt to present their CSR activities as motivated by 'altruistic' reasons, this particular case reveals a frank and candid rationale—risk mitigation and compliance. We interviewed the CEO of an industrial estate in the outskirts of Bangkok. The industrial estate houses about 500 factories that include automotive and textile manufacturers. The CEO is a former governor of the province, and he indicated that his former position helped him work with the local government officials and the community residents in the area, as he was also aware of the issues in the area. So, when he was hired to run the estate, one of his conditions was for the executive to listen to him as "I would like everybody to be in a win–win position." Identifying himself as the pioneer of CSR in the company, he also confided that if the company forced him to do something that will disadvantage the local residents, he won't do it and he will quit.

He viewed CSR as a framework for community engagement: "I tried to explain that CSR is not only giving. We need to have a relationship with the community. We need to engage them." However further discussions revealed that community engagement was employed as a means to mitigate company risks and ensure compliance from its internal stakeholders.

According to him, many of the complaints lodged against the company by residents in the surrounding neighborhood include traffic congestion, high density and pollution. The estate's area of responsibility covers five to ten kilometres within the estate and is located across two provinces. The CEO advised the estate's location on the east is critical because of its accessibility to and from other provinces. This meant that the traffic congestion is not only due to the vehicles travelling in and out of the estate, but other vehicles who traverse the highway.

The residents and some local NGOs had expressed their concerns with the management because the traffic conditions have affected the environment of the nearby residential area. The CEO said that before he took on the role, the NGOs led the residents to express their disapproval and mobilized resistance activities. After two years of negotiation, they were able to work together by establishing a traffic committee comprising "local residents, traffic police, NGOs, provincial government officer, local government officials (village leader and appointed district head) and company representatives. The problem is discussed in the council meeting and ends there. Now they are ok with my company."

For instance, one of the problems raised by the community related to the traffic jams at certain hours of the day, specifically during the start and end of work shifts. So, the committee discussed several options and some of the solutions they agreed is to stagger the work hours and for local residents to help with directing the traffic, with the company paying for their wages. The CEO admitted however that these solutions did not completely eradicate the traffic problem because of factors they cannot control "such as driving manners of the driver." However, despite complaining about the environmental pollution, residents in the area found opportunities to sell products that generated supplementary income.

The CEO also indicated that ongoing negotiations with community groups and NGOs are part of their risk mitigation strategy. He intimated some displeasure with NGOs who often lead the attacks against the company.

> NGO usually attacked (company). They want big news. Targeting (company) receives bigger news than targeting factory. Usually well-known factory like Honda or Toyota have good standard. I think that big news earned them the fund.

The standards he referred to were the environmental pollution standards that were required of factories and industrial estates. His initial response was to suggest that because the area is under the Thai government's Department of Environmental Control, any factory that is found to fail the pollution standards will be closed down. However, he then clarified that it is the estate's responsibility to ensure that the tenants—which are the factories—followed the standards according to the law. To maintain the appropriate environmental standards, the company has created an "environmental control system. The system is for measuring, air, noise and water pollution." He revealed that there are ...

> ... industrial department staff, (company) staff and facility control staff that deal with those who violated the environmental standard. If investigation found the violation, then the factory will be temporarily closed down. The closing time is depending on the law.
> 
> (CEO, THNC3)

The industrial estate seems to take responsibility for ensuring compliance of environmental standards because it is in the estate's interest to keep the tenant factories operating and ensure their rental income continues.

The use of CSR as risk mitigation is also employed in the company's expansion plans. When asked if CSR and community engagement tactics are employed to minimize risks, the CEO replied, "Exactly. Moreover, we want to expand the area. Locals were doing agriculture and fish farms before (company) came. Landlords want to sell the land to (company)." He revealed that the impending expansion has caused problems with the residents who will be forced to move out because they will need to be relocated and find alternative means of livelihood. While he did not go into details, he acknowledged that the expansion is causing problems that are now the subject of meetings between the estate, the landlords and the residents. As part of this exercise and to demonstrate notions of transparency, they have invited the community to visit the estate two times a month. Those invited include opinion leaders, students and local government officials.

As gleaned from the previous statement, community engagement tactics appear to involve negotiation and attempts at transparency. While he conceded that both the company and the community residents may suggest CSR activities, albeit the latter often "required help for their living," he made it clear that certain community project proposals cannot be supported by the company. For instance, at one point, the community wanted the company to fund the cleaning of the canal. The CEO said that they did not have the budget for that so instead, the local residents provided the 'labor' and the company provided food and equipment in the endeavor. He also stressed that while the company had allocated budgets for CSR and community projects, he was not going to support projects that "are not necessary or are already funded by the government."

Other 'support' involved sponsorships and philanthropic activities. At the time of the interview, his company already funded activities that support "religious festivals, education, housewives' groups, handicapped children's sports and special events such as Father's Day" and the like. When asked how support of projects is prioritized, he disclosed that

> part of the budget is fixed for special occasion every month by the calendar (e.g. children's day, Thai new year, etc.). Other part of the budget is for contingency situation ... such as flooding relief or sponsoring the occupation (*sic*) field trip.

While much of the initial CSR programs involved community relations, the CEO also divulged recent attempts to focus on his internal stakeholders. These internal stakeholders include their tenants, factories in the estate who also have their own CSR activities, but only at a small scale like providing t-shirts, etc. The tenants raised concern that once they combined their efforts and respective budgets with the estate's CSR activities, the factories' branding opportunities will be minimized, if not lost. The CEO admitted that negotiations were still underway at the time of the interview.

In addition to the leaseholders, he also planned to "*enforce* CSR activities within (company's) 200 staff" (emphasis by researchers). He confessed that employee engagement is still a new concept in his organization, having just started two to three months earlier.

> Staffs (*sic*) didn't really know what to do. MD ordered the staff to open the booth supporting Children's day activities.
> Interviewer: They liked it?
> It was an order. The activities are both weekday and weekend.

The language used by the CEO indicates the company's largely top-down and compliance-oriented approach to CSR. When asked why the company embarked on an employee engagement strategy, the CEO said it was to have a 'complete' CSR program. Then in the same breath, he conceded that "CSR is also a requirement from the stock market." While he added that publicizing their activities through the media is the responsibility of the public relations department, he also said that they produce a sustainability report as part of their compliance efforts.

## Summary

As this chapter shows, CSR in Thailand emerges from an intrinsic understanding of sustainable development inspired by its late King Bhumibol Adulyadej. The late King has been associated with 'sustainable development' long before the term became fashionable based on his Sufficiency Economy philosophy (Maxwell, 2016). This philosophy continues to be demonstrated through various royal projects and learning centers in urban and rural areas around the country. Many retail outlets in the capital city sold various products that promoted social enterprises (e.g., bee farms, organic soap products) produced by rural farmers. Our local partners directed our attention to these as examples of CSR in Thailand.

In addition to differing perceptions of CSR, there are also clear indications from our interviews that not many understand or even recognize what CSR is. While the THNC representatives' CSR knowledge was sophisticated in its integration of participatory strategies drawn from the international and community development field, the THMNC's retail store assistant manager was unclear of what CSR was despite being familiar with her company's ethical work with local communities. Similarly, the informal and formal village leaders as well as the NGO leader were very aware of sustainability issues and community development, but they do not see these as CSR.

Thus, CSR as a term, reflects a corporate-centric concept employed as mechanisms for reputation-building, community development and risk mitigation. Undoubtedly, the corporations' investments of time and participatory approaches to community engagement are reaping benefits for their reputation, as these 'best practices' have led us to identifying them for this study. And while the village leaders expressed gratitude for the corporation's projects, they also voiced a sense of weariness in the telling and re-telling of their 'success stories' as part of the corporation's public relations strategies.

As the cases in this chapter indicated, companies diffuse community resistance through long-term, community development approaches or intensive community engagement discussions. CSR programs are also employed by the private sector to minimize risk to company operations. It would seem that if companies provide employees and the community residents opportunities to make a living or better living conditions through their CSR activities, they expect less resistance or complaints against the company. With less resistance companies then gain the community's social license to operate. At the same time, corporations need to continually be sensitive and mindful of exploiting the goodwill that has been generated over time with their community partners.

On the positive side, CSR in Thailand is likewise being used by corporations as a platform for sustainable development that strategically aligns not only with their business goals but also with deference to the edicts of the late King. This deference is a manifestation of the Thai people's values of paternalism and hierarchy that are wittingly or unwittingly exploited by the corporations. Despite some elements of top-down, compliance efforts, CSR in Thailand integrates and values relationship building with Buddhist beliefs of 'giving' and respect while maintaining a low profile (Sthapitanonda & Watson, 2015).

As such, CSR has spawned a Thai interpretation of community relations that required time-consuming immersion in the communities by corporate staff to build trust, transfer knowledge, experience the difficult lives of economically marginalized hill tribes and empower the villagers to sustain the development efforts meant to uplift them. From reforestation, flood control, access to clean water and community stores that sold produce from which profits are returned to the producing communities to employment of people with disabilities, these are compelling stories that will live in the annals of CSR and community relations history in Thailand; one that made all the difference between what matters for both the communities and the companies that are doing good work.

# References

Central Intelligence Agency. (2017). Thailand. *World Fact Book*. www.cia.gov/library/publications/the-world-factbook/geos/th.html.

Chapple, W. & Moon, J. (2005). Corporate social responsibility (CSR) in Asia: A seven-country study of CSR web site reporting. *Business & Society*, 44 (4), 415–441.

del Rosario, R. (2011). Corporate social responsibility in Southeast Asia: An eight-country analysis. *Research Report*, Makati, Philippines: Asian Institute of Management.

Ekachai, D. & Komolsevin, R. (1996). Public relations in Thailand: Its functions and practitioners' roles. In Culbertson, H. & Chen, N. (Eds.). *International Public Relations. A Comparative Analysis*. New York: Routledge.

Ekachai, D. & Komolsevin, R. (1998). Public relations education in Thailand. *Public Relations Review*, 24 (2), 219–234.

Ekachai, D. & Komolsevin, R. (2004). From propaganda to strategic communication: The continuing evolution of the public relations profession in Thailand. In Sriramesh, K. (Ed.). *Public Relations in Asia. An Anthology*. (pp. 283–320). Singapore: Thomson.

Forsyth, T. & Walker, A. (2008). *Forest Guardians, Forest Destroyers: The Politics of Environmental Knowledge in Northern Thailand*. Seattle: University of Washington Press.

Halff, G. & Gregory, A. (2014). Toward an historically informed Asian model of public relations. *Public Relations Review*, (40), 397–407.

Hall, E. & Hall, M. (1987). *Hidden Differences*. New York: Doubleday.

Hallinger, P. & Kantamara, P. (2000). Leading at the confluence of tradition and globalization: The challenge of change in Thai schools. *Asia Pacific Journal of Education*, 20 (2), 46–57.

Herzfeld, M. (2002). The absent presence: Discourses of crypto-colonialism. *The South Atlantic Quarterly*, 101 (4), 899–926.

Hofstede, G. (1991). *Cultures and Organizations: Software of the Mind*. Berkshire, England: McGraw-Hill.

Jackson, P. (2005). Semicoloniality, translation and excess in Thai cultural studies. *Southeast Asia Research*, 13 (1), 7–41.

Kraisornsuthasinee, S., & Swierczek, F. W. (2009). Doing well by doing good in Thailand. *Social Responsibility Journal*, 5 (4), 550–565.

Leelakulthanit, O. (2014). Sustainability: The case of Siam Cement Group (SCG). *Journal of Business Case Studies*. 10 (4), 441–445.

Maxwell, D. (2016). Following King Bhumibol's sustainable development approaches. *Asian Correspondent*. Retrieved from https://asiancorrespondent.com/2016/10/following-king-bhumibols-sustainable-development-approaches/#D)#wpJaBK3Lf HdXARMm.97.

Minnesota Stormwater Manual. (2017). Sediment control practices – check dams, ditch checks, ditch dikes. https://stormwater.pca.state.mn.us/index.php?title=Sediment_control_practices_-_Check_dams_(ditch_checks,_ditch_dikes).

Pimpa, N. (2013). Poverty alleviation: Corporate social responsibilities approaches by multinational corporations in Lao PDR and Thailand. *Journal of Business and Policy Research*, 8 (1), 60–77.

Powell, L., Amsbary, J. & Hickson, M. (2014). The Wai in Thai culture: Greeting, status-marking and national identity functions. *Journal of Intercultural Communication*, 34.

Prachachart, T. (2005). Thai companies and CSR: For PR rather than for social contribution. www.tisi.go.th/clip_news/news028html. In Srisuphaolarn, S. (2013). From altruistic to strategic CSR: How social value affected CSR development – A case study of Thailand. *Social Responsibility Journal*, 9 (1), 56–75.

Redmond, M. (1998). *Wondering into Thai Culture*. Bangkok, Thailand: White Lotus Books.

Servatamorn, S. (1977). Education in Thailand: From old to new. *World Education Monograph Series*, 2. ERIC Reproduction Document Service No. ED 170 878.

Srisuphaolarn, P. (2013). From altruistic to strategic CSR: How social value affected CSR development – A case study of Thailand. *Social Responsibility Journal*, 9 (1), 56–75.

Sthapitanonda, P. & Watson, T. (2015). "Pid Thong Lang Phra" – The impact of culture upon Thai CSR concepts and practice: A study of relationships between NGOs and corporations. *Asia Pacific Public Relations Journal*, 16 (1), 42–72.

Tantivejakul, N. (2014). Thailand. In Watson, T. (Ed.). *Asian Perspectives on the Development of Public Relations: Other Voices. National Perspectives on the Development of Public Relations*. London: Palgrave Pivot.

World Bank. (2017). Thailand. https://data.worldbank.org/country/thailand?view=chart.

Yodprutikarn, P. (2006). The development of CSR in business organization management process: The first phase – the study of characteristics, components and development tools. *Final Report*. Bangkok: The Thailand Research Fund.

# 7 Blurring CSR/PR boundaries

Transactional approaches in Vietnam

## Country context

*Economic, political/historical context*

Inhabiting the Red River valley, the first Vietnamese were a homogeneous group that established a wet rice culture some 4,000 years ago (Hoang & Bui, 1979). Vietnam's history is littered with battles for sovereignty and like other armed conflicts "were both devastating and a source of wealth and cultural infusion" (Shultz, 2012, p. 10). Among the foreign powers that left indelible imprints on the country's national character are China, Cham and Khmer kingdoms, Mongols, France and the United States.

France occupied Vietnam from 1858 until 1887 when it became part of French Indochina. Although it declared independence from France after World War II, it remained under French rule until 1954 when Ho Chi Minh's communist forces drove the French out of the country. Not all of Vietnam came under communist rule though. The 1954 Geneva Accords divided the country into the communist North with Hanoi as the capital and the non-communist South with Saigon as the capital. Despite massive U.S. economic and military support throughout the 1960s, South Vietnam failed to sustain its resistance against the North Vietnamese and two years after the withdrawal of U.S. armed forces in 1973, it yielded to the communist North (CIA, 2017).

The Socialist Republic of Vietnam was born soon after the political and administrative unification of the country. A decade of anemic economic growth and increasing international isolation followed. The impetus for change was the 1986 government *"doi moi"* (renovation) policy, which propelled the transition of this densely populated developing country with its centrally planned, agrarian economy to a quasi-market-based economy. Here's a nation that has deftly isolated its economic and political systems without diminishing the government's ability to suppress political expression (del Rosario, 2011).

With an annual GDP growth of 6.3 percent and a burgeoning middle class, Vietnam is committed to integrate itself to the global economy. Its membership in a number of international institutions, notably ASEAN (1995), WTO (2007) and the TPP (2015), has spurred the influx of MNCs to the country. The fruits of economic integration, however, are not always sweet. Despite successes in certain areas particularly the MDGs, the growing gap between the middle class and the poor was increasingly noted in international reports (World Bank, 2014). Meanwhile, although foreign direct investment provided an important source and motive to economic development in the country, complaints and charges against malfeasances by MNCs have also proliferated (Hieu, 2011).

## Cultural and social context

The country's ethnic profile consists of a large majority of Kinh (Viet) at 85.7 percent and a sprinkling of Tay, Thai, Muong, Khmer, Mong and Nung, each at less than 2 percent. Vietnamese is the official language and English is the preferred second language. Some French, Chinese and Khmer are also spoken.

While there is a visible Buddhist (7.9 percent) and Catholic population (6.6 percent), the majority (81.8 percent) have no religious affiliation (CIA, 2017). Some Vietnamese still practice Caodism, a religion unique to Vietnam.

Like the other countries in the mineral-rich Mekong Delta, Vietnam grapples with social fault lines of class, gender, etc. It still faces the challenge of attaining a more inclusive growth.

As a collectivist society, the family and the village are the primary units of social organization. A mix of Confucian and Buddhist values that resulted from China's nearly 1,000 years of colonial rule is also evident in Vietnamese culture. Despite the society's march toward modernization and global integration, Vietnamese still hold dear the following traditional values that shape their societal roles and behaviors: *Ly Do* (reason), *Hieu* (filial piety), *On* (moral debt), *De* (proper relationships), *Nghia* (righteous path), *Tinh* (emotional spontaneity), *Nhan* (compassion), *Dieu* (relative versus absolute harmony), and *Chan Ly* (absolute standard) (Jamieson, 1995; Shultz, 2012).

## Public relations

Modern corporate PR in Vietnam is said to be introduced by MNCs in the mid-1980s. Before then, PR in this erstwhile war-torn country came in the form of political campaigns aimed at bolstering the new Democratic Republic of Vietnam after 1945. When the reunified Socialist Republic of Vietnam was established in 1975, propaganda was again used by the socialist government to shore up citizen support for its rebuilding and national unity efforts (Van, 2011; Doan & Bilowol, 2014).

The relatively young PR industry suffers from a number of misperceptions due to a lack of understanding of what it is and the confusion with advertising. Another common mistake is associating attractive bar girls pouring champagne or beer and "offering other services in Vietnam" (Doan & Bilowol, 2014, p. 485) as PR staff (Linh, 2012).

Empirically, a 2000 study (McKinney, 2000, 2006) found that PR is misunderstood along the narrow confines of guest relations, events management and "the business of entertaining officials." Hang's (2010) survey of Vietnamese PR practitioners likewise showed a heavy emphasis on media relations and event management. The same study reported a deeply entrenched "envelope culture" wherein PR professionals pay journalists to publish news releases and attend press conferences. Domm (2016) also cited the continuing expectations among journalists notably in Vietnam and in other Asian countries such as Malaysia and the Philippines to receive payments for positive news media placements. To professionalize Vietnamese PR, Hang (2010) recommended more education and training, establishment of a professional association and code of conduct as well as a legal framework.

Loan (2011) admitted that while PR in Vietnam is a borrowed Western concept, its localized practice is guided by two principles: knowledge of local culture and the importance of personal connections. The centrality of interpersonal relationships in and outside of the workplace thereby blurring the lines between personal and professional relationships with all the associated ethical complications that would raise some red flags among Western practitioners was also underscored in Doan and Bilowol's work (2014). Hang (2000) however contends that because these relationships are based on trust and personal integrity, this personal relationship building and maintenance are legitimate aspects of Vietnamese and for that matter Asian-style PR.

## Corporate social responsibility

If PR is a young industry in Vietnam, CSR is at its infancy and like PR the practice is mainly driven by MNCs but with the added participation of development organizations primarily from Western donor countries and other international agencies (Hamm, 2012). It appears that CSR is a new millennium phenomenon in Vietnam brought about by globalization. The concept and practice have also generated increasing attention from both domestic practitioners and scholars in recent years.

The Vietnamese government promoted CSR using its legislative authority. New regulations on environment and an agenda for sustainable development have been issued in addition to the formal establishment of the environmental police authority. Although specific measures responding to social and environmental misbehaviors are regulated, the government does not require companies to formally issue CSR reports (Hieu, 2011).

Outside of the corporate realm, civil society institutions such as the NGOs in the country have yet to play an effective role in promoting and evaluating CSR (Gray, 1999; Sidel, 1997). Although CSR partnerships between NGOs and businesses exist in Vietnam, they are still nascent and progressing slowly (Sison & Hue, 2015). The NGO community more importantly has yet to serve as watchdogs to corporate social irresponsibility, which can be challenging given the low level of public trust on NGOs in the country (Dang & Tri, 2013).

The relative difficulty of implementing CSR in Vietnam stems from the fact that most local firms understand and undertake CSR as a philanthropic activity (Long, 2015). Moreover, most of the local companies, unlike the big MNCs, lack the capacity and resources to implement CSR and meet international standards. This condition was earlier reported in a 2012 survey of Vietnamese businesses done by the Vietnam Academy of Social Sciences which found that many local companies failed to meet minimum CSR standards. Among the common business offenses were a "lack of basic employee benefits and deliberately causing environmental damage" (Bilowol & Doan, 2015, p. 826).

Indeed, Tencati, Russo and Quaglia (2008) corroborated the findings that the monetary and non-monetary costs of CSR compliance of international standards "may prove to be unsustainable and prohibitive for many enterprises ..." (p. 526). These researchers concluded that while CSR makes business sense in countries like Vietnam, fostering rather than imposing sustainable efforts is recommended together with the building of innovative multilateral partnerships involving companies, local authorities, civil society and other international agencies as well as a "demand-driven educational agenda" (Tencati et al., 2008, p. 529).

From the Vietnamese consumer's perspective, on the other hand, CSR is seen as fulfilment of economic, philanthropic, environmental and societal responsibilities (Bui, 2010). For countries like Vietnam, a strong state is considered an enabler in the promotion of CSR. Advancing CSR growth "either through legislation or by simply promoting the entry and creation of NGOs could help create a climate conducive to CSR" (del Rosario, 2011, p. 14).

MNCs and technical partners also help in promoting CSR by creating benchmarks, encouraging local enterprises to adapt international standards and providing financial and technical support. CSR although still viewed by some quarters of Vietnamese society as simply PR or image/brand enhancement, has in many ways helped alleviate the lack of adequate state resources to fund social initiatives by focusing on livelihood generation, education and health services (del Rosario, 2011).

## The melding of PR and CSR

Vietnam presents a curious case of cross-pollination between PR and CSR. Bilowol and Doan (2015) in fact suggested that MNCs have a role in developing Vietnam's PR industry through CSR. As noted earlier, the PR industry is typically about media relations and product publicity focusing on the growing middle class as the target audience (Bilowol & Doan, 2015) but there's increased recognition of the symbiotic relationship between PR and CSR.

In Vietnam, it is not unusual to find advertisements of both local companies and MNCs that showcase CSR activities using rational and emotional appeals to market their products in the media. In addition, as news media agencies have gained more financial autonomy in recent years, commercial news phenomenally proliferated including various forms of infomercial (Coe, 2014).

With intensified economic integration and with the growing need for socially responsible business practices, the business sector in Vietnam has indeed looked to CSR as part of strategies to legitimize their activities because collective acceptance of a particular social issue by related stakeholders afforded them legitimacy. Media visibility could be used as both a tool and an indicator of business legitimacy (Baum & Powell, 1995).

## NGOs and CSR

A recent study revealed that business perceptions of NGOs in Vietnam are ambivalent (Dang & Tri, 2013). Most businesses surveyed thought NGOs were primarily about poverty alleviation. Moreover, most businesses thought international NGOs (INGOs) were trustworthy while only a third said the same of Vietnamese NGOs (VNGOs). This same study highlighted that VNGOs have the potential to engage more with Vietnamese businesses possibly through CSR and strategic philanthropy.

It has been argued that CSR is the private sector's response to pressure received from NGOs in the environmental sector. So, CSR from an NGO perspective will be fraught with various interpretations. On one hand, the NGOs' involvement in CSR has led scholars to question if this engagement reflects an "appropriation and co-optation of protest" by the business community (Burchell & Cook, 2013b). They posit that while co-optation is inevitable in the engagement process, it is still possible to maintain 'agonistic' relationships where both parties are 'allowed' to debate their notions of responsible business. The authors further contend that through continuous dialogue, NGOs can persist in holding businesses to account and vice versa.

While CSR remains a fairly new and contested concept to NGOs, it seems that they can easily warm to the idea. For starters, CSR has been seen as a catalyst for NGOs and business to form partnerships. However, a successful partnership is contingent on whether the parties share common views of the nature of their collaboration.

## CSR perceptions and engagement

This chapter takes readers to the nuts and bolts of NGO and business engagement in some of Vietnam's CSR programs. To provide context for the relationship building, CSR engagement and partnership formation we will dredge the stakeholder perceptions of CSR from the vantage points of the NGO, corporation and the community. The main questions this chapter will address are: (1) how NGOs engage with business particularly in the context of CSR and (2) what, if any, partner selection process do they undertake.

## NGO perceptions of CSR

NGOs primarily view CSR as a means to achieve their philanthropic objectives. However, through their increasing engagement with MNCs, they are showing signs of expanding their knowledge on the other CSR aspects such as employee volunteer programs. This is certainly true in Vietnam. Funded primarily by international agencies, the two NGOs in our study are involved in capacity-building programs. With this as their main objective, they continually were seeking resources, both financial and human, for their programs. This is how corporates get involved.

In searching for program donors, NGO1 surveys websites of MNCs operating in Vietnam and looks for alignment with the companies' CSR strategy. Based on the survey, NGO1 would then develop a project proposal:

> ... that we think is in line with what they are looking for, because we have done some research on their website, we've read their past engagements, or we know about their business, and we think that this project is a good fit. We will prepare a presentation for them, and go in to try to have a meeting, to talk with them about it. Or send it to them by email if they're harder to reach in person. We try to present it so that there is an opportunity for a win–win scenario, so either offering corporate employee volunteer opportunities, or PR opportunities, or ... like giving it a good image....

NGO1 has in the past developed a program wherein corporate staff "work two to four hours per week for four months" and share their professional skills such as communication and financial management for fundraising with local non-profit organizations. Previously they sought help on creating marketing and communication materials.

On the other hand, NGO2 started a partnership with a VNMNC in the financial sector and they co-developed a three-year program to improve the education infrastructure of a community and provide scholarships to children. Instead of the VNMNC just funding the whole project outright, they engaged their global employees, clients and suppliers to participate in funding the program.

> One dollar match one dollar scheme you can say. Like if they raise one dollar from their clients, or from their staff members, then [MNC] will match one dollar.... They draw attention from those 4,000 staff members, and ... raise funds within their [MNC] team, but it's also from like you know anyone else that [MNC] can get in touch with their clients and suppliers.
>
> (Project officer, NGO2)

While this NGO engages with several corporate entities primarily as funding donors, the project officer highlighted this particular MNC because she considered their work relationship as indicative of a 'real partnership.' While the MNC approached the NGO in this instance, they conceptualized the program and fundraising strategies together, building on their respective strengths.

Although CSR in Vietnam is still nascent and often equated with philanthropy and predominantly marketing oriented (Hamm, 2012), NGOs have identified how CSR is evolving to include employee engagement in capacity-building programs. Critical to the evolution of CSR in Vietnam is the nature of the partnership and how these partnerships are forged.

## *Personal connection remains key to finding CSR partners*

Finding corporate partners is always a challenge for any NGO. In Vietnam, NGOs use a variety of approaches to find a suitable corporate partner for their projects. Our respondents agreed that often NGOs initiated the relationship building with business. They often employed a combination of three methods: (1) cold call project proposals, (2) organize events and (3) leverage personal connections.

Because the CSR proposals they develop do not always produce the desired result, NGOs would resort to using PR tactics specifically event management. At these events, which could take the form of a competition or cocktail party, NGOs invite potential business partners and discuss future collaboration more informally.

> So, what we really need is to open the door to a conversation. We just launched a product, we piloted it this year and the whole purpose is to try and help the corporates think more about what they give and how they give.
> 
> (CEO, NGO1)

The CEO explained that while organizing events could secure some one-off donations it rarely generates long-term partnerships. She recounted an incident when she hosted a cocktail party for a former ambassador and invited key corporate representatives with whom they haven't had previous success. These corporates donated on the spot but did not ask about longer-term partnerships:

> So those kinds of people you just get them in the room and they give money and they don't ask questions point blank. You want them to ask, you want them to follow up. They just give the money for now.
> 
> (CEO, NGO1)

Personal connections, however, seemed the most effective channel in pursuing business–CSR partnerships. For example, the NGO2 representative revealed that the partnerships with two MNCs resulted from her former director's personal network. As previously noted, personal connections and interpersonal relationships are at the core of PR/CSR practice in Vietnam. With this NGO, the former director knew the former MNC CEO and this connection eventually led to the partnership. Interestingly the partnership continued long after these two individuals have moved to their next assignment. This implies that while personal connections are good starting points, the project's sustainability is driven by joint ownership and control of the process.

Board membership also seems to pave the way for developing these connections. The respondent from NGO1 narrated how her own membership in one board enabled conversations with other board members.

> I was on the board with one of the CFO ... I'm on the board of another NGO, it's a start-up NGO. It matches career developments for young Vietnamese. And so, through some of those conversations. But I knew him from before because he was working for [company name]. And we were talking and he said he was interested, "can you come in and meet to introduce what you do because we were looking for something more meaningful." He was trying to push the company to do something a bit more strategic than what he had seen in the past.

Personal connections with board members also help establish relationships. The NGO leader remarked that a leading local food manufacturer became their committed partner because she knew a member in the company's board of management. She also mentioned an occasion when her husband, who is a businessman and a board member of another company, introduced her to a potential partner.

> So, he introduced us ... we went to them. We thought they would be interested because it was education-themed. We don't have a connection we just thought they would be interested, and they were.

While the conversations can be serendipitous, this study shows that the role of the Board of Trustees in Vietnam went beyond being "guardians" to protect and provide broad direction to NGOs to achieve its aims. Board members bring with them important social capital that can be leveraged for corporate partnerships. To ensure that these connections remain strong and that the projects are sustainable, the two NGOs have since invited their key partners on their respective boards.

### *Choosing the 'right' corporate partner*

Effective CSR often involves social partnerships but getting the right social partners can be difficult (Crane & Seitanidi, 2014). Many times, partnership dialogues ran into an impasse due to differences in perceptions about partnership expectations, understanding of CSR and organizational values.

## Blurring CSR/PR boundaries  145

Therefore, it was important to examine how NGOs perceived their roles in the partnership and how they selected their corporate partners.

The NGO2 representative said that trust, professionalism and transparency were paramount in securing NGO partnerships with businesses. Accurate reporting of budget expenditures and auditing are critical to establishing trust with their donors. She especially stressed transparency as an important criterion although she also interpreted transparency in the context of accountability.

> … because of the long track record of success of [NGO name], they (corporate partner) think that we are transparent, effective, in terms of changing lives of the children and doing the successful things for our own projects so that's the reason why they picked [NGO name]. And when they came and met us the first time, they shared more from our side about our work (sic) and they make the questions very frank, very straightforward questions about risk management and about corruption, you know all those questions relating to those issues.

Aligning NGO programs with corporate objectives is also critical in partner selection, especially in the absence of personal connections. In one instance, the NGO program supported the marketing objectives of their corporate donor. The respondent narrated how they wanted to extend the relationship with the Vietnamese company. The company challenged them saying,

> … we'll give you 50,000 dong for every selfie photo that somebody takes on the website that says "I support education" and then they put the hashtag with the [NGO program name] and [company name] and they said they would give us 50,000 up to 500 pictures. We got 800 pictures, it was right before mooncake season. It was great marketing for their company and it was great for us actually it really spurred community activism in Vietnam.
>
> (NGO2)

Although this example demonstrates what may be construed as corporates' 'co-optation' of the NGO (Burchell & Cook, 2013b), the NGO did not seem to mind the additional exposure they got from the increased consumer audiences they generated through the marketing communication/product publicity effort. It does highlight the difference between how local companies and MNCs appropriate CSR. It also shows the co-mingling of CSR and corporate PR to achieve organizational objectives at the time of the partnership.

### NGO engagement with local and multinational companies

Engagement between NGOs and companies have been described as: transactional, transitional and transformational (Bowen, Newenham-Kahindi &

Herremans, 2010). *Transactional engagement* is characterized by one-way, one-off charitable provision of funds or volunteers where control of process is primarily from the corporation; *transitional engagement* occurs when both parties participate and benefit but the process is initiated and controlled by the corporation; and *transformational engagement* ensues when both parties co-create projects, share control and generate mutual benefit.

Our NGO respondents revealed the different challenges in engaging local and multinational companies in CSR. Long-term strategic CSR programs that offer win–win benefits for both parties are more likely to occur with MNCs than with domestic partnerships. While it was more difficult to discuss joint CSR projects with local companies, some MNCs also did not adequately train their staff on their CSR strategy, which posed some challenges. For example, a respondent said that some MNCs "don't train the people staffing the CSR position or the PR marketing position to really believe in it, to believe in how it can impact their company, they're just told to do something." She continued,

> Online it sounds great but when you go talk to them they're looking for a charity activity. You know there's no real dialogue about (what) they're going to do, something really strategic or that's in line with what their website says, so I find that it's really who you talk to.

Approaching the 'right' leader or decision maker who understands CSR goes a long way in developing potential partnerships. But since local companies still have a loose understanding of CSR and how they can leverage CSR for their business, finding the 'right' person can be a challenge.

On the other hand, this 'loose understanding' of CSR by local companies presents opportunities as they tend to be more open to inputs from the NGOs. In this instance, NGOs enjoy more latitude to recommend and even "educate" local companies on CSR strategies.

> I see the local companies with much greater opportunity because they don't have strict structures of what they fund or don't fund. The companies I know, I can't go into Nike because they only fund women's empowerment so if we have something on women I'll go to Nike but most of the time we don't. So, I find that the Vietnamese company is much more open so there's more opportunity for us because we can help them design something.

According to both respondents, local and multinational companies both expect social partnership outcomes to generate PR effects and branding benefits. For instance, respondent 2 described how one of their partners is sponsoring a huge school building project with them.

> They are celebrating their 15 years in Vietnam. So, it's not just a building school project but it also supports their PR activities. They run it as a

reality show and they work with [state media agency] to make a TV program, a TV series about the work. I think it's good. It benefits their brand, their corporation, it also benefits the community....

Similarly, the respondent from NGO1 laments that companies they approach tend to send them to the PR/marketing department because of their narrow view of CSR opportunities for the whole organization's reputation.

## Partnership engagement strategies

The interviews revealed different patterns of NGO perceptions of their corporate social partnerships. NGO1 reported how corporates approached them for purely instrumental corporate-centric reasons. For example, some companies would ask them to do something for their corporate identity program, saying "Can you set us up with an NGO to paint the school or to pick up trash or to do something?" These types of company requests have "no value to NGOs. It has great value to the companies but nothing.... All the NGOs complain about them.... We struggle with groups like that because they're usually looking for something that they can show the next year."

The NGOs also reported that their local business partners seemed to prefer lump sum donations and left it at the discretion of the NGOs to utilize the fund. While this provided NGOs more flexibility and freedom with budget and planning, it also resulted in low engagement of local companies in planning and implementing CSR projects. In sum, it was much like "Here is the money, you go and do a good job and let us know what it is about." Kolk (2014) described this as a form of social investment from the business perspective, which was popular as an in-kind support via donations.

According to respondent 2, the types of partnership strategies sometimes depend on the level of corporate support. If a third MNC partner only provides support that is about a fifth of what the other two partners are providing, the engagement with the third partner is less. This means that the amount of funding or equivalent input from the corporation determines the type of partnership and subsequent engagement strategy.

While most engagement between NGOs and corporates was *transactional* where firms preferred to donate funds or sponsor events, there seemed to be elements of transitional and transformational engagement. To illustrate, respondent 2 compared the different engagements they had with two MNCs.

One of their partnership programs reflected a more *transitional* approach where the idea of the program and its implementation were primarily developed by the MNC. The company approached the NGO with a ready-made plan for developing a reality show using the NGO's school building program. The company then contracted a media agency to produce the reality show to promote their sponsorship. During the show, the NGO was barely mentioned, despite doing much of the legwork, undertaking surveys, monitoring the project, communicating and working with the community. The MNC who funded the project retained branding rights.

> ... we do get mentioned within the film. We do get interviewed. And during the interview, we take the opportunity to brand ourselves by wearing our t-shirts with logo. But an official (said), we are not allowed to put in our logo in there because [state media agency] and [private production] promotion, the producer of that program, they work with [MNC name]. And they said that this program is marketing for [MNC].

She admits however that this particular project was on its first year, and they have expressed their concerns to the MNC's CSR person regarding the need for more NGO visibility and participation.

The other project with another international financial institution reflected a more *transformational* engagement approach. She recounted how the other MNC treated them as a real partner, consulting and collaborating with them at every turn. This joint partnership involved both parties from start to finish.

> ... anytime they would like to launch anything on our side, anything that go out, they discuss with [NGO name].... It is a very mutual respect (*sic*), there's mutual partnership and if they use any pictures of the children they contact us.... And we contact the local community to get their permission as well. So, with [MNC] we work together on developing, designing the projects together, fund raising strategy for it and monitor the implementation of the project and reporting as well. So that's how we work together.

Moreover, the respondent empathically said that the school building site was chosen by the NGO, not the company.

> ... actually, just one point to make it clear, we don't do our work at a certain place at the request of the donors. So, the partnership with [MNC] it's just at the very good timing we just identified the new project area and then we got the request from [MNC] to focus our work at a certain place.

As these examples show, NGO approaches to corporate engagement take various forms depending in part on the corporate attitude toward community engagement and their PR/marketing as well as community relations objectives. While mostly transactional, there are signs that co-construction of CSR programs through transformational engagement is emerging. These differences lead to questions of how NGO manage conflicts with their corporate CSR partner.

## Communication is key to corporate engagement

Managing partnerships clearly requires resources and synchronization of interests between the NGO and the corporate stakeholders. As Tulder and Pfisterer (2014, p. 105) posit, "The smaller the fit, the bigger the chance of misalignment, role conflicts and skewed development trajectories." Simultaneously, the more corporate partners an NGO has, the more strategic they have to be with managing the relationships. One NGO respondent remarked that to manage partnerships well, the NGO needed to design ways of constantly and effectively communicating with the companies. For example, the NGO and the MNC in the finance sector started their partnership by openly discussing each other's needs and capabilities.

> We [the NGO] have got already in our list of where we'd like to focus our resources, and then they [the corporations] come in and say, well we would like to work with you and we would like to focus our resources in a certain place as well. So here we know where we'd like to work and we are looking for funders and they said that they are looking for the place to work so we match it together.

It seemed that the NGOs understood well that they must balance the "give and take" to create a space for CSR partnerships with corporations. While the NGOs recognize their own organizational expertise, knowledge of and existing connections with communities as well as their experience in developing, implementing and evaluating community development projects, their knowledge of corporate PR based on CSR is limited.

In our case study, the NGO representatives admitted that at times they felt some CSR projects were heavily geared toward building corporate image through immediate relief services, which were not conducive for long-term community development. Thus, there were signs that the NGOs had to make compromises to satisfy their business partners.

## NGO roles in CSR engagement

The preliminary findings indicate that the NGO takes on different roles when engaging with corporates in CSR programs. With local companies, the NGOs drove the CSR program as found in previous studies (Arenas et al., 2009). But this study uncovered that NGOs played the role of educator to local companies by providing information and advice on community engagement strategies. With MNCs, the NGOs participate in knowledge sharing and have regular interactions. While some MNCs are showing signs of entrusting NGOs by co-owning the CSR program development, NGOs in Vietnam are still often viewed as middle agents delivering charity support to those in need (Dang & Tri, 2013).

Not all MNCs used this approach with partnerships. Other MNCs seemed to focus more on using CSR as a PR and staff education tool. In most cases,

NGOs initiated NGO–business relationships by approaching corporations with proposals for joint CSR projects. Occasionally, corporations would initiate discussions but only when prior personal relationships between the NGO staff members and corporate members existed. Here, it was notable that personal relationships played a key role in cultivating organizational relationships, particularly the utilization of Board of Trustee members' social network. This finding indicated that in emerging economies such as Vietnam, civil society served as an external driver to initiate stakeholder activism to CSR as discussed by Visser (2008).

In the main, NGOs use two major types of engagement with their corporate partners—as a 'beneficiary' and as a 'partner.' When NGOs take the more traditional role of 'beneficiary' they tend to have less authority in the design of the CSR program. When the companies respond to NGO proposals and see a fit with the company leader's perception of "social good deeds," the NGO would receive a funding package. While the NGOs welcome this type of involvement, it reflects a more transactional and instrumentalist approach to CSR by both parties. Moreover, it also reveals a patriarchal decision-making process in determining CSR partners. For the company, associating with the NGO gives them credibility and legitimacy to their CSR program. For the NGO, associating with the company provides legitimacy, wider audience exposure and much-needed funds.

## Corporate perspective

For this perspective, we interviewed representatives from two local companies and three MNCs operating in Ho Chi Minh City. For MNCs, interview respondents included senior executives consisting of a Chief Operating Officer, a CSR director and a communication manager. For the local companies, we interviewed three Board of Management members for one company and the CEO for the other. Except for the interview with the Board of Management, which was conducted in Vietnamese, the rest of the interviews were in English. For the interview with the local food production company, the Vietnamese research partner led the interview and translated for the non-Vietnamese research partner. However, translations were minimized to enable a smooth interview flow with the respondents.

We found the participants' perceptions and communication of CSR take different forms depending on the company ownership and the leadership's vision of CSR. Three major themes emerged from our analysis: local companies focus on employee well-being, MNCs focus on visible and strategic CSR, and both local and multinational companies frame their CSR within the context of social and national development.

## CSR is "for our employees' well-being"

Local companies perceive CSR as a framework for helping employees and as an extension of their 'familial' responsibility. This was the case with our first local company, a fairly big-sized, private company, which has been in the market for over ten years. Although different members of the Board of Management, who were in charge of overall management, human resources, production, and research and development (R&D) were interviewed their responses were consistent in meaning. We group the responses into two salient themes: organizational responsibility and commitments, and "family spirit."

Senior executives of the local companies indicated that the way they practice their 'social responsibility' is by ensuring that the employees are satisfied with their working conditions to the degree that they are happy to stay with the company for a long time. To illustrate this, VNNC respondent 1 reported that the company's overall CSR strategy involves implementation of policies affecting employees' working conditions, such as working in a hygienic and safe environment and providing medical and labor insurance as well as protective gear. For them, organizational responsibility is about fulfilling and going beyond all items in the national labor law regarding employee rights and welfare. When asked about the company's approaches to social responsibility, one VNNC representative read from an annual report containing quantitative data on employees and their working conditions. The approach simply is good employee relations that meet both labor mandates and PR/CSR expectations.

Furthermore, when describing social responsibility, one VNNC manager kept referring to their achievement in meeting the ISO for product quality and interpreted it chiefly as a result of good labor conditions and employee welfare. Corroborating this perspective, a company member said:

> We take the safety and well-being of our staff very important. We developed a culture in which our employees feel very satisfied with the working condition so that they can stay here and work for long time.

The narrative consistency continues on the company's website where it reiterated that: "Despite the downturn of the economy [name of the company] continuously strives by all means to maintain production and sustain the jobs for employees…"

VNNC's focus on the family is a value espoused by the managers and employees, often expressed through treating employees like family members, and ensuring that they achieve a reasonable work and family balance. For example, the respondent stressed how the company chose to locate the corporate employee housing in the suburb where most workers reside. This way, the employees do not have to travel long distances and take more time away from their families. Such an effort was seen by the managers as a paragon of CSR because not many companies are committed to such an initiative. They said, "The decent housing condition provided by our company to our employees reflects our company's commitment to overall social responsibility."

Another board member added that the company even sponsored buses to bring employees to their home communities during the Lunar New Year holiday. In Vietnam, the Lunar New Year is an occasion that employers use as a traditional way to appreciate their stakeholders, particularly employees. This gesture, according to the board members, has now been institutionalized as company policy and culture. The company website section for organizational culture discussed it explicitly:

> The management board of [company name] pay special attention to nurturing, solidifying, and creating favorable conditions for all company members to build and develop [this] culture....

The above narratives were cited by the company board members as the main reasons for the company's growth from 11 staff in 2003 to 1,300 employees in three factories by 2012. To them, staff loyalty, employee retention and expansion were clear evidence that the company did well in creating and sustaining its "social responsibility" toward its own employees.

### CSR is "giving back to our community"

VNNC2, a smaller enterprise, focused its CSR on both internal and external stakeholders. VNNC2's CEO articulated that his company's approach to CSR combined philanthropy and traditional community support. He stated that CSR is a way to pay back the community. His company's approach to CSR is strategic in that the company used resources from its network of professionals, including employees and family to work on community projects in various parts of the country. The projects range from helping build bridges in flood-stricken areas and school libraries, donating food, books and school supplies as well as training the teachers. Personal networks were reported to be important in diffusing CSR ideas and activities.

One of their projects is to provide internships to young people so they can "give them some (work) experience." The CEO used a personal network of fellow business club members to harness resources. For example, he spearheaded a start-up project to provide not only experience but also the infrastructure in the form of a network of professionals who act as mentors: "We bring successful business people and provide young entrepreneurs with free one-on-one mentoring." When asked why they undertook CSR activities, he said, "We have to pay back our community. That's our responsibility."

Regarding CSR communication, the CEO mentioned that they do CSR without having to show their company brand: "We just do it, we are a small company so we don't have millions to spend. But we ask other SMEs to join so we name the project as the fund...but we are anonymous in that fund."

Indeed, the company website does not mention any CSR activities. However, a careful examination of the company's online CSR publications would lead to a business club where the CEO is a pioneering member. Still, the descriptions are mostly implicit and the word "corporate social responsibility" is not used at all. The CEO stated:

> Charity for SME and in Vietnam is a part of life ... so we don't ask if it's a legal thing or not. We just do it. I think in Vietnam, giving and helping the other is part of life.

When asked where this thinking might come from, the respondent said "it doesn't matter if you're Buddhist, Khmer or Christian, Vietnamese are brought up to help each other."

To the CEO, this sense of community and mutual support should be a tradition. This idea was salient in his story about how and why he and his business colleagues bring their children to their charity work. He says that during their annual charity event, which could well be in the rural areas, "the rich kids live with the [poor] children and we provide them the experience so they learn how to give ... so they can share [feeling] with the poor kids in the middle of nowhere."

Despite differences in CSR methods and outlook, the two local company cases reflect a basic collectivistic sense of family and community in Vietnam (Jamieson, 1995). In both cases, the leaders focused on the immediate internal and local stakeholders in a communal and geographical sense. In Vietnam, charity begins at home, the corporate home that is. We found almost no account on the grand perspective; for example, a concern for the global environment or international labor issues that are often the staple of Western CSR mandates.

The interpretation of and approach to CSR seemed more intrinsic and intuitive. Their motivation often comes from their value of helping each other and their families. As such they do not feel they need to promote their CSR activities as it detracts from the authenticity and value of their intention. As the representatives of VNNC1 hinted, if CSR is about the company's immediate stakeholders, then they are directly working on it. And that such a responsibility has to come from within; in other words, the employees and immediate communities around have to be well supported.

## CSR as strategic communication

In contrast to local company cases, the respondents from three MNCs saw CSR as an integrated part of their business strategy. They shared their different projects within the company, with their employees and those in partnership with an NGO or charity organization. For the MNCs, CSR was a strategic part of organizational communication, which resulted in different degrees of media exposure.

Included in these are employee volunteer programs where they allocate a day in the year when their employees are 'released from work' to perform community service. For VNMNC1, this 'global day of service' is part of the MNC's global strategy, but has since been referred to on its website as a 'regional day of service.' The company provides employees one to two days of paid leave when they undertake a corporate-sponsored volunteer activity, which is often in partnership with an NGO. Enabling 'employee volunteers' through these sponsored activities fulfils the partnership terms between the corporation and the NGO.

However, when asked when this volunteer work is scheduled, the respondent from VNMNC 1 said, "Usually during the weekend." This response raises questions on whether 'volunteer' time actually uses up the employees' family time instead of work time. The VNMNC1 respondent however said that if their employees want to volunteer elsewhere in their own personal communities or projects they can still do so although that is not 'counted' as part of the company's employee volunteer program. VNMNC2 and VNMNC3 follow a similar model of enabling their employees to volunteer on one of the company's sponsored projects.

In addition to providing employee volunteers in partner projects, MNCs offer funding and funding opportunities to their preferred partners. For example, VNMNC1 partnered with a VNNGO1 to co-develop a project to raise funds for education. Since the company is in the financial sector, they not only gave financial support but also promoted the project to their employees, suppliers and clients. In doing so they substantially increased the funding base.

Quite expectedly, this partnership activity is well publicized in the company website and that of the partner NGO satisfying implicit PR and reputational motivations. Given that the VNMNC1 is a global company with shareholders, reporting on their CSR programs and activities is also part of their transparency and accountability measures. Thus, the websites of the MNCs clearly articulate CSR as a key corporate undertaking. VNMNC1's local website heralds their engagement with the community stating their CSR initiatives and local partnerships with a "focus on developing the local communities we serve." VNMNC3's CSR commitment, which appears on its landing page "supports the communities around the world in which our employees live and work through our established CSR entities and via company-sponsored volunteer initiatives."

CSR activities are definitely used as media events with the purpose of increasing public visibility of their corporate brands. For example, VNMNC2 reported that they work with newspaper companies because

> they are good with community support projects. However, they usually come to us and suggest to share the costs. And you get the company name in the media for good things with less money spent as you would have to sponsor otherwise.

The sponsorship events and partners however undergo risk assessment to ensure congruence with corporate image and objectives. For example, when VNMNC2 was approached to fund a bridge building project, they refused to do so:

> Our selected projects are mostly sensitive to any predictable crisis. It means when we smell that a project would relate or end up with risks, which would bring our reputation down, we never choose them. For example, some people asked us to sponsor bridges. While this may be a great idea, bridges are very vulnerable to potential crisis. What happens if a bridge bearing our company name falls down the river? No matter what reason, our name is associated with the crippled bridge and that would really damage the company.

The VNMNC2 respondent admitted that since her organization is a corporate foundation, "we do not have an independent website because we are only the charity arm of the company." As a corporate foundation, which she confided is difficult to establish in Vietnam, they have to spend the funds allocated for the foundation and its programs. As part of the project funding requirements, they undertake project evaluations that involve site visits, photos and Key Performance Indicator (KPI) reports. The respondent however confessed that they do not undertake impact evaluation.

For example, we sponsor pupils' scholarship program, each pupil received about three or four million VND. And that is a one-off activity. We do not know if the kids did better with our money or not. We found it hard to monitor and evaluate that over time.

The lack of impact evaluations raises questions on CSR's effectiveness. While MNCs have been found to be best placed to progress PR practice in Vietnam through CSR, they have not developed a sophisticated and meaningful approach to CSR (Bilowol & Doan, 2015; Hamm, 2012). Instead the efforts still reflect a largely marketing/PR-oriented approach to CSR that is aimed at generating goodwill among the communities in which the businesses operate.

## *CSR as social development*

Like in Indonesia and the Philippines, we found throughout our Vietnam interviews that MNC participants often explicitly referred to their CSR projects as contributing to the development of Vietnam, which reflects a nation-building CSR paradigm. Three of the four of MNC respondents emphasized that building community primary schools was not just about supporting the targeted communities but also symbolically representing the MNCs' commitment to support the country's effort to improve education and literacy, which are key indicators in the UN MDGs and SDGs. This and other evidence lead us to another common theme that emerged from the research and directs attention to how CSR contributes to social development, if at all?

Although the respondents from both local and global companies viewed CSR within the context of capacity building, the MNCs expressed commitment to sustainable development such as alleviating poverty, improving education and health, and saving the environment, albeit minimally. By directing their CSR efforts on supporting education and employment, local and global companies believe they are enacting social responsibility by ensuring livelihood opportunities exist for the poor and underprivileged members of their communities.

As such the CSR projects often involve building schools or libraries, offering scholarships, donating books and school supplies. MNCs however have also offered training and educational programs on financial literacy and employee well-being in line with their respective business strategies.

While Vietnam has a literacy rate[1] of 94.5 percent (CIA, 2018), companies still see education as a key factor in economic development. However, the current form of measuring literacy might not be a sufficient indicator of a country's human development. UNESCO (2008) suggested that,

> There are different literacy practices in different domains of social life, such as education, religion, workplaces, public services, families and community activities. They change over time, and these different literacies are supported and shaped by different institutions and social relationships.
>
> (p. 11)

National development initiatives undertaken as CSR projects in remote areas or as one respondent described "in the middle of nowhere," rely on assistance from the private sector because the government is unable to provide all the resources required. For instance, government authorities identify the location for the education-oriented charity project, provide the land and school building but the furniture and school equipment/materials are auspiced by the private sector and partner NGO through fundraising. Efforts like these, also known as public–private partnerships, demonstrate the cooperation between social institutions, including governments, corporations and NGOs.

Striving a balance between their global CSR strategies and their local environmental conditions is a concern expressed by the MNC respondents. They report that finding this balance is difficult but achievable because they often leverage their financial capacity in negotiating with government and NGOs. Despite MNCs' growing interest in social partnerships (Sison & Hue, 2015), they still exercise considerable 'financial' power in getting their preferred priorities implemented.

For example, all MNC participants expressed firmly their priorities on school buildings and student scholarships while rejecting proposals related to other community development initiatives outside of their corporate interests. When asked if they would support proposals to clear landmines left during the Vietnam war and provide assistance to landmine victims, the MNC participants quickly turned the idea down as the ideas would "likely expose my companies to unforeseeable risks."

The MNC's provision of 'employee volunteering opportunities' to company-sponsored projects, and low-risk, high-visibility building projects exhibits a highly strategic and transactional approach to CSR. Given that one MNC allocated 5 percent of the company's profit toward CSR activities, of which 70 percent was used for internal proposals, one can infer that CSR is employed as a 'strategic mechanism' to meet corporate interests. Because these CSR strategies employ top-down approaches from overseas headquarters, it is understandable that local managers would be cautious of CSR proposals departing from their global priority framework.

## Summary

The various perspectives and experiences of NGOs and corporations in Vietnam reveal that CSR practices are largely transactional. NGOs use CSR as a mechanism for identifying and targeting potential corporate partners who might contribute financial or human resources to their programs. Private-sector organizations, both local and multinational, view CSR as a means to contribute to national development and to strengthen their strategic interests.

While CSR is currently perceived as primarily a marketing activity or a form of 'enlightened' employee relations, image management and community relations, the potential exists for a more nuanced community engagement approach. An intimate knowledge of local culture combined with the trust placed on interpersonal relationships may provide practitioners with a useful framework. This community-centered approach involves the participation of community 'beneficiaries' in co-constructing the CSR program. Community participation in developing these programs will empower them and avoid perpetuating a resource dependency on corporations and other benefactors.

The cases disclose that the intrinsic community orientation in the local culture may need to be considered and integrated into corporate CSR programs. Balancing local knowledge with global standards continues to be a challenge for both local and multinational companies. Western CSR is a relatively new concept although the philosophy underpinning it is not new to many Asian cultures such as Vietnam. While filial and kinship values influence approaches to philanthropy and CSR programs, paternalistic overtures are also manifest. The emphasis on ensuring livelihood and employee well-being is rooted in the paternalistic, and somewhat elitist, belief that those in authority will provide for those with lesser means.

The research confirms that companies are providing real tangible benefits to disadvantaged communities through infrastructure projects and scholarships however the intangible benefits and long-term impact have not been measured. Moreover, while the CSR objectives and projects are often noble, they currently suggest a transactional approach where corporations are the 'benefactors' and communities the 'beneficiary.' This benefactor–beneficiary dichotomy needs to be examined in the context of empowerment and authentic social development. Future research can explore these relationships and whether CSR actually enhances and encourages resource dependency.

## Note

1 Literacy rate is defined as the percentage of the population 15 years and over who can read and write.

## References

Aguinis, H. & Glavas, A. (2012). What we know and don't know about corporate social responsibility: A review and research agenda. *Journal of Management,* 38 (4), 932–968.

Aras, G. & Crowther, D. (Eds.). (2010). *NGOs and Social Responsibility.* Bingley, UL: Emerald Group Publishing Limited.

Arenas, D., Lozano, J. M. & Albareda, L. (2009). The role of NGOs in CSR: Mutual perceptions among stakeholders. *Journal of Business Ethics,* 88, 175–197.

Arvidsson, S. (2010). Communication of corporate social responsibility: A study of the views of management team in large companies. *Journal of Business Ethics,* 96 (3), 339–354.

Bansal, P. & Roth, K. (2000). Why companies go green: A model of ecological responsiveness. *The Academy of Management Journal,* 43 (4), 717–736.

Bartlett, J. L. & Devin, B. (2011). Management, communication and corporate social responsibility. *The Handbook of Communication and Corporate Social Responsibility* (pp. 47–66). West Sussex: John Wiley & Sons.

Bator, M. & Stohl, C. (2011). New partnerships for a new generation of corporate social responsibility. In Ihlen, O., Bartlett, J. & May, S. (Eds.). *The Handbook of Communication and Corporate Social Responsibility.* (pp. 399–421). Oxford: Wiley Blackwell.

Baum, J. A. C. & Powell, W. W. (1995). Cultivating an institutional ecology of organizations: Comment on Hannan, Carroll, Dundon, and Torres. *American Sociological Review,* 60, 529–538.

Berger, P. L. & Luckmann, T. (1966). *The Social Construction of Reality.* New York: Freeman.

Bilowol, J. & Doan, M. A. (2015). Multinational corporations' role in developing Vietnam's public relations industry through corporate social responsibility. *Public Relations Review,* http://dx.doi.org/10.1016/j.pubrev.2015.06.004

Bhattacharyay, B. N. (2010). Infrastructure for ASEAN connectivity and integration. *ASEAN Nath Bhattacharyay,* 27 (2), 200–220.

Birkin, F., Cashman, A., Koh, S. & Liu, Z. (2009). New sustainable business models in China. *Business Strategy and the Environment,* 18, 64–77.

Bortree, D. (2014). The state of CSR communication research. *Public Relations Journal,* 8 (3), 1–8.

Bowen, F., Newenham-Kahindi, A. & Herremans, I. (2010). When suits meet roots: The antecedents and consequences of community engagement strategy. *Journal of Business Ethics,* 95, 297–318.

Bui, T. L. H. (2010). The Vietnamese consumer perception on corporate social responsibility. *Journal of International Business Research,* 9 (1), 75–87.

Burchell, J. & Cooke, J. (2013a). Sleeping with the enemy? Strategic transformations in business-NGO relationships through stakeholder dialogue. *Journal of Business Ethics*, 113 (3), 505–518.

Burchell, J. & Cooke, J. (2013b). CSR, Co-optation and resistance: The emergence of new agonistic relations between business and civil society. *Journal of Business Ethics*, 115 (4), 741–754.

Centre, V.-N. R. COMINGO, VUFI and PACCOM. From www.ngocentre.org.vn/content/comingo-vufo-and-paccom.

Central Intelligence Agency. (2017). Vietnam. *World Fact Book*. www.cia.gov/library/publications/the-world-factbook/geos/vm.html.

Charmaz, K. (2000). Grounded theory: Objectivist and constructivist methods. In Denzin, N. K. & Lincoln, Y. S. (Eds.). *Handbook of Qualitative Research* (2nd edn.). Thousand Oaks, CA: Sage.

Cheung, D., Welford, R. & Hills, P. (2009). CSR & the environment: Business-supply chain partnerships in Hong Kong & the PRDR of China. *Corporate Social Responsibility and Environmental Management*, 16.

Christensen, L. T., Morsing, M. & Thyssen, O. (2011). The polyphony of corporate social responsibility: Deconstructing accountability and transparency in the context of identity and hypocrisy. In Cheney, G., May, S. & Munshi, D. (Eds.). *The Handbook of Communication Ethics* (pp. 457–474). New York: Routledge.

Clifford, J. (1990). Notes on (field) notes. In Sanjek, R. (Ed.). *Fieldnotes: The Making of Anthropology* (pp. 47–71). Ithaca, NY: Cornell University Press.

Coe, C. A. (2014). Minding the metaphor: Vietnamese state-run press coverage of social movements abroad. *Journal of Vietnamese Studies*, 9 (1), 1–35.

Crane, A. & Seitanidi, M. M. (2014). Social partnerships and responsible business: What, why and how? In Seitanidi, M. M. & Crane, A. (Eds.). *Social Partnerships and Responsible Business: A Research Handbook* (pp. 1–13). New York: Routledge.

Dang, G. & Tri, P. M. (2013). *Corporate Philanthropy and Corporate Perceptions of Local NGOs in Vietnam*. Retrieved from Hanoi.

Dartey-Baah, K. & Amponsah-Tawiah, K. (2011). Exploring the limits of Western corporate social responsibility theories in Africa. *International Journal of Business and Social Science*, 2 (18), 126–137.

del Rosario, R. (2011). Corporate social responsibility in Southeast Asia: An eight-country analysis. *Research Report*, Makati, Philippines: Asian Institute of Management.

Doan, M. A. & Bilowol, J. (2014). Public relations and professionalism in Vietnam – Vietnamese PR practitioners' perceptions of an emerging field. *Public Relations Review*, 40 (3), 483–491.

Dobers, P. & Halme, M. (2009). Corporate social responsibility and developing countries. *Corporate Social Responsibility and Environmental Management*, 16 (5), 22.

Domm, G. (2016). Public relations practice in the emerging 'powerhouses' of Southeast Asia: Some views from within. *Public Relations Review*, 42, 641–653.

Duong, H. T. (2014). The future of corporate philanthropy. *Saigon Times*, 36, 62–63.

Edelman. (2015).Trust around the world. *2015 Edelman Trust Barometer*. Retrieved June 5, 2015 from www.edelman.com/2015-edelman-trust-barometer/trust-around-world/.

Elving, W. J. L., Golob, U., Podnar, K., Ellerup-Nielsen, A. & Thomson, C. (2015). The bad, the ugly and the good: New challenges for CSR communication. *Corporate Communication*, 20 (2), 9.

Golob, U., Poddnar, K., Elving, W. J., Nielsen, A. E., Thomsen, C. & Schultz, F. (2013). CSR communication: quo vadis? *Corporate Communications: An International Journal,* 18 (2), 176–192.

Gray, M. L. (1999). Creating civil society? The emergence of NGOs in Vietnam. *Development and Change,* 30, 693–713.

Hagen, R. (2002). Globalization, university transformation and economic regeneration: A UK case study of public/private sector partnership. *The International Journal of Public Sector Management,* 15 (3), 204–218.

Hallahan, K. (1999). Seven models of framing: Implications for public relations. *Journal of Public Relations Research,* 11 (3), 205–242.

Hamm, B. (2012). Corporate social responsibility in Vietnam: Integration or mere adaptation. *Pacific News,* 4–8.

Hang, D. T. T. (2010). *PR Industry in Vietnam.* Hanoi: Labor and Society Publisher.

Hew, D. & Soesastro, H. (2003). Realizing the ASEAN economic community by 2020: ISEAS and ASEAN-ISIS approaches. *ASEAN Economic Bulletin,* 20 (3), 292–296.

Hieu, P. D. (2011). Corporate social responsibility: A study on awareness of managers and consumers in Vietnam. *Journal of Accounting and Taxation,* 3 (8), 162–170.

Ihlen, Ø., Bartlett, J. & May, S. (2011). Conclusions and take away points. In Ihlen, Ø., Bartlett, J. & May, S. (Eds.). *The Handbook of Communication and Corporate Social Responsibility* (pp. 550–571). Oxford: Wiley Blackwell.

Jamali, D. (2010). The CSR of MNC subsidiaries in developing countries: Global, local, substantive or diluted? *Journal of Business Ethics,* 93, 181–200.

Jamali, D. & Keshishian, T. (2009). Uneasy alliances: Lessons learned from partnerships between business and NGOs in the context of CSR. *Journal of Business Ethics,* (84), 277–295.

Jamieson, N. L. (1995). *Understanding Vietnam.* University of California Press.

Kellow, A. (2000). Norms, interests and environment NGOs: The limits of cosmopolitanism, *Environmental Politics,* 9 (3), 1–22.

Keyton, J. (2006). *Communication Research: Asking Questions, Finding Answers.* New York: McGraw-Hill.

Kolk, A. (2014). Partnerships as panacea for addressing global problems? On rationale, context, actors, impact and limitations. In Seitanidi, M. M. & Crane, A. (Eds.). *Social Partnerships and Responsible Business: A Research Handbook* (pp. 15–43). New York: Routledge.

Lee, S. Y. (2015). Samsung Display to invest extra $3 billion to boost Vietnam output. Retrieved from www.reuters.com/article/2015/08/07/us-samsung-elec-vietnam-display-idUSKCN0QC02G20150807.

Lindlof, T. R. & Taylor, B. C. (Eds.). (2002). *Qualitative Communication Research Methods* (2nd edn.). Thousand Oaks: Sage.

Linh, T. (2012). Bar girls. Retrieved from www.congan.com.vn/?mod=detnews&catid=702&id=463937.

Loan, T. H. V. (2011). Public relations in Vietnam: History in the making. Paper presented at the International history of public relations conference. Bournemouth University, July 6–7.

Long, C. U. (2015). The impact of market orientation and corporate social responsibility on firm performance: Evidence from Vietnam. *Academy of Marketing Studies Journal,* 19 (1), 265–277.

Long, S. (2014). Safety in number: ASEAN invites comparison with the EU. *The Economist.*

Mak, A. (2009). Public relations in Vietnam: The development under the Doi Moi policy. *Modern Asia,* 14 (2), 122.

Matten, D. (2006). Why do companies engage in corporate social responsibility? Background, reasons and basic concepts. In Hennigfeld, J., Pohl, M. & Tolhurst, N. (Eds.), *The ICCA Handbook on Corporate Social Responsibility* (pp. 3–46). The Atrium, Southern Gate, Chichester: John Wiley & Sons Ltd.

McKinney, B. (2000). Public relations in the land of ascending dragon: Implications in light of the US/Vietnam bilateral trade agreement. *Public Relations Quarterly,* 45 (4), 23–26.

McKinney, B. (2006). Public relations in Vietnam: A six-year perspective. *Public Relations Quarterly,* 51 (2), 18.

O'Riordan, L. & Fairbrass, J. (2008). CSR—Theories, models and concepts in stakeholder dialogue—A model for decision-makers in the pharmaceutical industry. *Journal of Business Ethics,* 83 (4), 754–758.

Oruc, I. & Sarikaya, M. (2010). Non-governmental organizations as outsourcing in corporate philanthropy.

Pedersen, E. R. G. & Pedersen, J. T. (2013). The rise of business-NGO partnerships. *Journal of Corporate Citizenship,* (50), 6–19.

Poret, S. (2014). Corporate-NGO partnerships in CSR activities: Why and how. Retrieved May 22, 2015 from HAL Sylvaine Poret. Corporate-NGO partnerships in CSR activities: why and how? cahier de recherche 2014–21. 2014. <hal-01070474>

Richter, J. (2004). Public-private partnership for health: A trend with no alternative? *Development,* 47 (2), 43–48.

Runckel, C. (2015). Asia opportunities: Asean Economic Community (AEC) in 2015. Retrieved from www.business-in-asia.com/asia/asean_economic_community.html.

Samii, R., Van Wassenhove, L. N. & Bhattacharya, S. (2002). An innovative public private partnership: New approach to development. *World Development,* 30 (6), 991–1008.

Shukla, A. (2010). First official estimate: An NGO for every 400 people in India. *The Indian Express.*

Shultz, J. (2012). Vietnam: Political economy, marketing system. *Journal of Macromarketing,* 32 (1), 7–17.

Sidel, M. (1997). The emergence of a voluntary sector and philanthropy in Vietnam: functions, legal regulation and prospects for the future. *Voluntas: International Journal of Voluntary and Nonprofit Organizations,* 8 (3), 283–302.

Sison, M. & Hue, D. T. (2015). CSR Communication and NGOs: Perspectives from Vietnam. Paper presented at the 3rd International CSR Communication Conference, Ljubljana, Slovenia.

Son, N. T. (2014). The purpose of business existence: The difference between CSR, corporate charity and cause marketing. *Forbes Vietnam,* 7, 40–41.

Tencati, A., Russo, A. & Quaglia, V. (2008). Unintended consequences of CSR: Protectionism and collateral damage in global supply chains: The case of Vietnam. *Corporate Governance. The International Journal,* 8 (4), 518–531.

Tran, A. N. (2011). Corporate social responsibility in socialist Vietnam: Implementation, challenges, and local solutions. *Labor in Vietnam* (pp. 119–159). Singapore: Institute of Southeast Asia Studies.

Tulder, R. B. & Pfisterer, S. (2014). Creating partnership space: Exploring the right fit for sustainable development partnerships. In Seitanidi, M. M. & Crane, A. (Eds.).

*Social Partnerships and Responsible Business: A Research Handbook* (pp. 105–124). New York: Routledge.

United Nations. (2002). *Report of the World Summit on Sustainable Development: Johannesburg*, South Africa. New York: United Nations.

U.S. State Department (2012). Fact Sheet: Non-Governmental Organizations (NGOs) in the United States. Retrieved May 15, 2015 from http://iipdigital.usembassy.gov/st/english/texttrans/2012/01/20120130171036roma0.1718823.html#axzz3qHRPItEn.

Van, L. (2011). Public relations in Vietnam: History in the making. Paper presented at the International history of public relations conference. Bournemouth University, July 6.

Van Niekerk, A. J. (2010). Governance from below and global governance: Accommodating change. In Aras, G. & Crowther, D. (Eds.). *NGOs and Social Responsibility* (pp. 33–55). UK: Emerald Group Publishing Ltd.

Wiriyapong, N. (2015). Investors keen on Asean but sceptical about AEC. *Bangkok Post*. Retrieved from www.bangkokpost.com/print/564587/.

Wong, L. (2008). Corporate social responsibility in China: Between the market and the search for a sustainable grownth development. *Asian Business & Management*, 8, 129–148.

World Bank. (2014). *Vietnam development report 2014: Skilling up Vietnam: Preparing the workforce for a modern market economy.*

Yaziji, M., & Doh, J. (2009). *NGOs and Corporations*. Cambridge: Cambridge University Press.

# 8 Conclusion
## Connecting the narratives

### Summary of findings

*Narratives of community and collaboration*

The field research undertaken in the six countries reveals a commonality around the intrinsic value of community—helping others, sharing one's wealth with those less fortunate, not leaving people behind and supporting a greater good—which have been integrated or reconfigured to Western conceptualizations of CSR. While intrinsic culture values of collectivism (Hofstede, 2001) and communitarianism (Leeper, 1996), kinship and filial relations (Herrera & Roman, 2011) common to many Asian countries have been identified by other scholars as contributing to CSR, limited attention has been given to how these values shape and influence stakeholders, especially community 'beneficiaries,' perceptions and enactment of CSR. In particular, we were interested in how these cultural values may have informed how community stakeholders communicated and negotiated with corporate and government representatives.

Moreover, the impact of external forces such as the global standards of the Global Reporting Initiative or International Standards Office, also play a part in how multinational and domestic companies interpret and enact CSR in their respective organizations. These standards also influence how multi-sectoral alliances are developed between the private sector, national, state and local governments, NGOs and civil society organizations, and community organizations.

The narrative of community spirit resonated in all of the research sites we visited. Whether 'community' was defined in geographical terms (our neighbors), or in superior–subordinate relations (employees), or in terms of social inequality (marginalized women and at-risk youth; disabled and elderly), the respondents articulated a strong sense of 'helping others.' In fact, the local language of some of the countries, language being the main communicative element in human relations, has a word for this community-centeredness and mutual aid. The Philippines, for example, has *bayanihan* and Indonesia's, Malaysia's and Singapore's *gotong-royong* all denote the sense of communal helping of one another. Each country's value system somehow seems to influence this spirit of 'not leaving anyone behind' that according to the CEO of the PHMNC is not about a particular religion but a "sense of humanity."

In this regard, we found various levels of collaboration, cooperation and co-optation across the region. Most of the community and corporate representatives spoke about the relationships and partnerships they have developed across the private, government, civil society and community sectors through CSR programs. Undoubtedly the private-sector organizations have found, others may call it 'exploited,' opportunities to engage with community stakeholders either directly or through the local NGOs where government institutions have otherwise been absent or inadequate. This confirms the focus on community development programs also referred to as the 'governance gap' (Hirschland, 2006; Waldman et al., 2006).

To address these interconnections, various engagement strategies have been employed by the different sectors. For instance, we found that community relations officers in Indonesia, the Philippines and Thailand employed by the multinational companies had previously worked in NGOs. Community relations officers with NGO experience provide corporations with critical network information about local community touch points, and a 'trusted' mediator who can span both the corporate and NGO boundaries. While this strategy may be viewed as collaboration by some, critics may view it as 'co-optation' (Burchell & Cook, 2013). Regardless, joining forces with other stakeholders is becoming a necessity with increasing societal expectations and diminishing resources.

Scholars and practitioners agree that collaboration is the key to addressing sustainable development and other social issues such as poverty, public health and education (Austin, 2000; Armitage, Berkes & Doubleday, 2007; Vazquez-Brust, Sarkis & Cordeiro, 2013). Certainly, multi-sectoral and multi-stakeholder collaboration scaffolded by values of co-creation and inclusion is necessary to achieve the sustainable development goals. Social issues and their solutions are not, and should not be, exclusive to particular ideologies. The idea behind collaboration, "dissensus," pluralism, requisite variety and dialectics is an openness to listen and learn from different perspectives. Dialogic communication facilitates this process and we must aim to engender a safe and nurturing environment for this dialogue to occur for all participants, regardless of their background.

Partnerships between the private-sector and non-profit organizations go through a 'collaboration continuum' with three stages: philanthropic, transactional and integrative (Austin, 2000). In the philanthropic stage, the relationship tends to be one-way where the business takes the role of 'benefactor' and the recipient group the 'beneficiary.' This type of collaboration is characterized by limited engagement and fit. Transactional collaboration reflects a mutually beneficial relationship between the business and the non-profit organization. During this stage, the two parties identify a similarity in its values, increase their interactions and leverage this exchange for their respective benefits. The third stage of integration is described as the point when the organization's boundaries disappear and notions of 'them' and 'us' shift to 'we' when they do things together. At this point, the relationship goes beyond the leaders and advocates and involves most organizational members. In many private-sector organizations, 'integrating' CSR into their business strategy is the ultimate goal.

However, further work on the collaboration continuum produced a fourth stage—transformational (Austin & Seitanidi, 2012). According to the authors, transformational collaborations involve partners learning about their social needs and roles in meeting those needs and could take the form of collaboration which benefits a large segment of the society (Austin & Seitanidi, 2012). Because this type of collaboration promotes interdependence and collective action, the transformative effects of collaboration go beyond social, economic and political systems but also within organizations and their individual employees. The experience of the Singapore corporation with 'engagement as research' and Indonesia's culturally strategic community engagement approaches are testaments to the transformational effects of collaborative CSR. Thailand's immersive experiences for corporate employees where staff live with the farming villages imbued the employees with a deeper appreciation of the produce they sell in their "community stores" aside from learning new things such as the process of collecting the produce.

While CSR remains a fairly new and contested concept to NGOs, it seems that they can and some have warmed to the idea. For starters, CSR has been seen as a catalyst for NGOs and businesses to form partnerships. Some NGOs are discovering that CSR programs are opportunities to engage with corporations. While they are extremely selective in their choice of corporate partners, some NGOs are open to aligning and re-aligning some of their programs to enable the collaboration to proceed, as is the case in the U.S. NGO based in Vietnam. However, a successful partnership is contingent on whether the parties share common views of the nature of their collaboration.

While increased engagement between NGOs and businesses has resulted in collaborative partnerships, there are benefits and risks for both parties. For companies, the benefits of engaging with NGOs include risk mitigation and local access. Working with NGOs enables companies to "head off trouble, accelerate innovation, foresee shifts in demand, shape legislation, and set industry standards" (Yaziji & Doh, 2009, p. 129). This was apparent in our communities in Indonesia and Thailand where the corporate representatives initially experienced resistance from the village leaders. Moreover, through the help of NGOs who have established social capital through relationships with key community leaders, corporations gained access to and local knowledge of communities who granted the social license to operate.

For NGOs, collaborating with business provided them with access to financial and structural resources in an area of increased competition. Partnership with companies who they could see as allies to their cause could provide them with much needed resources (Yaziji & Doh, 2009). Corporate engagement can provide NGOs with a broader platform for their advocacy as well as access to business expertise needed for their social programs. The access to financial and structural resources were clearly identified by the NGO partners in Singapore, Vietnam and Indonesia. For instance, in Singapore, one of the social enterprises that partnered with a major financial institution started off as a grant recipient, then became an event supplier, that snowballed to events of the institution's clients, and also became a site for the institution's employee volunteer program. This multi-layered partnership model with the financial institution enabled the social enterprise to grow quicker than it had imagined.

This multi-sectoral engagement through corporate social responsibility has been dubbed by an Indonesian scholar as a form of 'collaborative social responsibility' (Kartikawangi, 2017). She proposes that 'collaborative social responsibility' is where the corporation, government, society and media work together on CSR as "equal partners." While 'equality' of power within these partnerships may be contested, we have found that corporations, especially MNCs, are cautiously 'co-sharing' power and control with selected NGO partners. Sthapitanonda and Watson (2015, p. 70) refer to this type of engagement between corporations and NGOs as a form of 'managed distance.' The authors suggest that corporations enact 'managed distance' as an extension of a paternalistic relationship while NGOs view 'managed distance' as "the retention of (the) freedom to operate and campaign, uncontaminated by the influences of corporate interests" (Sthapitanonda & Watson, 2015, p. 70).

The need for NGOs to establish some sort of 'independence' and 'impartiality' is also related to their regard for their reputation. While one NGO in the Philippines was keen to establish their financial independence from the corporation (who provided funding to kick start the micro financing project), other NGOs in Indonesia, the Philippines and Thailand seem not to be ready for their corporate partners to complete the engagement. For instance, the corporate partner in Indonesia has already discussed their exit strategy from the cooperative, but the village leaders insisted they are not ready yet as they still need further business expertise training especially while they apply for 'organic' certification. Similarly, the NGO in Thailand had already won awards and grants on its own, but has expressed that the corporate partnership gave them a certain level of 'comfort and confidence.' The community leaders in the Southern Philippines, who demonstrated initiative and energy, echoed this embedded partnership arrangement with their corporate partners.

Partnerships come with risks for both the NGO and the corporation. For NGOs, choosing the 'wrong' partner threatens their credibility and legitimacy especially among their key stakeholders. That is why the NGOs in Vietnam were careful about choosing their corporate partners. At the same time, the international NGO headed by the American woman used her knowledge of CSR and whether a particular corporation had a CSR program, as a means to engage with particular corporations. NGOs' involvement in CSR in this manner has led scholars to question if this engagement reflected an "appropriation and co-optation of protest" by the business community (Burchell & Cook, 2013b). The authors posit that while co-optation is inevitable in the engagement process, it is still possible to maintain 'agonistic' relationships where both parties are 'allowed' to debate their notions of responsible business. The authors further contend that through continuous dialogue, NGOs are able to continue to hold businesses to account and vice versa.

For corporations, the risks of partnership include security of sensitive information that is shared with NGOs, increased public scrutiny and its perceived 'public relations' advantage (Yaziji & Doh, 2009). However, the corporations we interviewed saw the benefits of community and employee engagement through CSR over and above the 'risks.' In particular, the corporation in Thailand was initially concerned about the forests surrounding the plant as fire hazards that also affected the surrounding villages. The drought experienced by the community impacted not only business operations but more importantly the villagers' livelihoods. It was through the intervention of the local NGO representative to broker an arrangement between the corporation and the villagers to co-create several CSR activities. In addition to engaging the villagers to build the 'check dams,' the corporation also trained the villagers to measure and research about their water levels. This information was shared as both the community and corporation deemed it vital to monitor their water resources.

Thus, the narratives of collaboration and cooperation among communities continue to inform and shape CSR programs. Undoubtedly power relations still exist but community stakeholders are not naïve; they are aware and cognizant of the 'soft' power they hold and exercise when the need arises. Moreover, sensitive and authentic communication is needed to skilfully navigate and negotiate these power dynamics across all stakeholder groups.

## *Narratives of women as community leaders*

In many of the communities we visited, the women leaders played a major, albeit subtle, part in the collaborations between corporate entities and communities. We observed this during our visits with Indonesian farming communities, among the Vietnamese teachers, in the Philippines' disaster community and Thailand's informal village leader. These observations are valuable when juxtaposed with the predominantly patriarchal society in which these communities are located.

While previous scholars have highlighted the absence of marginalized voices in CSR practice, there has been limited attention given to the role of women in CSR. The few that exist however focus on the role of women's NGOs as actors in CSR practice (Grosser, 2016) or how CSR programs might integrate more gendered and feminist approaches (Grosser & Moon, 2005; Larrieta-Rubín de Celis, Fernández de Bobadilla-Güemez, Alonso-Almeida & Velasco-Balmaseda, 2017). Other studies have examined the role of women in community resistance and activism (Ikelegbe, 2005; Mukhopadhyay, 2017). Limited attention has been given to exploring the narratives of women empowerment through CSR programs.

In examining the voices of community 'beneficiaries' of CSR, we found that women exercised community leadership in two ways. First, by being open to exploring opportunities to earn additional sources of livelihood; second by their willingness to learn new skills and technologies.

The women's willingness to explore new sources of livelihood was a common theme mentioned by our male and female respondents. While the women's role as providers have often been subjugated to the traditional role of men as breadwinners in the family, our research revealed that women exercised an innate entrepreneurial spirit. When opportunities to generate income, albeit supplementary, to support their families were offered, they did not hesitate to participate and take advantage of the opportunity. This was particularly clear in the Indonesian case when the INDMNC approached the women to explore new ways of integrated and organic farming, which the men had initially resisted or dismissed. The women's ability to demonstrate to the male farmers that planting herbs and learning about waste management generated additional income convinced the latter to reconsider the INDMNC's CSR initiatives around organic farming. Moreover, the women's additional income had dissuaded them to leave their village to find work in the cities or even overseas. The general manager of the cooperative in the Philippines also reported that many of his members were women who borrowed money to start microbusinesses such as a *'sari-sari'* (convenience) store or dressmaking services. He proudly reported also that these women were good creditors who paid on time.

The women's openness and willingness to try and learn new skills and technologies to improve their current circumstances reflect courage and leadership. In addition to the above examples, the female community leaders in the disaster community in the Philippines learned new skills including masonry and carpentry to help build their new houses. In Thailand, while the formal village leader was male, the informal village leader was female and she was instrumental in promoting the value of the THNC's check dam project. By demonstrating how the improved water collection in the mountains led to a regular water supply in the villages and to their homes, she has since become an important voice in the community.

It is not a rarity to see women from developing countries venturing out for overseas work in increasing numbers. In the Philippines, almost half of the migrant workers are women. They are filling jobs in the services sector as nannies or maids in foreign lands (Santos, 2014). Thailand, on the other hand, is both a significant labor-sending country in the international market as well as a major labor-recipient among the Southeast Asian countries (Pholphirul, 2012). While the majority of overseas Thai workers are men, Thai women account for about 16 percent of the country's labor outflow. And like the Philippines, overseas Thai women tend to work in private households. They also are in the entertainment industry and service sector such as restaurants (Global Slavery Index, 2016). Necessity and the willingness to sacrifice to provide a better future for their families often drive the exodus from home and community to other countries. Internal migrations also occur typically from rural and urban areas so CSR interventions that create new livelihood opportunities close to home that women are prepared to avail of such as the one in Thailand allowed the woman village leader to stay home.

The value of empowering women in the communities has also underpinned the Singapore coffee academy's focus on providing free training to vulnerable women and at-risk youth. Led by a female entrepreneur, the social enterprise provides a holistic approach that combines professional coffee-making training with life and emotional management and physical training. They have proudly 'graduated' several women—single mothers, some may only have completed primary or high school—and have since found full time work in cafes and restaurants around Singapore.

Shifting the narrative towards women empowerment is a critical component of many of the CSR programs. Some corporations have discovered the potential of women to become 'CSR champions' albeit accidentally, while others have deliberately focused their programs for marginalized women. When women become the 'object' or 'focus' of the CSR program, there is also the risk of perpetuating the 'stereotype' that women need 'protection' or 'help.' In disaster contexts in particular, Bradshaw (2013) suggests that women take on the role of the 'protector' and the 'protected.' Similarly, she proffers that in the development discourse, women's protection is centered around poverty or women's role in caring for others. However, she cautions that assuming women want to be involved in the reconstruction or take the role of providers can be problematic as these could add risk to their current status at home.

> In particular, it is important to understand that the participation of women is not, in itself, automatically or necessarily a good thing for them. Rather, participation should be a choice and should bring benefits to those who participate—practical and strategic. When participation becomes an obligation, it should be questioned. The fact that women may not want to participate should be examined and understood in relation to their perception of priorities and risks
>
> (Bradshaw, 2013, p. 184)

What this study however confirms is that women were instrumental in enabling CSR initiatives to gain ground and prosper. We have demonstrated how the inclusion, articulation and amplification of women's voices in the CSR and community development discourse through their communicative, persuasion and negotiation skills with the various actors with whom they engage have generated positive results. While women's 'efficiency' in delivering programs may be considered as valuable skills, it is important to note that shifting responsibility to women needs to be rewarded and recognized.

In postcolonial societies with feudal systems of thought and paternalistic tendencies still evident, the disruption of traditional power arrangements such as the economic and social empowering of women and similar populations of the repressed and dispossessed necessitate a certain level of willingness by all actors in the CSR process not only to recognize the power differentials and cede some control but also to understand why and how it doesn't have to be a zero-sum game. The *gawan ng paraan* (we will find a solution or a compromise) mentality in the Philippines and the huge social expectation for reciprocity in these Southeast Asian countries inherently make strategic CSR collaborations possible.

## Narratives of sustainability and social development

As mentioned in the beginning of this book, critical to the enactment of many CSR programs is the notion of sustainability and sustainable development. While sustainability is the goal or aspiration, sustainable development is the process to achieve the goal. In 1987, the World Commission on Environment and Development released the Brundtland Report which defined sustainable development as the development which "meets the needs of the present without compromising the ability of future generations to meet their own needs" (Brundtland, 1987, p. 16). Early iterations of the concept focused on three pillars: social, environmental and economic which have also translated to the Triple Bottom Line (people, planet and profits). However, the current Sustainable Development Goals (SDGs) comprise 17 focal areas that range from poverty alleviation to gender equality, clean water to responsible consumption and production and climate action to peace and justice. This framework, along with its predecessor Millennium Development Goals (MDGs), has been used by corporations and governments to drive their social responsibility activities.

Interestingly several of the countries in this study have integrated social responsibility in their legislative and regulatory frameworks. As illustrated in Table 1.1, Indonesia and the Philippines have introduced a law that required corporations to allocate resources toward CSR activities. Some countries, such as Thailand, are driven by the ISO 26000 and the Global Reporting Index (GRI) requirements.

While the private-sector organizations in this study have espoused social responsibility as a key platform for their business operations, many of them have claimed that their focus on social responsibility precede the introduction of CSR in their respective countries. The companies are major players in the manufacturing, transport and logistics, financial, hospitality and education industries in their respective countries, and as such, are committed to sustainable business futures. Some even claim their businesses are critical participants in nation building. These corporations have indeed invested and focused their CSR programs on livelihood and enterprise development activities the most. Social programs that involve education, training and volunteering come next, and then followed by environmental and disaster relief and rehabilitation programs. Philanthropic activities still continue but are often associated with either scholarships or donations to disaster victims.

In contrast community stakeholders' notions of sustainability focus on ensuring the future of their family, their farming communities and their livelihood. Their narratives highlight the need to ensure they have the means to generate income, stay on their land and improve their lot through education and training for them and their children. Listening to their narratives, we hear strong references to their faith, whether they are Muslim or Christian, or their cultural beliefs to guide them to 'do the right thing.' For instance, in Thailand where most are Buddhists and where the late King Bhumibol Adulyadev was a respected conservationist, the initially skeptical farmers became convinced that protecting the environment including the water sources protects their communities and their livelihood. In Vietnam where religion is not practised, respondents referred to alms giving or helping less fortunate family or community members.

Except for Singapore, the economies of the countries in the study are still considered 'emerging' despite their impressive growth rates which in the past five years have been higher than Western developed countries such as the U.S., U.K. and Australia. The 'emerging' status of the five countries influence how much of CSR is perceived and designed as part of nation building. For instance, the national company in Indonesia, which is in the transport and logistics industry, clearly articulated that their CSR focus is on nation building, which they operationalized through the provision of training, jobs and employment.

## Narratives of power: the bibingka approach

To ascertain how power is enacted during the interactions between corporations, government, NGOs and community stakeholders, we asked our informants who initiated the CSR programs three questions: who provided inputs, how they negotiated differences of opinion, and how they managed their cross-sectoral partnerships.

As previously mentioned, corporations often provided resources and networks which NGOs and community agencies found extremely valuable. Governments offered some infrastructure and regulatory frameworks that can facilitate, or hinder, the implementation of community and social development initiatives. NGOs took on different roles depending on who they are working with, but often served as cultural mediator akin to the boundary spanning role. For instance, corporations would access, co-opt or employ NGOs to gain access to local community leaders and members and provide contextual intelligence. As discussed in our Indonesia, Singapore and

Philippine case studies, the CSR managers used to work with NGOs or have backgrounds in social work and community development. Local village leaders and residents on the other hand would work with local NGOs to get advice and often represent them in consultations and negotiations with corporate representatives.

These relationships among the three sectors—business, government and civil society—reflect the relationships identified in the UN Global Compact. This cross-sectoral interaction is also reflected in the Melbourne Model of the UN Global Cities Programme where cities work with government and business to enable sustainable development and the achievement of the ten Global Compact principles (https://citiesprogramme.org/our-framework/the-melbourne-model/). While cross-sectoral collaboration is being touted as a relatively new framework for engagement, particularly for complex global issues such as climate change, poverty alleviation and public health, there have been previous examples of 'interactive' engagement between state and society-centered groups.

In the communicative interactions between the private, public and civil society sectors within the CSR space, we have observed the exercise of 'top-down' power by national governments, international agencies (UN and GRI) and the Malaysian university as well as the 'bottom-up' power by community residents and farming communities. These two dimensions signify the 'power over' and 'power to' relations suggested by Berger (2005) in his critical reflections on public relations. However, one of the elements he mentioned, 'power with,' is a crucial component in the relationships we found in the case studies in this book, and which we already discussed earlier. Reflective of the collaborative nature of the interactions among the three sectors,

> **power with** relations are in play when members advocate or support decisions or decision-making processes that are non-coercive, self-reflective, inclusive of other points of view, and consider public relations to be an important relationship variable.
>
> (Berger, 2005, p. 16)

From our end, we draw from our Philippine roots and Filipino scholars in the land and gender and development sector (Capeling-Alakija, 1993) in proposing a cross-sectoral collaboration framework called '*bibingka*' strategy or principle.

In his paper on land reform in the Philippines, Borras (1998) referred to the symbiotic interaction between state reformists from above and autonomous societal actors from below as the '*bibingka*' strategy. As he explained,

> *Bibingka* is a native Filipino rice cake baked in a homemade oven of two layers with charcoal smolders in each layer, on top of and underneath the cake ... [highlighting] the situation that the state and society are marked

by often heated simultaneous conflicts between pro- and anti-reform forces at different levels.

(Borras, 1998, cited in Franco & Borras, 2009, p. 219)

Borras (1998) mentioned that there were several factors that enabled the success of the land reform case study including the strategic positioning of the state reformists and the alliances created by the societal actors. These factors combined to develop a coalition against non-reforming landlords.

In the gender and development arena, the '*bibingka*' principle has been applied by the United Nations Development Fund for Women (UNIFEM) to describe the process of linking women at the grassroots level with the policymakers. Acknowledging that the term, '*bibingka*' principle was proposed by a women's group leader, UNIFEM Director Capeling-Alakija suggested:

> For sustainable development, we need to create a fire at the bottom— empowering people and communities so that they can negotiate effectively on their own behalf. At the same time, we must build a fire at the top, convincing policymakers that it is in everyone's best interests to have a healthy population and a healthy environment and that women must be involved in order to keep the flame alive.
>
> (1993, p. 36)

In the context of this book, we propose that the '*bibingka*' approach to CSR involves the interplay of institutional power (from above) and community power (from below). However to incorporate the 'power across' dimension, we would like to propose a variation to the '*bibingka*' metaphor. We propose that the 'fire' from the top and the bottom are not sufficient to keep the embers going. It needs to be fanned by 'air' from the sides, which in the Philippine context is done manually. Otherwise the rice cake will not be cooked to perfection. Continuing with the baking process analogy, the top-down and bottom-up heating process may be referred to as the 'normal' radiant heat process, and circulating the hot air may be referred to as the 'convection' process. The horizontal winds in the illustration represent discursive and negotiated powers that may occur such as potential foment, changing mindsets and power influences. The *bibingka* in the middle is meant to communicate that the perception, design and enactment of CSR are "cooked" by the various energy/power sources.

Following this metaphor, we propose that the perception, design and enactment of CSR in the selected Southeast Asian countries as exemplified by the case studies in each of the countries involved negotiated and discursive power between institutions (government, private-sector organizations), community actors (village leaders, residents) and cultural intermediaries (NGOs, advocacy groups and media).

174  *Conclusion*

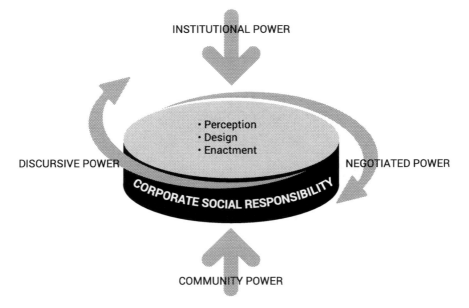

*Figure 8.1* "*Bibingka*" approach to CSR.

## Rethinking the narrative of 'beneficiaries'

One of the main themes that resonated with us during the research and the writing of this book is the need to rethink the notion of 'beneficiaries.' In more traditional terms, 'beneficiaries' refer to people or groups of people who receive "money or advantages." During disaster relief efforts, people who have lost their family members, homes and their belongings and who are then provided material goods and temporary housing are referred to as 'beneficiaries.' In philanthropic programs, beneficiaries may refer to recipients of scholarships, funding for school buildings, free health care and the like.

This type of 'provider–recipient' relationship however reflects a paternalistic dynamic that assumes the power of the provider and the passiveness of the recipient.

In the cases discussed however some of the 'provisions' have taken the form of knowledge transfer or training programs as was evident in the 'check dam' building in northern Thailand, or the 'herb garden' as social enterprise for women in Indonesia. In the disaster community in the Philippines, the provision took the form of 'psycho-social' interventions. The current 'beneficiary' terminology seems to reinforce the 'dependency' model where wealthier states (or individuals) tend to exploit less developed and poorer states (or individuals) by keeping the latter in a deficit mode. Sonntag (2001, p. 3502) suggests that dependency occurs when "certain economies depend on others to buy or sell raw materials and manufacture." He also recounted that the term 'dependency' became controversial when related to development studies particularly in Latin America and the Caribbean as it highlighted the inequities between the 'producers' and the 'manufacturers' during the modernization era. The notions of 'dependency' however take on a different meaning in the era of globalization particularly within the context of China and the Western developed nations. While development studies focus on empowerment, mobilization and active participation in decision making (Larsen, Sewpaul & Hole, 2014; Martinez-Cosio & Bussell, 2012; Rubin & Rubin, 2007), limited attention has been given to revisiting the notion of 'beneficiary.'

What seems to be missing in the international development and CSR discourse is that the so-called 'provider' is actually a 'beneficiary' as well. As the definition indicated, benefits can take the form not only of money but 'advantages,' or what we can refer to as 'intangible benefits.' As our cases showed, the corporations who engage with their community stakeholders through CSR programs are reaping major reputational and operational benefits. These benefits may include: a 'positive' reputation as a good corporate citizen which many claim on their corporate websites; community protection from potential saboteurs of corporate facilities and equipment; and overall reduced costs by avoidance of conflicts and crises with community stakeholders. Moreover, some corporations through their authentic and meaningful CSR and community engagement activities also receive valuable, and in many ways critical, information about the local communities that could be a form of 'competitive advantage.' Once the local communities determine the trustworthiness of the corporate and NGO partners and allow them entry to their villages and people, and in some cases build a 'social fence' around the corporate premises, corporations can observe and access the 'local wisdom' to their advantage. Thus, knowledge or in this case 'wisdom' transfer becomes two way, and reflects a different power dynamic.

We would argue that the discourse around beneficiaries needs to change. In particular, we propose that beneficiaries are not seen as 'passive' nor be automatically assumed to be the 'recipients' of a corporation's or a government's largesse. Instead we argue that the term 'beneficiary' needs to be unpacked when used for the 'intangible benefits' received by corporations, governments and NGOs in their engagement with community stakeholders. Reframing the 'beneficiary' concept is one way to shift the paradigm in existing power structures between institutions and community residents and individuals at the local level. Articulating that institutions are 'beneficiaries' as well highlights that the 'giving' and 'receiving' relationship is not merely based on 'instrumental' artifacts such as money, scholarship, access to education and good health, but also 'intangible' assets such as local wisdom, reputation and social harmony.

## Implications for practitioners

Based on the perspectives of the various actors discussed in this book, we would argue that the integration of participatory approaches with strategic communication that respect multiple perspectives is integral to meaningful enactment of CSR programs. To address inequities of power particularly for poor, marginalized and 'unheard' community members, we need to actively promote authentic dialogue. Authentic communication or dialogue is defined as "founded on the experience of direct, unmediated contact with others" (Craig, 1999, p. 138) or from the phenomenological perspective, as one that "requires congruency between the experience and the expression" (Craig, 1999, p. 141).

In public relations scholarship, authenticity has been defined as 'conforming to fact' (Page, 2007, p. 15); consistency (Molleda, 2010); good character, sincerity and moral autonomy (Stoker & Rawlins, 2010) and ethical leadership, genuineness, transparency and truthfulness (Bowen, 2010). They argue that authenticity and ethical practice are keys to developing trust. At a time when trust of institutions, including NGOs, is eroding (Edelman Trust Barometer Global Report, 2018), communication practitioners from all sectors need to work together and work harder at regaining credibility with their stakeholders.

Regaining credibility and trust involves being aware of how other people in the relationship might think about or perceive an issue, which is the basis of co-orientation theory. Co-orientation occurs when "two or more individuals are oriented to one another and to something of mutual interest" (Broom, 2013, p. 195). In the context of organization–public relationship, co-orientation suggests that: (1) congruency exists between the organization's views on an issue and its estimates of the public's views on the issue, and similarly with the public's views on an issue and its estimates of the organization's views on the issue; and (2) there is agreement and accuracy between the organization and public's views of each other. However instead of aiming simply for consensus, as co-orientation theory suggests, we could also aim toward 'dissensus' (Holtzhausen & Voto, 2002) or 'agonistic pluralism' (Burchell & Cook, 2013). Burchell and Cook (2013, p. 749) propose adopting Mouffe's (1999) framework of 'agonistic pluralism' which is a position wherein "conflicts exist between 'adversaries' who oppose one another but who regard each other as holding 'legitimate' views." Agonistic pluralism acknowledges difference and conflict that will lead groups to interact and make decisions. While these interactions do not necessarily have to result in consensual decisions (Burchell & Cook, 2013), engaging in a continuing dialogue that aims to present conflict, rather than contain the issue, enables NGOs and activists to continue the pressure and influence as well as promote responsible business practices.

As development communication scholar Waisbord (2014) argues, strategic communication needs to be integrated in participatory perspectives that "links communication, collective action and politics" (p. 149). He suggests that instead of information dissemination and top-down persuasion, participatory principles be integrated in problem definition, where multiple actors define and negotiate the social problem, goals selection, strategy and tactic development and in assessing motivations for change. At the same time, communication practitioners must be mindful of appropriating and co-opting the sustainable development language into neo-liberal and managerial contexts because doing so could be construed as inauthenticity.

In addition, we must reconfigure practitioner roles as 'experts' to that of 'facilitators' (Waisbord, 2014; Wilkins 2014). By playing a facilitative role, practitioners enable communities to discuss and define the problems, identify the approaches and solutions from a context that is appropriate to their local environment. External 'experts' are often criticized for trying to impose their 'best practice' knowledge and processes, which may not necessarily be appropriate for the local culture and context.

Instead, we echo the call of critical public relations scholars (Bardhan & Weaver, 2011; Curtin & Gaither, 2012) who advance the reframing of public relations toward social justice and highlighting the value of communication as a process of meaning making:

> communication practitioners ... serve as cultural intermediaries to create shared meanings, or discourses surrounding globalization issues, thus legitimizing certain norms and values.
> (Curtin & Gaither, 2012, p. 11)

Curtin and Gaither (2012) suggest that when "corporations, governments, NGOs and activists work together, diplomacy becomes an attainable standard that trumps the unilateral interests of one organization" (p. 310). Communication practitioners play an integral role in redirecting or recalibrating organizational and public discourse towards social justice issues as well as in building relationships between these global actors to drive social change.

Facilitating and advocating for meaningful social change is a critical role that communication practitioners can play in pursuit of the Sustainable Development Goals, whether they are working in a corporate, government or non-government organization. The practitioners' communicative skills, strategic approach, cultural and contextual intelligence and abilities to traverse the languages of business and community, provide an opportunity to contribute toward global advocacies. In addition, we reiterate the opportunities for practitioners to reconsider the agency of critical conscience (Sison, 2010). The practitioner as critical conscience agent ensures that through the dialectical process, all parties are able to process the issues and not be pressured by expediency, commercial interests or management demands. In addition to their commitment to the dialectical process, agents of critical conscience welcome and promote debate, critiques and new ideas as well as exercise moral courage (Sison, 2010, p. 331).

As the case studies have shown, social justice and human empowerment are ideologies that are not exclusive to NGOs or activist groups. Governments and civil society around the world are acknowledging that the magnitude and complexity of social problems require a collaborative approach. Businesses, whether they are large multinational conglomerates, small or medium companies or social enterprises, are actively integrating social justice and social responsibility in their operations. Regardless of whether these motives are altruistic or commercial, the private sector's extensive resources and global infrastructure are necessary to scale up local community projects that could produce systemic change.

However, we must continue to be vigilant in keeping all organizations accountable and transparent. Constant communication between governments, civil society and the private-sector organizations must occur and communication practitioners must participate at the start, during the planning stage, including contributing to the formative research of any project. Reconceptualizing the role of communication practitioners as facilitators and enablers of the participatory process is needed. They should not simply be called to implement a program, manage the media or manage a crisis. Trust and goodwill with stakeholders, particularly those who may be located at a distance or often invisible, need to be nurtured and cultivated. These positive relationships, built over time, are critical to the sustainability of the business and the livelihoods of the communities in which they operate. Thus, a community- and culture-oriented approach that privileges dialogic relationships underpin the future of CSR communication and practice. We believe that it is only through nuanced and culturally sensitive research, listening, negotiating and interpreting, can we engender inclusive communication that will empower all citizens regardless of their position or role in life to address the global issues that we all face.

We hope that the suite of cases in this book gave eloquence to the lived versions of CSR as interpreted and implemented in a less-studied part of the globe, a region that might rightfully claim that this Western concept actually has roots in Eastern cultures. And, by amplifying and validating the once feeble or even unheard voices as exemplified through the CSR programs of the selected ASEAN countries, we become empowered to realize and harness our roles as facilitators and enablers of truly participatory processes at the confluence of CSR, PR and development communication. In doing so and by democratizing CSR and promoting inclusiveness and social justice for sustainable development of communities and individuals, we become better versions of ourselves, our work and the organizations we represent in the profound and urgent task of building a better future and world for all.

# References

Armitage, D., Berkes, F. & Doubleday, N. (Eds.). (2007). *Adaptive Co-Management: Collaboration, Learning and Multi-Level Governance*. Vancouver: UBC Press.

Austin, J. E. (2000). Strategic collaboration between nonprofits and business. *Nonprofit and Voluntary Sector Quarterly,* 29 (1 Supplement), 69–97.

Austin, J. & Seitanidi, M. (2012). Collaborative value creation. *Nonprofit and Voluntary Sector Quarterly,* 41 (6), 929–968.

Bardhan, N. & Weaver, C. K. (2011). *Public Relations in Global Cultural Contexts: Multi-Paradigmatic Perspectives*. London: Routledge.

Berger, B. K. (2005). Power over, power with and power to relations: Critical reflections on public relations, the dominant coalition and activism, *Journal of Public Relations Research,* 17 (1), 5–28.

Borras, S. M. Jr. (1998). *Bibingka strategy to land reform and implementation: autonomous peasant mobilizations and state reformists in the Philippines*. ISS Working Paper Series/General Series (Vol. 274, pp. 1–88). Erasmus University Rotterdam.

Bowen, S. A. (2010). The nature of good in public relations: What should be its normative ethic? In Heath, R. L. (Ed.). *The Sage Handbook of Public Relations* (pp. 569–583). Thousand Oaks. CA: Sage.

Bradshaw, S. (2013). *Gender, Development and Disasters*. Cheltenham, UK: Edward Elgar Publishing.

Broom, G. M. (2013). Co-orientation theory. In Heath, R. L. (Ed.). *Encyclopedia of Public Relations,* 1, 195–198. Thousand Oaks, CA: SAGE Publications Ltd.

Brundtland, G. H. (1987). *Report of the World Commission on Environment and Development: Our Common Future*. Retrieved from www.un-documents.net/our-common-future.pdf.

Burchell, J. & Cook, J. (2013). CSR, co-optation and resistance: The emergence of new agonistic relations between business and civil society. *Journal of Business Ethics,* 115 (4), 741–754.

Capeling-Alakija, S. (1993). The bibingka principle: Women between the fires. *Harvard International Review,* 16 (1), 34–37.

Craig, R. T. (1993). Communication theory as a field. *Communication Theory,* 9 (2), 119–161.

Curtin, P. A., & Gaither, T. K. (2012). *Globalization and Public Relations in Postcolonial Nations: Challenges and Opportunities*. Amherst, NY: Cambria Press.

Edelman. (2018). *2018 Edelman Trust Barometer Global Report*. Retrieved from https://cms.edelman.com/sites/default/files/2018-01/2018%20Edelman%20Trust%20Barometer%20Global%20Report.pdf.

Franco, J. & Borras, S. (2009). The 'September thesis' and rebirth of the 'open' peasant mass movement in the era of neoliberal globalization in the Philippines. In Caouette, D. & Turner, S. (Eds.). *Agrarian Angst and Rural Resistance in Contemporary Southeast Asia*. (pp. 206–226). Abingdon, Oxon: Taylor & Francis Group.

Global Slavery Index. (2016). How many people are in modern slavery in Thailand? www.globalslaveryindex.org/country/thailand/.

Grosser, K. (2016). Corporate social responsibility and multi-stakeholder governance: Pluralism, feminist perspectives and women's NGOs. *Journal of Business Ethics,* 137 (1), 65–81.

Grosser, K. & Moon, J. (2005). Gender mainstreaming and corporate social responsibility: Reporting workplace issues. *Journal of Business Ethics,* 62 (4), 327–340.

Herrera, M. E. B. & Roman, F. L. (2011). *Corporate Social Responsibility in Southeast Asia: An Eight Country Analysis*. Retrieved from Makati City, Philippines: www.researchgate.net/publication/275026528_Corporate_Social_Responsibility_in_SouthEast_Asia_An_Eight_Country_Analysis.

Hirchsland, M. J. (2006). *Corporate Social Responsibility and the Shaping of Global Public Policy*. New York: Palgrave Macmillan.

Hofstede, G. (2001). *Culture's Consequences. Comparing Values, Behaviors, Institutions and Organizations across Nations*. Thousand Oaks, CA: Sage.

Holtzhausen, D. & Voto, R. (2002). Towards a postmodern research agenda for public relations. *Public Relations Review*, 28 (3), 251–264.

Ikelegbe, A. (2005). Engendering civil society: Oil, women groups and resource conflicts in the Niger Delta region of Nigeria. *The Journal of Modern African Studies*, 43 (2), 241–270.

Kartikawangi, D. (2017). Symbolic convergence of local wisdom in cross–cultural collaborative social responsibility: Indonesian case. *Public Relations Review*, 43 (1), 35–45.

Larrieta-Rubín de Celis, I., Fernández de Bobadilla-Güémez, S., Alonso-Almeida, M. & Velasco-Balmaseda, E. (2017). Women's occupational health and safety management: An issue for corporate social responsibility. *Safety Science*, 91, 61–70.

Larsen, A. K., Sewpaul, V. & Hole, G. O. (2014). *Participation in Community Work: International Perspectives*. Milton Park, Abingdon, Oxon: Routledge.

Leeper, K. A. (1996). Public relations ethics and communitarianism: A preliminary investigation. *Public Relations Review*, 22 (2), 163–179.

Martinez-Cosio, M. & Bussell, M. (2012). Private foundations and community development: Differing approaches to community empowerment. *Community Development*, 43 (4), 416–429.

Molleda, J. C. (2010). Authenticity and the construct's dimensions in public relations and communication research. *Journal of Communication Management*, 13, 223–236.

Mouffe, C. (1999). Deliberative democracy or agonistic pluralism? *Social Research*, 66 (3), 745–758.

Mukhopadhyay, M. (2016). Mainstreaming gender or "streaming" gender away: Feminists marooned in the development business. In Harcourt, W. (Ed.). *The Palgrave Handbook of Gender and Development*. London: Palgrave Macmillan.

Page Society, A. W. (Ed.). (2007). *The Authentic Enterprise*. New York: The Arthur W. Page Society.

Pholphirul, P. (2012). Labor migration and the economic sustainability in Thailand. *Journal of Current Southeast Asian Affairs*, 31 (3), 59–83.

Rubin, H. J. & Rubin, I. (2007). *Community Organizing and Development* (4th edn.). Boston: Pearson/Allyn & Bacon.

Santos, A. (2014). Who takes care of Nanny's children? https://pulitzercenter.org/projects/asia-philippines-uae-dubai-paris-nanny-overseas-migrant-labor-work-children.

Sison, M. D. (2010). Recasting public relations roles: Agents of compliance, control or conscience. *Journal of Communication Management*, 14 (4), 319–336.

Sonntag, H. R. (2001). Dependency theory. In Smelser, N. J. & Baltes, P. B. (Eds.). *International Encyclopedia of the Social & Behavioral Sciences* (pp. 3501–3505). Palo Alto and Berlin: Elsevier.

Sthapitanonda, P. & Watson, T. (2015). "Pid Thong Lang Phra" – The impact of culture upon Thai CSR concepts and practice: A study of relationships between NGOs and corporations. *Asia Pacific Public Relations Journal*, 16 (1).

Stoker, K. & Rawlins, B. (2010). Taking the B.S. out of PR: Creating genuine messages by emphasizing character and authenticity. *Ethical Space: The International Journal of Communication Ethics*, 7, 61–69.

Vazquez-Brust, D. A., Sarkis, J. & Cordeiro, J. J. (2014). *Collaboration for Sustainability and Innovation: A Role for Sustainability Driven by the Global South?* Greening of Industry Networks Series. Dordrecht: Springer.

Waisbord, S. (2014). The strategic politics of participatory communication. In Wilkins, K., Obregon, R. & Tufte, T. (Eds.). *The Handbook of Development Communication and Social Change*. (pp. 147–67). London: John Wiley & Sons Ltd.

Waldman, D. A., Sully du Luque, M., Washburn, N. & House, R. J. (2006). Cultural and leadership predictors of corporate social responsibility values of top management: A GLOBE study of 15 countries. *Journal of International Business Studies*, 37, 823–837.

Wilkins, K. G. (2014). Advocacy communication. In Wilkins, K., Obregon, R. & Tufte, T. (Eds.). *The Handbook of Development Communication and Social Change*. (pp. 57–71). Hoboken: Wiley-Blackwell.

Yaziji, M. & Doh, J. (2009). *NGOs and Corporations*. Cambridge: Cambridge University Press.

# Index

Page numbers in **bold** denote tables, those in *italics* denote figures.

advocacy NGOs 8
agonistic pluralism 176
Ahmad, Z. A. 56
Aquino, Corazon 75
aspirational CSR talk 55, 70
Associated Chinese Chambers of Commerce and Industry of Malaysia 60
Association of Foundations (AF), Philippines 77–78
Association of Southeast Asian Nations (ASEAN) 5; Socio Cultural Community Blueprint 2025 5
Australia 4, 5
authentic communication 176

Badan Amil Zakat National 28
*Barisan Nasional* 50
Baydoun, N. 52
Beautiful Gate Foundation 64
beneficiaries of CSR programs 9, 174–175; corporations as 9, 68–69, 95, 175
Berger, B. K. 172
BERNAMA 53
Bhumibol Adulyadej, king of Thailand 117, 134, 171
*Bibinka* strategy 172–173, *174*
Bilowol, J. 139, 140
Blowfield, M. 11
Bok, D. 56
Bolante, M. P. 93
Borras, S. M. Jr. 172–173
boundary spanners 43, 171–172
Bourdieu, P. 15
Bradshaw, S. 169
Broom, G. M. 176

Brundtland Report (1987) 170
Brunei 5
Bruning, S. D. 11, 12
Buddhism 118, 119, 120, 121, 135, 138
Burchell, J. 167
Bursa Malaysia 54
Burson-Marsteller 67, 100
business–NGO relationships 8–9, 15

capacity building: through education and training, Indonesia 30, 34–37, 39–40, 44; Vietnam 142, 143
Capeling-Alakija, S. 173
Carroll, A. B. 56
Castells, M. 81
Catholics/Catholic Church: Philippines 76, 78; Vietnam 138
Chapple, W. 2, 3, 4, 120
China 4, 5, 65, 75, 137, 138, 175
Christensen, L. T. 55
civil society 2, 3, 4, 5, 9, 12, 21, 163, 164, 172, 178; Indonesia 29; Malaysia 50; Philippines 78, 95; Singapore 101, 114; *see also* NGOs
Clark, C. 11
class relations 15; Malaysia 52; Philippines 76–77
co-optation 141, 145, 164, 167
co-orientation theory 176
collaboration 163, 164
collaboration continuum 164–165
collectivism 7, 163; Malaysia 52; Philippines 77, 78; Thailand 118; Vietnam 138
colonial pasts 5, **6**, 13; Indonesia 25, 26–27, 29; Malaysia 49, 57, 70

communication 15, 176–177; authentic 176
communication practitioners: as critical conscience agents 177; as facilitators 177, 178; implications for 176–178
communication technology 2
communitarianism 163
community: focus on 5, 7–11; narrative of 163–164, 167
community development 1, 3, 4, 7, 11–13, 15, 16, 18, 20; and corporate social responsibility (CSR) 12–13; definition 11; and public relations (PR) 12
community involvement 7
community nurturing 7
community organizing 7
community relations officers 164
community service projects, university CSR programs, Malaysia 56, 65–67
community-based organizations (CBO) 38
compliance-oriented approach, Thailand 131–134
Cook, J. 164, 167
Corporate Responsibility Institute (CRI), Thailand 120
corporate social responsibility (CSR) 1, 3–4; as aspirational talk 55, 70; *Bibinka* strategy to 172–173, *174*; as business tool 3; communication management model of 11; and community development 12–13; critical approach to study of 14–15; definitions of 2, 10–11; as development tool 3–4; and emerging economies 3; and public relations (PR) 11; as Western construct 3; *see also under individual countries*
corruption: Indonesia 29; Philippines 78, 95
Craig, R. T. 176
critical conscience 177
critical-cultural theory 14–15
CSR Malaysia 54
culture 2, 15
culture industries 15
Curtin, P. A. 177

Daymon, C. 16, 17
del Rosario, R. 140
dependency 174–175
disabled people 106–107, 111, 113, 130

disaster relief 171, 174; Philippines 88–93; Singapore 111–112
dissensus 164, 176
Doan, M. A. 139, 140
Doh, J. 8, 165
Domm, G. 139
Duterte, Rodrigo 75
Dutta, M. 13–14

Earth Hour movement 67
education, CSR in *see* university CSR programs
education and training programs 171; Indonesia 30, 34–37, 39–40, 44; Malaysia university CSR programs 61, 64–65; Philippines 79, 82, 84–85; Singapore 111, 113; Thailand 120; Vietnam 155, 156
elderly people 106, 109–110, 113
employee engagement: Singapore 104; Thailand 129–131, 133–134, 165
employee volunteerism, Singapore 102–104
employee well-being, Vietnam 151–152, 156, 157
empowerment 11, 45, 86, 90–92, 125–126, 178; of women 167–170
environmental-related CSR: Malaysia university CSR programs 67–68; Singapore 111, 113; Thailand 120–129
Eric White Associates 52
ethnic relations, Malaysia 50, 51–52, 54, 57

familial approach to community engagement 41–42, 46
farming programs, Indonesia 31–34, 40–44, 46
focus groups 17–18
Frynas, J. G. 3–4, 11, 15
fundraising, Malaysia 62, 64–65

Gaither, T. K. 177
GDP growth rates 4, **6**
Global Compact Network Singapore 101–102
Global Corruption Barometer 95
Global Reporting Initiative (GRI) 54, 163, 170
globalization 2, 11, 101
*gotong royong* 58–59, 163
govenance gap 3, 164
government 2, 3, 4, 5, 171, 172

government PR: Indonesia 27–28; Malaysia 52–53; Philippines 79; Singapore 99–100; Thailand 119
Gramsci, A. 13

Habibie, B. J. 27
Habitat for Humanity Malaysia 62
Hagen, R. 9
Haley, U. 99
Hall, E. & Hall, M. 118–119
Hallahan, K. 7
Hang, D. T. T. 139
Heath, R. L. 7
Herzfeld, M. 118
Hill and Knowlton 100
Hirschland, M. J. 3
Hofstede, G. 7, 52
Holloway, I. 16, 17
Hopkins, M. 15
Horkheimer, M. 15
Human Development Index 4–5
Hutton, J. 10

Ife, J. 11
inclusive business 30, 31
individualism 7
Indonesia 25–48, 164, 165; civil society 29; colonial past 25, 26–27, 29; corruption 29; cultural and social context 26–27; demographic and media data **6**; historical, political and economic context 4, 25–26; Human Development Index 5; kinship relations 26, 46; and Malaysia confrontation 49, 53; patronage 19; *priyayi* ideals 29, 29; public relations practice 27–28; religious influences 26, 28, 29, 45–46; research respondents **19**; tradition and innovation dynamics 29; women's role and status in 26; *Zakat* Management Law 28, 46
Indonesia Business Links 29
Indonesia, CSR development 28–29, 170
Indonesia, CSR perceptions 29–37; community stakeholders 31–34; corporate 30–31, 34–37; inclusive business view 31; nation building view 30
Indonesia, CSR programs: beneficiary–benefactor relationship 45; cultural influences on 29, 45–46; education and training 30, 34–37, 39–40, 44; livelihood and enterprise development (farming) 31–34, 40–44, 46; NGO partners 38, 39, 40, 46; partnership and engagement processes 37–40, 41–44, 46, 165; power relations 40–45; women's influence on 33–34, 41, 42–43, 46, 168
Indonesia Global Compact Network 28–29
Institute of Public Relations Malaysia 52, 53
Institute of Public Relations of Singapore (IPRS) 100
integrative collaboration 164, 165
International Association of Business Communications Philippines (IABC Philippines) 79
international development agencies 12
International Institute of Social Studies 80
International Public Relations Association (IPRA) 79
International Standards Office 163
interpretive approaches 17
Islam: Indonesia 26, 28, 29; Malaysia 50, 52, 54; Philippines 76
ISO 26000 101, 120, 170

Japan 27, 52, 53, 98
Jimena, J. 56

Kartikawangi, D. 166
Kemp, M. 29
Kenan Institute of Asia 120
Kidney Foundation 64
kinship relations 163; Indonesia 26, 46; Vietnam 157
Kramer, M. R. 110
Kruckeberg, D. 7
Kucerova, R. 56
Kurian, P. 13

League of Corporate Foundations (LCF), Philippines 78
Ledingham, J. A. 11, 12
libraries, community, Malaysia university CSR 62–64
Loan, T. H. V. 139
Locks for Hope Initiative 65
Low, L. 99
Lwin, M. O. 100

Macapagal, Gloria 75
Mahathir bin Mohamad 49, 53

Malaysia 49–74, 98, 163; authoritarian culture 70; civil society 50; class relations 52; collectivist culture 52; colonial past 49, 57, 70; cultural and social context 51–52; demographic and media data **6**; economic and historical context 4, 49; Environmental Quality Act (1974) 54; ethnic relations 50, 51–52, 54, 57; Human Development Index 5; and Indonesia confrontation 49, 53; political context 50–51; power distance 52; public relations practice 52–54; religion 50, 51, 52, 54; research respondents **19**
Malaysia, CSR development 54
Malaysia Global Compact Network 54
Malaysia, university CSR programs 56–71; beneficiaries 68–69; community service projects 65–67; environmental-related CSR 67–68; fundraising and philanthropy 64–65; and *gotong royong* concept 58–59, 65; New Village (NV) activities 59–64, 69–70
Malaysian Association of Practicing Opticians 65
Malaysian Chinese Congress 50
Malaysian Indian Congress 50
Marcos, Ferdinand 75, 79
marginalized communities 108, 113
Megawati Sukarnoputri 28
Mehta, S. R. 57
Memmi, A. 13
mentoring 41, 42, 43
Millennium Development Goals (MDGs) 3, 4, 45, 170
Moon, J. 2, 4, 120
Mouffe, C. 176
Muijen, S. C. A. H. 56
multiculturalism, Singapore 99, 100
Munshi, D. 13, 14

Najib Razak 49
nation building 3, 30
National Trades Union Congress, Singapore 101
National Tripartite Initiative for CSR, Singapore 101
Newell, P. 3–4
NGOs (non-governmental organizations) 3, 164–167; advocacy 8; as boundary spanners 171–172; and business relationship 8–9, 15, 165–167; definition 7; independence/ impartiality 166; numbers 8 operational/development 7; reputation 166; as stakeholders 8; *see also names of NGOs and under individual countries*
Ni, L. 7

Ogilvy PR 67

Pal, M. 13
Pang, A. 100
partnership and engagement processes: Indonesian CSR programs 37–40, 41–44, 46, 165; Vietnamese NGOs and business 141–150
paternalism 1, 79, 135, 157, 166, 170, 174
patronage: Indonesia 29; Thailand 121
Peet, G. L. 52
Pfisterer, S. 149
philanthropic collaboration 164
philanthropy 2, 3, 46, 171, 174; Malaysia 64–65; Philippines 78; Thailand 120, 121
Philippine Business for Social Progress (PBSP) 77, 78, 82, 86, 93, 163
Philippines 1, 49, 75–97, 164; civil society 78, 95; class relations 76–77; collectivist culture 77, 78; Corporate Social Responsibility Act (2011) 80; corruption 95; cultural and social context 76–77; demographic and media data **6**; economic, political/ historical context 4, 75–76; Human Development Index 5; public relations practice 78–79, 80, 81; religion 76, 78; research respondents **19**; women 168
Philippines, CSR development 77–78, 170
Philippines, CSR programs: disaster relief 81, 88–93; education 79, 82, 84–85; multisectoral involvement 86, 94; philanthropy as hallmark of 78; as risk mitigation strategy 86–88, 93; social enterprise 81, 82–84; as social/ community development 80–95; sustainable development projects 81–86
PLDT, *Gaby Guro* educational program 79
Political Action Party (PAP), Singapore 99
populism 5
Porter, M. E. 110

# Index

postcolonial approaches 2, 13–14
poverty alleviation/reduction 3, 7, 15
Powell, L. 118
power, narratives of 171–173
power distance: Malaysia 52; Thailand 118
power relations 2, 14, 15; Indonesian CSR programs 40–45; power across relations 173; power with relations 172
Prayut Chan-ocha 117
Prieto-Carrón, M. 15
Propaganda Movement, Philippines 78
public relations (PR) 1; and community development 4, 12; community-centered approach 5, 7; and corporate social responsibility (CSR) 11; critical scholarship 2, 177; definition 10; Indonesia 27–28; Malaysia 52–54; Philippines 78–79; postcolonial approaches to 13–14, 80, 81; Singapore 99–100; Thailand 119; Vietnam 138–139, 140–141, 155
Public Relations Society of America 10, 119
Public Relations Society of the Philippines (PRSP) 79
Public Relations Society of Thailand 119

qualitative research approach 16; interpretive 17

reforestation projects, Thailand 122, 124, 125, 126
religion: Indonesia 26, 28, 29, 45–46; Malaysia 50, 51; Philippines 76, 78; Singapore 99, 101; Thailand 118; Vietnam 148; *see also* Buddhism; Catholics/Catholic Church; Islam
representation 14
reputation, NGO 166
research approach 16–20
research respondents **19**
resistance to CSR initiatives 40–41
risk mitigation 165; Philippines CSR programs as 86–88, 93; Thailand CSR programs as 131–134
Rizal, Jose 78

sampling approaches 17
Sarabia-Panol, Z. 79
Servatamorn, S. 118
shared values approach 102, 110–112

Singapore 17, 98–116, 165; civil society 101, 114; cultural and social context 98–99; demographic and media data **6**; Enabling Masterplan 113; historical, political and economic context 98; Human Development Index 5; multiculturalism 99; public relations 99–100; religion 99, 101; research respondents **19**; women's empowerment in 169
Singapore Compact for CSR 101
Singapore, CSR development 100–101; and globalization 101; and government 101
Singapore, CSR enactment 102–115; disaster relief 111–112; employee volunteerism 102–104; environmental issues 111, 113; shared values approach 110–112; skills training 111–113; social entrepreneurship 102, 104–110, 112, 113, 115, 166
Singapore Employers Federation 101
Singapore International Foundation Social Entrepreneurship program 106
Sison, M. D. 79
small and medium-sized enterprises (SMEs) 104, 105, 114
social change 81, 94, 106, 177
social development 170–171; definition of 80–81; Philippines CSR as 80–95; Vietnamese CSR as 155–157
social enterprise/entrepreneurship: Philippines 81, 82–84; Singapore 104–110, 112, 113, 166; Thailand 129–131
social exchange theory 12
social justice 177, 178
social mapping 37–38, 46
Soekarno 25, 27
Sonntag, H. R. 174–175
Spivak, G. 13, 14
Srisuphaolarn, P. 120
stakeholder engagement 8, 9
Starck, K. 7
Sthapitanonda, P. 166
strategic CSR 150, 153–155, 157
subaltern classes 2, 13
Suharto 25, 27
sustainable development 164, 170–171, 173
Sustainable Development Goals (SDGs) 2, 3, 4, 45, 164, 170, 177
sustainable development projects:

Philippines 81–86; Thailand 121–131, 134–135

Tan, E. K. B. 101, 114
Tan, V. 93
Technical Education and Skill Development Agency (TESDA), Philippines 90
Tencati, A. 140
Thai Industrial Institute 120
Thailand 117–136, 164, 165; Buddhist values 118, 119, 120, 121, 135; collectivist culture 118; cultural/social context 118–119; demographic and media data **6**; economic, political/historical context 117–118; Human Development Index 5; patronage 121; philanthropic practice 120, 121; power distance 118; public relations practice 119; research respondents **19**; women 168–169
Thailand, CSR development 120–121, 170
Thailand, CSR perspectives and practices 121–134, 167, 171; community empowerment 125–126; community stores 129–131, 165; employee engagement and social enterprise 129–131, 133–134, 165; negotiating with communities 126–129; NGOs 121, 123, 125, 126, 127, 128, 129, 131, 132; reforestation project 122, 124, 125, 126; risk mitigation and compliance 131–134; sustainable community development 121–131, 134–135; water project 122–125, 127, 129, 167–168
Thailand Research Fund 120
Thaksin Chinnawat 117
training programs *see* education and training programs
Trans-Pacific Partnership 5
transactional collaboration 164–165
transactional engagement 145, 146, 147
transformational collaboration 165
transformational engagement 145, 146, 148
transitional engagement 145, 146, 147–148
Transparency International, Corruption Perceptions Index 95
Triple Bottom Line 170
Trump, Donald 5
Tulder, R. B. 149

United Malays National Organization (UMNO) 50, 51
United Nations Development Fund for Women (UNIFEM) 173
United Nations (UN) 7; Global Cities Programme 172; Global Compact 12, 29, 172; Human Development Index 4–5; Millennium Development Goals (MDGs) 3, 4, 45, 170; Sustainable Development Goals (SDGs) 2, 3, 4, 45, 164, 170, 177
United States (US) 4, 5
university CSR programs 55–56; *see also* Malaysia, university CSR programs

Vietnam 17, 137–162, 171; collectivist culture 138; cultural and social context 138; demographic and media data **6**; economic, political/historical context 4, 137–138; Human Development Index 5; kinship relations 157; public relations 138–139, 140–141, 155; research respondents **19**
Vietnam Academy of Social Sciences 140
Vietnam, corporate perspective on CSR 150–157; employee well-being 151–152, 157; giving back to the community 152–153; social development, contribution to 155–157; strategic interests, contribution to 153–155, 157
Vietnam, CSR development 139–140
Vietnam, CSR and NGO community 139–140, 141, 142–150; choosing the 'right' corporate partner 144–145, 166; communication, importance of 149; local versus multinational companies 145–147; NGO roles in CSR engagement 149–150; partnership engagement strategies 147–148; personal connections and partnership formation 143–144
volunteerism 171; employee, Singapore 102–104; student, Malaysia 56, 66–67

Wahid, Abdurrahman 27–28
Waisbord, S. 176–177
water projects, Thailand 122–125, 127, 129, 167
Watson, T. 166
Weber Shandwick 67
Widodo, Joko 25, 27, 28
Willett, R. 52

women 173; as community leaders 167–170; Indonesia 26, 33–34, 41, 42–43, 46, 168; migrant workers 168–169; Philippines 168; Thailand 168–169
Women's Candidacy Initiative, Malaysia 50
World Bank 7, 80–81

World Commission on Environment and Development 170
World Vision Malaysia 64

Yaziji, M. 8, 165
Yeo, S. L. 100
Yinglak Chinnawat 117
Yudhoyono, Susilo Bambang 28